Martha
Locke 79

4216

THE GROWTH OF CHRISTIAN PERSONALITY

A STUDY OF THE PUPIL
For teachers of religion in home and school

By

WILFRED EVANS POWELL

Professor of Religious Education,
Phillips University

A textbook in the Standard Leadership Training Curriculum
outlined and approved by the International Council
of Religious Education

Printed for
THE TEACHER-TRAINING PUBLISHING ASSOCIATION
By
THE BETHANY PRESS
St. Louis, Mo.

CONTENTS

To my Mother and Father
in grateful appreciation of
the early years

AUTHOR'S INTRODUCTION

This book is described in the sub-title as "A Study of the Pupil." A pupil is "a person of either sex or of any age under the care of a teacher." The discussion, therefore, does not deal exclusively with childhood but treats of matters that relate to all periods of life. The volume is planned particularly for use in training classes of church school leaders but it is hoped that it will be helpful to other teachers also, especially those who are engaged in the all-important educational enterprise of being parents. Religious education can never be very effective until there is the fullest co-operation between home and school.

Where the book is used as a text by a training class it will be well for both the leader and the members of the class to note the following suggestions:

1. The reader should have in mind, from the beginning, the general plan of the book. This can be secured by reading over carefully the table of contents, paying special attention to the questions given with the titles of the chapters. These questions, together with those in the body of the book which constitute the chapter sub-divisions, are intended to stimulate something of the problem-solving attitude. They should make for definiteness of thinking, and may be found helpful in reviewing.

2. At the close of each chapter there are a number of additional questions and some topics for report and investigation. This material is a definite part of

the course and is not to be considered merely supplementary. The class discussion may well be based largely upon these reports and questions. The items called for will, no doubt, suggest other lines of investigation which it will be profitable for the class to follow. The leader should make definite assignments from among the suggested topics, and a number of written reports should be required.

3. The effective church school teacher has the habit of observation and constantly makes note of things done and said by the pupils. It is very desirable that those who are pursuing this course keep a notebook in which such observations may be recorded to be used as a basis for report to the training class. In addition to the particular matters listed at the close of each chapter, there will be many other observations of human behavior that may contribute much to the class discussion. These might well include notes on the activities of the pupil at home, school, church, play, and work, and special attention should be given to the pupil's problems, interests, social behavior, religious attitudes, and character achievement. The following works contain helpful suggestions for securing and recording observations of human behavior, especially the behavior of children. They illustrate, also, the kinds of things the teacher will be interested in observing. *Co-operative Study of the Religious Life of Children*, by Hartshorne (Religious Education Association, pamphlet); *The Junior*, by Chave (University of Chicago Press); *The Project Principle in Religious Education*, by Shaver (University of Chicago Press), chapter vii; *Childhood and Character*, by Hartshorne (Pilgrim Press), chapter iv, and

pages 241-264; *Case Studies for Teachers of Religion,* by Watson (Association Press).

4. If the members of the training class are unfamiliar with psychological terms, it may be well for the leader of the group to go over certain parts of the text with the class. Perhaps chapter two should be treated in this way and possibly some sections of chapters seven and eight. In a work of this kind it is quite impossible to avoid the use of some technical terms and, while the number of such words has here been reduced to a minimum, the student who has no acquaintance with psychology may experience a little difficulty in following the discussion at certain points. Most of the terms, however, are explained in the text at the place where they are first introduced. By consulting the index at the close of the book the student will be able to find these explanations and will soon become familiar with the expressions used.

5. Where the books in the reference lists at the close of the chapters are available, the course may be expanded indefinitely. There is an abundance of material for twenty lessons, so that double credit may be earned if the class desires to do the extra work. The references bear directly upon the topics discussed in the respective chapters and they have been limited to a few authors so that the books may be more readily secured. If the course is expanded so as to give double credit, there should be available at least four or five of these books in the different fields touched upon: In *psychology,* preferably Gates, *Psychology for Students of Education,* or Woodworth, *Psychology: A Study of Mental Life;*

in *education*, preferably Chapman and Counts, *Principles of Education;* in the general field of *religion,* such a book as Baillie, *The Roots of Religion in the Human Soul,* or Brightman, *Religious Values,* or Pratt, *The Religious Consciousness;* and in the general field of *religious education,* one or two books such as Coe, *A Social Theory of Religious Education,* Weigle, *The Training of Children in the Christian Family,* and Shaver, *The Project Principle in Religious Education.* For double credit an increased amount of observation and written work should, of course, be required.

At the close of the book there is a bibliography of some fifty volumes for the use of those who may wish to make a more thorough study of the field opened up by this course. The list includes not only the books referred to in connection with each chapter but also a number of additional works on psychology and character development. It need hardly be said that, among the titles included, a number of very different viewpoints are represented.

This book is small. It would not be fitting for it to be weighted down with a long list of acknowledgments. Yet the author's dependence upon others has been very great. His indebtedness to former teachers, to many writers and publishers, and to friends and counselors, is here thankfully recognized. Further acknowledgements are made in connection with the quotations used throughout the book.

W. E. P.

Arlington, Mass.
Christmas, 1928.

CHAPTER I

THE PLACE OF THE PUPIL

What Is the Place of the Pupil in Education?

If you are a teacher in the church school, this course does not mark the beginning of your study of the pupil. You have been compelled at times to give a good deal of thought to the members of your class in seeking to understand them and in planning lessons suited to their needs. In this pupil study you may, or may not, have sought the guidance of books. But if you have taken your work seriously, the effort to understand your pupils has cost you both time and energy. Many things have happened in the lives of the boys or girls which have led you to ask questions regarding them. And the questions were not always easy to answer. Why does that boy act so selfishly? Why does this one learn so much more rapidly than the other members of the class? Why are the children noisy during the worship period? Is it just because they are children, or is there something wrong about the way the service is conducted? Why did the boys listen so attentively to the story last Sunday? Why was John so non-co-operative in the games today? Have the lessons on ''working together'' failed to affect him? I wonder if my teaching is really making any difference in the lives of my pupils? How can I help them to attain a genuinely Christian personality?

Questions such as these must frequently occur to the thoughtful teacher and any serious effort to answer them makes necessary a study of human nature. The teacher can be successful only as he seeks constantly to know and to understand the members of his class.

It is the purpose of the course of study upon which you are now entering to help you to understand the pupils whom you now teach, or whom you expect some time to teach. Only a beginning can be made in this series of lessons. The teacher must continue to study the pupil as long as he remains interested in teaching. But there are some fundamental matters concerning human nature, how it develops, and what can be done with it, that form the basis of any adequate understanding of the interesting people who make up our church school classes. To these matters chief consideration will be given in this book.

9

It will be necessary, first of all, to make a brief analysis of the work in which you are engaged as a church school-teacher, or in which you hope to engage if you are preparing to teach, in order to make clear the significant place of the pupil in what is being done. In this chapter, therefore, the questions to be discussed are: (1) What is education? (2) What is religious education? (3) What are the main factors in the educative process? (4) Why is the pupil of such importance in education? and (5) How shall the teacher study the pupil?

WHAT IS EDUCATION?—

The best teachers no longer think of education as merely the imparting of knowledge, or as the training of the mind. It is much more than that. The pupil might gain knowledge if he were shut up in a room alone with his books, but he could not be properly educated in isolation. Education is, in the main, a social process; that is, it takes place while the pupil is in fellowship with others. And it is concerned not just with the intellect, but with all that makes up the life of the pupil—his habits, thoughts, feelings, will, attitudes, purposes and ideals.

In one sense the education of the child begins in his earliest years. The many influences which play upon him and to which he responds, in his home, in his play group, and elsewhere, contribute toward it. And all of the changes that are made in his life as he grows from babyhood to maturity are, in this broad sense, his education. What the school seeks to do, however, is to control for a time the conditions under which he lives so that desirable changes will be made and undesirable ones will be prevented.

In its more restricted sense, then, education is the conscious "production and prevention of changes"[1]

[1]Thorndike, *Education,* p. 2.

in the pupil that will enable him to share intelligently, efficiently and happily in the life of society. It does not aim merely to prepare him for the future —although it cannot be blind to his future—but it seeks to help him, where he now is, to live more richly and worthily.

It is but putting the matter another way when we say that the purpose of education is best expressed not in terms of knowledge, but of character and personality. ''The question to be asked at the end of an educational step is not, What has the child learned? but, What has the child become?''[2] Yet if we do not think of learning too narrowly, it may be said that what the child becomes is what he was at birth, plus what he has learned. Such learning, however, does not come about by means of instruction alone, but by living; not merely by the acquiring of information, but by the sharing of experience. Education takes place as the pupil becomes more and more able to share happily and efficiently in the life of the home, the school, the community, the nation, and the world. And through this process some kind of personality is attained.

WHAT IS RELIGIOUS EDUCATION?—

The church school-teacher is engaged in the work of education. He belongs to the company of men and women who in public school, in private school, in home and church, are helping the boys and girls of the nation to grow in character and personality, and to find satisfaction and happiness in genuine social living. But the special interest of the church

---

[2]James P. Munroe, *The Educational Ideal,* p. 2.

school-teacher is in an education that is religious—
and Christian. What, after all, is religious education? How may it be distinguished from education
in general?

These questions are important. But if the conception of education which has been suggested in this
chapter were carried out thoroughly, under ideal conditions, there would be no need to raise them. The
whole of education would then be religious for it
would help the pupil to live an adequate life in all
his relations both to his fellows and to God.

Practically, however, general education means the
instruction and training provided by the public
school. And the public school is limited in the scope
of its education because it must serve a state, the
citizens of which hold to a great variety of religious
beliefs and, in some cases, deny the value of religion
altogether. The practical question, therefore, becomes: How does the work of the teacher of religion differ from that of the public school-teacher?

It would be an error to make the work of these
two servants of society appear to be in conflict.
There is a unity about the whole task of education,
and the two institutions—the church school and the
public school—have much in common. Both of them
are interested in the development of character. Both
of them deal with the whole personality of the pupil
and not merely with his body, his mind, or his soul.
And both of them seek to achieve their purpose not
alone by the imparting of information, but by stimu-
lating and guiding the growth of the pupil through
personal contacts in a wholesome group life.

The teacher must be clear, however, as to the difference between a religious education that is Christian, and public school education which is, and at least at the present must be, less than Christian.

1. *Religious education is wider in its scope than general education.*—Its horizon takes in the whole world. For the most part, public education today seeks to make good citizens of the nation. Religious education, if it is Christian, aims at world citizenship, and, although the two ideals are not necessarily in conflict, they are by no means identical. The kingdom of God does not have national boundaries. The brotherhood of man must embrace all peoples.

2. *Religious education seeks a higher goal than general education.*—The state may be satisfied if, by means of its schools, it can build a society in which justice shall rule. The schools of the church must not stop short of the reign of love. The character which is the goal of their efforts is Christian character. They have not reached their goal until the pupils strive to meet all life-situations "in the spirit and way of Christ."[3] They have not completed their task until there has been built a society that is ruled by love.

3. *Religious education helps men to know God and thus secures a more complete adjustment of the individual to his world than that which is made possible by general education.*—It takes into consideration both human and divine relationships. It views the world as God's world and has something to say about the character and purpose of the One in whom "all

[3]Shaver, *The Project Principle in Religious Education*, p. 40.

things consist'' (1 Colos. 1:17). It brings the pupil not only into efficient and happy participation in the affairs of men, but into fellowship with God.

WHAT ARE THE MAIN FACTORS IN THE EDUCATIVE PROCESS?—

The discussion thus far will have suggested that many factors contribute to the complex process of education. It is especially important that this truth should be realized by the church school-teacher for whom the formation of character is such a central aim. Character cannot be developed merely by things learned from books—not even from the Bible itself. The process involves much more than the lesson-story, blackboards, and maps. ''The first concern of education,'' says Professor Coe, ''is not a textbook or anything that printers' ink can convey, but the persons with whom the pupil is in contact, and the sort of social inter-actions in which he has a part.''[4] The whole life of the church school contributes toward those changes in the pupil which really constitute his religious education. The teaching of religion does not take place in the thirty-minute period of instruction alone, but the lesson is being taught, for good or ill, by all of the activities of the school; by its worship, its play, its discipline, its organization, and its sharing in the enterprises of the church and of the community.

It should be noted also, that other factors may counteract the work of formal instruction. The teacher's aim, in a given lesson, may be to teach reverence. The story may be prepared with this

[4]Coe, *A Social Theory of Religious Education,* p. 19. Chas. Scribner's Sons, N. Y. Used by permission.

objective in mind. Yet the atmosphere of the class-room, the fussiness of the teacher, the cramped position of the pupils, or the disorderly way of conducting the affairs of the class, may in a manner much more effective than the spoken word of the teacher, create attitudes that are directly opposed to those which the lesson is intended to cultivate.

In order to indicate something of the contribution of the various factors to education, a fivefold summary of them may be made. An analysis of a concrete teaching situation would suggest, as the five main factors in the teaching process, (1) the pupil, (2) the teacher, (3) the lesson materials, (4) the methods of teaching and of class management, and (5) the surroundings or environment. Each of these factors includes a great many elements and they all contribute to the final result. The part played by the teacher, for example, may be analyzed into *personality* and *teaching skill*, and these, in turn, may be broken up into the numerous traits and abilities that constitute them. In a similar way any of the other factors may be analyzed into their constituent elements and these may be viewed as to their contribution to the whole process of education.

The efficient teacher understands the part played in the teaching process by each of these factors and he knows something of how to control them so as to attain the real objectives of his teaching. He knows what qualities in a teacher tend to make his work effective. He knows how to evaluate and select lesson-materials. He can use methods of teaching and of class-management which, in themselves, contribute toward the development of character. He realizes how much the personal contacts of the pupil with other pupils, and with the teacher, may mean in the achievement of the aims of religious education, and how important even the physical surroundings of the room may be. And, most important of all, he understands human nature and knows how to deal with it. There is nothing in the equipment of the efficient teacher that is of more vital significance than this knowledge of those whom he teaches. First of all, the teacher must know the pupil.

WHY IS THE PUPIL OF SUCH IMPORTANCE IN EDUCA-
TION ?—

The conception of education which has been given in this chapter will already have suggested the important place of the pupil in the work of the church school-teacher. Two or three facts, however, must be given special emphasis here.

1. *The pupil supplies the material with which the teacher works.*—He comes to the class-group equipped with certain instincts, impulses and tendencies to activity, which make education possible. "The little human animal," to use Professor Weigle's expression, "is born going." And it is with this active individual, whether child, youth, or adult, that the teacher must deal. Only as he lives with his pupils in fellowship and understanding, is his work likely to be effective. For his real materials are not books, and maps, and blackboards, but human beings with impulses, desires, prejudices, hopes and fears. The chief concern of the teacher must always be not things, but persons; not textbooks, but pupils.

2. *The pupil is "the great objective" in religious education.*[5]—He not only supplies the "raw material" for the teacher's work, but he is himself the measure of the teacher's success. The results of one's teaching, at the end of the church school year, are to be measured by the changes the class has made in the lives of the pupils during the period in which they have been members of the group. Do they have a better knowledge of Christian principles? Have they any finer appreciation of the world in which they live? Has their sense of fellowship with God become more real? Are they more responsive to the teachings of Christ? Are they more just, more truthful, more reverent, more loving?

Questions such as these will test the effectiveness of the work of the teacher. He has not reached "the great objective" unless changes in the direction of Christian character have been wrought in the lives of his pupils.

3. *The potentialities that lie within the pupil make social progress possible.*—The child does not have to begin his spiritual adventure where the race began it. The racial heritage, in religion as in other realms, can be communicated to him by teaching. Even at an early age he may know something of the higher life as it was revealed in the person of Jesus Christ.

Moreover, the child may build upon the past. The wise teacher will strive to stimulate his pupils so that they will not merely reproduce his own ideas and attitudes, but will seek to go beyond him. He will desire them to become more thoroughly Christian than he himself has been. And he will think

[5]Betts, *How to Teach Religion*, p. 30.

of his objectives not merely in terms of the individual pupils, but of society. He will aim at the development of personality, but also at social progress. He will seek, by his teaching, to build a better world—to make more real the kingdom of God on earth.

This wider social view of education emphasizes again the central place of the pupil in the teaching process. It rests upon the social nature of the individual and upon his capacity to change, to learn, and to grow. It calls for an understanding by all those who teach, of the potentialities of human nature.

How shall the teacher study the pupil?—

The teacher, it is clear, must know and understand human nature. But how can this knowledge and appreciation be gained? There are two ways of studying the pupil. The teacher may observe, directly, the behavior of those whom he teaches and of other persons with whom he comes into contact. He may, on the other hand, study the results of observations of human conduct that have been made by others, and gain from them a better understanding of his own pupils. The observations of others may be in the form of books, or they may be merely oral or written reports of things seen and heard in the home, the school, the play-ground, or the place of business.

An adequate knowledge of the pupil can be secured only by the use of both direct and indirect methods. The teacher may learn much concerning his pupils from books written by those who have made a study of human nature, such as works on child study and psychology, popular biographies, or the imaginative creations of writers who have known "what was in man.'' The child characters in the works of such authors as Tarkington, Stevenson, Mark Twain, and Howells, may well be studied by the teacher of children. A knowledge of the child may also be gained from parents who have an opportunity to observe him in the intimate relations of home-life. If the teacher can enlist the co-operation of the home, and can secure from it reports of the things children do and say, he should receive much help toward vitalizing his church school teaching.

But there is nothing that will contribute more to the proper understanding of the pupil than the first hand study by the teacher, of the boys or girls, the young people or adults, who make up his class group. If other factors remain the same, the more the teacher learns to know his pupils the better teacher he becomes. This knowledge, it is true, needs to be balanced by the wider and more systematic observations of others such as may be found in works on psychology. But nothing can take the place of the teacher's personal contacts and fellowship with his pupils, or of his thoughtful observation of persons of various ages, in the different situations of life.

This book, then, is only a part of the course upon which you are entering. The discussion in the lesson text must be somewhat abstract because it has to deal with the pupil in general terms. The chapters take up aspects of human nature that are roughly alike in all pupils. They give some of the results of experiment and observation by psychologists and other students of human nature. They present some of the basic facts and principles concerning the pupil, which all teachers need to know.

But the other part of the course is by no means less important than the reading of the text. It should consist in the thoughtful study of living pupils. Flesh-and-blood children, vigorous young people, and real men and women, are as much the materials of this course as they are those with which the teacher of religion must always deal. The facts and principles discussed in the text will have increasing value as they are studied in relation to concrete and definite situations in the lives of particular pupils. By following the suggestions for observation and investigation given in connection with each chapter, your study of the pupil may become, in reality, a study of life—the most fascinating of all subjects, and the one of greatest value to the teacher in the church school.

QUESTIONS—

1. In what sense may it be said that the education of the child begins in his earliest years?
2. How does education help the pupil to share intelligently, efficiently and happily in the life of society?
3. What do you mean when you use the term "religious education"? How does your view compare with that suggested in this chapter?
4. In what ways, other than those mentioned in the text does the work of the church school teacher differ from that of the teacher in the public school?
5. Why does religion have such a small place in public education?
6. Are the three "distinguishing marks" of religious education suggested by the author clearly apparent in the work of your church school?
7. What is the significance of the word "adjustment" as it is used in discussions of education?
8. How would you analyze the main factors in the teaching process into their constituent elements?
9. What reasons for the importance of the pupil in education would you add to those given in the text?

10. Does the program of your church school provide definite means of helping the teachers to understand their pupils? (Workers' Library, Parent-Teachers' Meetings, etc.)

REPORTS AND INVESTIGATIONS—

1. Give, in outline form, the main sources of information about the pupil that are available to the teacher.
2. List some of the chief problems encountered by the teacher in his work. In how many of them is the pupil directly concerned? Would a better understanding of the pupil help toward their solution?
3. Recall any specific instances known to you where a more adequate knowledge of the pupil has improved teaching efficiency.
4. If possible observe a church school class in session. Note especially the things done and said by the pupils during the class period. For how much of the time were the pupils active? Was their activity always that desired by the teacher? How was it directed?

REFERENCES—

Betts, George H., How to Teach Religion, chap. ii. Abingdon Press.

Chapman and Counts, Principles of Education, chaps. i and xvii.

Coe, George A., A Social Theory of Religious Education, chap. v. Scribners.

—, Education in Religion and Morals, chaps. v and vi. Revell.

Hartshorne, Hugh, Childhood and Character, chaps. i and iv. Pilgrim Press.

Shaver, Erwin L., The Project Principle in Religious Education, chap. iii. University of Chicago Press.

Thorndike, Edward L., Education, chaps. i-iii. Macmillan.

CHAPTER II

ORIGINAL NATURE

With What Equipment Does the Pupil Begin Life?
(General Characteristics and Neural Basis)

As a teacher you are dealing constantly with living pupils. Your work involves "the production and prevention of changes" in the lives of those who make up your class group. Whenever you teach effectively you either bring about desirable changes in your pupils, or you prevent undesirable ones from being made. Similarly, whenever the pupil learns; he does so by reason of changes of one kind or another which take place in him. That is what learning is.

But there are some things the pupil does not have to learn. They are a part of his very nature, and no learning of them is necessary. The baby does not have to be taught to suck, nor the boy—perhaps—to fight. The boy may have to be taught not to fight, or to fight in some other way than that which he spontaneously adopts, but the impulse to pugnacity is part of his native equipment.

Various terms are used to refer to this unlearned behavior of the child—instincts, original nature, native tendencies, and the like. It should be noted that the term "original nature" is here used in the psychological and not in the theological sense. Its meaning will be made clear in this and the following chapter. At present we are concerned merely to point out that the teacher's work is, to a great extent, dependent upon these natural tendencies of the pupil. If the activity to which they lead is in harmony with the Christian way of life, the impulses may be encouraged. If not, they must be modified. Intelligent dealing with pupils demands that the teacher understand the equipment with which they begin life.

But perhaps you are a teacher of older pupils. If so, you may feel that this approach to the study of human nature pushes the matter too far back; that it is too remote from your immediate concern with a class of adolescents, or of adults. It must be remembered, however, that these tendencies, although they become greatly modified by the varied experiences of individu-

als, persist throughout life and that the behavior of
human beings of any age, can scarcely be understood
without reference to them. Moreover, some of the tendencies, although they are rightly considered a part of
original nature, do not manifest themselves in the
life of the individual until a number of years after
birth.

Our study of the pupil may well begin, therefore,
with a discussion of original nature. We must ask:
(1) What is meant by original nature? (2) What is
the basis of the original tendencies in the nervous system? (3) What are the characteristics of instincts?
(4) What are some of the more important instinctive
tendencies? and (5) What other general tendencies are
of importance to the teacher?

WHAT IS MEANT BY ORIGINAL NATURE?—

Original nature is sometimes thought of as the
potential nature of the individual as it is at birth.
This conception is, however, not quite accurate. The
pupil's original nature is his native endowment, that
which he is, apart from any learning, or any environmental influences. And influences which must really
be considered environmental, may affect the individual while still in the foetal stage. An injury to the
foetus, for example, which might hinder, even permanently, the full development of the individual,
could not be considered a part of his native equipment. It is necessary to go further back than the
time of birth. Original nature is, rather, the nature
of the individual as it is, potentially, at the time of
the union of the germ cells which combine to produce
the new life. At that time, what may be called the
basic structure of the new life is set, or, to change
the figure, the capital with which it is to transact
the business of life is determined. Yet so plastic
is human nature, and so varied are the influences
which may be brought to bear upon it, that even to

a very modestly endowed individual, education may open up almost infinite possibilities.

The youngest child that comes to the church school has already passed through a long process of education. He has been active from the beginning of his life, and he has been learning from the time he first gave attention to sight or sound. But the basis of his learning has been the unlearned tendencies which make up his original nature. Without these, he could not have developed. And without them the teacher could not guide his further development. They represent not only the pupil's life capital; they are also the "capital with which teachers work."

Types of original tendencies.—There are several types of these original tendencies although it is quite impossible to make a rigid distinction between them. The most obvious division is, perhaps, that which may be made between tendencies which the individual possesses by reason of his being a member of a particular family, let us say; and those which belong to him because of his membership in the human race. The particular family inheritance of the pupil may give him the basis for certain special aptitudes like musical skill or facility in the use of language, or, because of some lack it may make these attainments almost impossible to him. These general tendencies are usually termed capacities. They will be considered more particularly in the chapter on "Individual Differences."

The present chapter is concerned with the other group of activities, or tendencies to activity, namely, those that are common to the race. All normal children are born with hearts that beat and with stomachs that digest food. These activities do not have to be learned and they go on without any conscious direction whatever. They are termed physiological responses. Likewise all normal children will wink involuntarily when the eye is threatened by a moving object, or will start at the sound of a sudden loud noise. Such actions are usually considered reflexes. There are also, in all normal children, certain larger, less rigidly fixed predispositions, to which the term instinct is applied. Tendencies to fight, to manipulate objects, to seek the company of others and to engage in love-making, belong in this third group of the responses which make up the racial inheritance of man. It is with this group, the instincts, that the teacher is most directly concerned.

WHAT IS THE BASIS OF THESE ORIGINAL TENDENCIES IN THE NERVOUS SYSTEM ?—

A proper understanding of original nature and of the use of native tendencies, involves a knowledge of their basis in the nervous system. Only the briefest sort of discussion of this topic is possible here.

In its simplest form the nervous system may be thought of as a vast number of thread-like fibres, or nerves, extending from and to every part of the body, and connecting with certain nerve centers known as the brain and the spinal cord. If the analogy is not pushed too far some similarity may be pointed out between this intricate mass of nerves and the wires of a telephone system in a large city. The brain and the spinal cord would then correspond to the "central" office where connections are made between one telephone and any other. The electricity passing over, or through, the wire, might be compared to the nerve current which passes along the nerve, as a "message" is carried from, let us say, the eye to the brain.

The nervous system is made up of three parts the significance of which can best be seen by the analysis of a simple human action. A child, for example, sees a bright object and grasps for it. What has taken place in his nervous system? First, the sense organ,

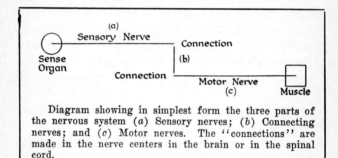

Diagram showing in simplest form the three parts of the nervous system (*a*) Sensory nerves; (*b*) Connecting nerves; and (*c*) Motor nerves. The "connections" are made in the nerve centers in the brain or in the spinal cord.

the eye, was stimulated by the light from the object and a nerve current was conveyed, by means of the optic nerve, to the nerve center in the brain.[1] In the second place, a connection was made in the brain between the end of this incoming nerve, and the beginning of an out-going one. The third stage in the process was the passage of the nerve current along this out-going nerve to the muscles of the hand, which resulted in the grasping activity.

The three parts of the nervous system are, there-

---

[1] In this particular case it would be in the "brain-stem," the upper continuation of the spinal cord.

fore: **(1)** the sensory, or incoming nerves; **(2)** the motor, or out-going nerves; and (3) the connecting centers in the brain or spinal cord. Together they make possible the sensitiveness of man to his surroundings and the great variety of responses which he can make to them. They are the neural basis of human behavior.

The analogy of the telephone system may again be used to make clear the importance of the brain and spinal cord in the neural make-up of man. Just as the central office makes possible the connection of any telephone with any other in the system, so the nerve centers in the brain or cord make possible a connection between the nerves coming from or extending to any part of the body. Because of this centralization of the nervous system, human behavior, instead of being merely impulsive, can become coordinated and unified.

Even the briefest discussion of the neural basis of original tendencies requires some further consideration of the structure of the nervous system. Man's neural equipment is much more complex than our brief description of it may suggest. A nerve, for example, is not just a single thread-like fibre, but is rather comparable to a telephone cable which contains many wires within an encasing tube. It is really a bundle of very minute fibrils called axons, and these are, in turn, branches or neurones. There are billions of neurones in the human body and the connections which we have been discussing are connections between many neurones. "A neurone is a nerve cell with its branches,"[2] and the junction be-

---

[2] Woodworth: *Psychology,* p. 32.

tween two neurones is called a synapse. (See diagram, below.)

Stimulus, response, and connection.—So far as the neural basis of behavior is concerned[3] (*see footnote on Behaviorism below*) it is possible to think of any of

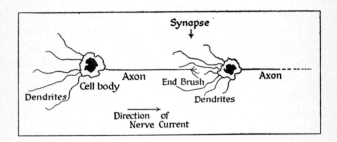

Two neurones in conjunction.—The short branches are the dendrites; the long thread is the axon which terminates in an end-brush.   The junction between the neurones is the synapse.   The arrow indicates the direction in which the nerve current passes from one neurone to another.

the pupil's actions in terms of the stimulus (the thing seen, or heard, or thought, and so forth); the response (the thing done, or said, or thought—as a conse-

[3]Note.—No commitment to the position of mere behaviorism is involved in this discussion.   All students of human nature agree that man's behavior has a neural basis and that one is helped in the study of original nature and learning by some knowledge of the structure and working of the nervous system.   The objective study of the behavior of the pupil in terms of "stimulus" and "response" should prove most valuable to the church school teacher.   It should tend toward concreteness and definiteness in his thinking and is really a good way to study children.   But the teacher cannot assume, with the behaviorist, that all of the observed responses of the pupil are due solely to habit mechanisms (that is, to fixed neural connections) in which conscious purpose and thinking have no determinative influence. To do so would rob him of power as a teacher and would take the heart out of his Christian message.   Some of the methods of the behaviorist may well be used in the study of the pupil, but the behavioristic philosophy cannot be accepted by the Christian teacher.   (For a brief but good discussion of this problem, see *Principles of Education* by Chapman and Counts, pp. 94-98.)

quence); and the connection or bond in the nervous system which makes the response possible. The connection means that something has taken place at the synapse so that the nerve current passes over the neurones involved in the observed response, instead of over some other neurones. It may do so because the path across the synapse has been made easy by learning, or it may do so because the path was already established in the original nature of the pupil. When a child, in response to the stimulus, "Where was Jesus born?" responds, "At Bethlehem," he does so because of learned connections. When he responds to a large black dog coming toward him by crying and clinging to the parent, he does so largely because of unlearned or original connections. The neural basis of the original tendencies is, therefore, in the synapses. The character of some of the synapses is fixed by inheritance. What the pupil is by original nature, he is because of the "preformed connections or tendencies to connections present in his nervous system."[4]

WHAT ARE THE CHARACTERISTICS OF INSTINCTS?—

Of the four types of unlearned tendencies, the teacher is perhaps most directly concerned in the use of the instincts and because of their importance in education they must be given some further consideration.

As has already been noted instincts are inherited tendencies to respond to certain situations in more or less fixed ways. But so also are reflexes and physiological responses. Are instinctive acts in no

[4]Norsworthy and Whitley, *Psychology of Childhood*, p. 22.

sense different from the winking of the eye or the beating of the heart? How may they be distinguished from other unlearned tendencies?

Let us be clear, first of all, that it is not necessary to assume a rigidly fixed line of demarkation between any of the types of original responses. They blend into each other and the differences between them are largely, though perhaps not wholly, differences in degree. The impulse to fight differs from the impulse to sneeze in that the former tendency is more complex, less definite, and more modifiable than the latter. Instincts, then, are the more complex original responses and in their functioning there is a larger element of conscious control than in the other forms of unlearned behavior.

Perhaps the clearest distinction between reflexes and instincts, however, is that made by Woodworth and others who find it to be a matter of the difference in quickness of response. The slower response in the case of the instinct, gives to it the quality of a "persisting tendency," whereas in reflex activity the response is almost always immediate. The normal eye, for example, responds immediately to the presence of light (reflex), but the youth who seeks the company of his fellows (gregarious instinct) may wander restless and dissatisfied for some time, before he reaches the goal of fellowship in the group. "What is characteristic of the instinct," writes Woodworth, "is the persisting 'tendency,' set up by a given stimulus, and directed towards a result which cannot be instantly accomplished."[5]

------

[5]*Psychology; A Study of Mental Life*, Woodworth, p. 109 Henry Holt and Co., N. Y. Used by permission.

Many problems are raised by recent discussion of the instincts. Some writers deny their existence altogether; some reduce their number to one or two fundamental drives such as sex or the impulse of the herd; while others continue to make rather lengthy lists of instincts and to suggest various ways of classifying them. Moreover the lists of different psychologists show little agreement as to details and in many cases there are clear contradictions in the items included. The layman is apt to be puzzled by the discussion and to feel that, where so much confusion exists, there can be little that has practical worth for him.

The attitude of the teacher.—But the study of instincts is not a profitless task for the church school teacher. For while he needs to be intelligent and informed about the whole matter, his attitude is essentially a practical one. Many of the intricate and technical matters discussed by the psychologist are not especially his concern. Yet from the discussion some conclusions emerge which the teacher may well have in mind.

1. Man is not equipped by original nature with a few rigidly distinct tendencies which can be conveniently labeled and which can be used to explain all human conduct. He inherits, rather, many tendencies which may be classified in various ways. The term instinct is used to designate certain groupings of these tendencies and of the emotions which accompany them. These groupings are somewhat, though not wholly, arbitrary, but they are of practical use in the study and control of behavior. They embrace tendencies which lead, in a general way, to-

ward some "end-result" that is more or less satisfying. A mother hearing the cry of her baby responds, perhaps, by running to the cot where the child is lying, picking the child up in her arms, looking at the clock to see if it is feeding time, carrying the baby to a rocking-chair, feeding it, and finally rocking it to sleep in her arms. Although, of course, many of these particular responses have been learned, the whole group of them is bound together by a native "persisting tendency" which is not satisfied until the child's needs have been met. This tendency we call the "parental instinct." The practical teacher is interested in knowing what situations arouse the instinctive tendencies, what kind of responses result from their stimulation, in what direction they lead, what emotions accompany them, and how they may be modified. A considerable portion of this book is given to the discussion of these matters.

2. While any knowledge of human nature may be of value to the teacher, that which is most necessary is not a detailed, scientifically accurate and complete list of the instincts, but is rather a knowledge of the more important native tendencies with which he will constantly be called upon to deal in his teaching work. No attempt is made, therefore, to list all of the instincts in this chapter. Only those are discussed which are important in the work of religious education.

3. From the point of view of the teacher it is not necessary to assume that the instincts include no elements which are the result of learning. It would be interesting to know what forms of human behavior are absolutely instinctive in the sense of being com-

pletely free from any of the influences of environment, and the scientific psychologist may well seek to experiment upon the problem. The teacher, however, does not need to be concerned if he has to admit a certain admixture of habit in his working list of the instincts. Modification of the original responses takes place from the earliest years of life and intelligence often operates in and through them, not in opposition to them. But the tendencies having an instinctive basis remain sufficiently definite to be studied and used, and their instinctive character gives to them an added drive which may be invaluable to the teacher in guiding the development of personality.

WHAT ARE SOME OF THE MORE IMPORTANT INSTINCTIVE
  TENDENCIES?—

For the teacher a convenient working list of the instincts may well include the following tendencies. Tendencies (1) to engage in general physical activity; (2) to fight; (3) to engage in sex behavior; (4) to engage in parental behavior; (5) to seek the company of others; (6) to be assertive; (7) to be submissive; (8) to avoid or seek to escape; (9) to seek to explore or be curious; (10) to seek the approval of others. This list, it will be noted, does not include the tendencies involved in responses to organic needs, such as eating, drinking, sleeping, breathing and the like. These reactions obviously have a basis in original nature but they represent the simpler forms of human activity with which the teacher is not so directly concerned. Moreover, many of the tendencies in this working list are really groupings of a number of minor responses and the form given to them here is largely for the convenience of the teacher. One who has followed carefully the discussion about the nature of the instincts will not be misled by its apparent finality.

For each of these tendencies there are stimuli that are sufficient to arouse them, and there are results in behavior which may be expected to follow from their stimulation if the conditions are favorable. The tendency to explore, for example, is aroused by a novel situation and, if it is not interfered with by counteracting tendencies, it results in the investigation, handling, testing and exploring of the unfamiliar thing. The instincts are discussed from this point of view in some detail in chapter three.

WHAT OTHER GENERAL TENDENCIES ARE OF IMPORTANCE
    IN THE WORK OF THE TEACHER?—

Original nature includes a number of other tendencies which are of importance to the teacher although they are not as readily classified into convenient groupings. They will be discussed as tendencies to be satisfied or annoyed, tendencies to mental activity, and tendencies to emotional states.

1. *Satisfiers and annoyers.*—The neural constitution of man is such that certain states are satisfying and others are annoying to him. This condition, just as truly as the active tendencies which have been noted, is a part of man's native endowment. It is the basis of his desires and motives and it has much to do with his ability to learn from experience. There are some satisfiers and annoyers that are practically constant and others which depend more largely upon the condition of the individual at the time they

are experienced. There are things which man seems to be born to like and others which he naturally dislikes.

In general, when instinctive behavior is aroused, it is satisfying for it to move smoothly along to the "end result" without interference. Interference is annoying. However, the condition of the individual must be considered. If a certain tendency has been sufficiently exercised, to stimulate it may indeed be annoying. One may be so tired by a round of social activities that he desires to be alone. To be forced into the company of others under such circumstances would be annoying. The "tendency to seek the company of others" is at the time not "ready" to act. Such facts as these led Thorndike to formulate certain principles of human behavior which he called the law of readiness. They are stated simply by Gates as follows: "(1) When an instinct is ready to act, for it to act is satisfying. (2) When an instinct is ready to act, for it not to act is annoying. (3) When an instinct is unready to act, for it to act is annoying."[6]

2. *Mental activity.*—In the list of native tendencies given above attention has been directed chiefly to the resulting behavior. All of these responses, however, involve mental as well as bodily activity. There is an awareness of what is going on and there is a succession of mental states which are more or less satisfying in themselves. Man possesses what has been called the "instinct of general mental activity." He finds satisfaction in merely having sensations and if the possibility of expressing his instinctive tend-

---

[6]Gates, *Psychology for Students of Education*, p. 153. The Macmillan Co. Used by permission.

encies in behavior is denied him, he may satisfy some of them in memory and imagination. If he cannot enjoy the company of others in bodily presence, he may find delight in well-chosen books which bring him into the fellowship of the "eternal court" whose society is "wide as the world, multitudinous as its days, the chosen and the mighty of every place and clime."[7]

In man, then, mental states may serve both as stimuli and as responses, and mental activity itself may be intrinsically satisfying. The particular connections which are made in these mental processes at any one time will be determined by the training and experience of the individual but there is a basis for such activity in original nature. To use the suggestive words of another, there are "original roots" for attention, perception, memory, imagination, thinking and learning.[8]

3. *The emotions.*—Most of the instinctive tendencies are accompanied by more or less characteristic emotional states but the emotions soon blend into each other and it is difficult to determine which of them are really primary. The tendency to fight seems generally, though by no means always, to be accompanied by the emotion of anger; that to escape by fear; that to sex behavior by love. It is clear that the basis for certain emotional states belongs to man's original equipment, but not a great deal is known as to what are the fundamental emotional reactions. Some psychologists maintain that there are very few of them and that all other emotional states are due to various

[7]Ruskin, *Sesame and Lilies.*
[8]Norsworthy and Whitley, *Psychology of Childhood,* p. 97.

refinements and combinations of such basic emotions as love, fear, and rage. Only in a rough and approximate way can the emotions be paired with the instincts. Yet the best explanation of the emotions seems to be that they are due "to sensations aroused by the bodily changes which follow directly upon the stimulation" of these and other tendencies.[9] There is thus a close relation between instinct and emotion.

The importance of the emotional states in the development of personality can scarcely be overestimated. "Were it not for these peculiar emotional disturbances life, if possible at all, would be lived or rather endured on a vegetative level. Man might derive benefit from the absence of certain harmful feelings attending the arousal of fear and anger, but he would lose the joys and thrills which accompany the satisfaction of other tendencies. These emotional disturbances furnish the drive and serve as the motivation of the elaborate lifelong process of habit formation upon which learning depends."[10]

In the following chapter consideration will be given to some of the emotions in discussing the tendencies with which they are usually united.

QUESTIONS—

1. What is meant by "original nature" as the term is used in this book?
2. What are some of the things that have already been learned by the youngest child entering the Church school?
3. How may the four types of original tendencies be distinguished? Give illustrations of each type.
4. Why is it difficult to determine what human tendencies are really instinctive?

---

[9]Chapman and Counts, *Principles of Education,* p. 62. Houghton, Mifflin & Co., Boston.

[10]Chapman and Counts, *Principles of Education,* p. 62. Houghton, Mifflin and Co., Boston. Used by permission.

5. Are there other native tendencies which you think should be added to the teacher's "working list" given in the text?

6. How do you detect the presence of emotion in another person? What emotions are most easily recognized?

7. Is the emotional life of the pupil a matter with which the teacher is concerned? Why?

8. What is the significance for education of the fact that certain states are satisfying and others are annoying to man?

9. Of what value to the teacher is a knowledge of the neural basis of behavior?

10. What do you think of the position that some of the *methods* of the behaviorist may well be used by the Christian teacher but that he cannot accept the behavioristic *philosophy?*

REPORTS AND INVESTIGATIONS—

1. Write out a brief statement showing that you understand the meaning of each of the following terms: (*a*) Nerve, (*b*) brain, (*c*) spinal cord, (*d*) sense organ, (*e*) sensory nerve, (*f*) motor nerve, (*g*) connecting center, (*h*) neurone, (*i*) synapse, (*j*) stimulus, (*k*) response, (*l*) behaviorism.

2. In the work of the church school class which you recently observed in session, (*a*) what would you say was intrinsically satisfying to the pupils? (*b*) What was annoying to them? (*c*) What gave them an opportunity for the expression of instinctive tendencies?

3. Give several instances from your own experience of the operation of the law of readiness.

4. Begin work on your "Observation Notebook" following the suggestions given in the Author's Introduction.

REFERENCES—

Chapman and Counts, Principles of Education, chap. v. Houghton Mifflin.

Gates, Arthur I., Psychology for Students of Education, chaps. ii-vi. Macmillan.

Norsworthy and Whitley, Psychology of Childhood, chap. iii. Macmillan.

Thorndike, Edward L., The Original Nature of Man, chaps. i, ii, and xiv. Teacher's College.

Woodworth, Robert S., Psychology, chaps. ii-vi. Henry Holt.

CHAPTER III

ORIGINAL NATURE (CONTINUED)

With What Equipment Does the Pupil Begin Life?
(Classification and Description)

The teacher's thinking upon the subject of original nature needs to be done in terms both of the general and of the particular. He must have as a background some understanding of the characteristics of native tendencies and of their basis in the nervous system. Without this knowledge his thinking will lack perspective and he is likely to make false inferences from his observations. On the other hand, the teacher's background of information, if it is to help him in his work, needs to be translated into the concrete. The teacher must ask: What do these things mean in terms of my own pupils and of the people whom I meet from day to day?

To help you in making this practical application of the matters considered in chapter two, another chapter is given to the discussion of ''original nature.'' The list of native tendencies with which you are already familiar is followed, and in the case of each instinct answers are suggested to such questions as these: What are some evidences of the existence of this tendency? What stimulus arouses the tendency? What responses are involved in it? Of what value is the tendency to the church school teacher?

In answering these questions some suggestions are given as to changes which need to be made in the responses if Christian personality is to be developed. Later chapters tell how these changes can be made.

1. TENDENCIES TO ENGAGE IN GENERAL PHYSICAL ACTIVITY—

Much of the pupil's learning, especially during the earlier years of his life, takes place because of his tendencies to general physical activity. The child seems to find satisfaction in mere bodily movements, in manipulation and in vocalization. Anyone who has observed a very young baby, during its waking hours, will require little argument to convince him of the instinctive character of these activities. Apparently both outward and inward stimuli arouse the responses and they are varied and almost continuous during the period of wakefulness. Quite early in the life of the individual there is noticeable a wriggling of the arms and legs, and soon the grasping and fumbling with objects that lie within reach becomes an all-absorbing occupation. Vocalization begins with gurgling and cooing and, in the course of time, as a result of environmental influences takes on the form of speech and song.

Children are thus naturally active and the tendencies which, in this brief discussion, we have grouped together as "general physical activity" are of no little concern to the church school teacher. Adults have been guilty of many crimes against childhood because of failure to recognize the child's instinctive need of, and right to, activity. And the Sunday school has often been one of the most serious offenders in this regard. On the one hand it has tried to make children keep still when they should have been active and has thus run counter to their native impulses. On the other hand it has failed to provide direction for the child's active tendencies and, since these impulses have a way of asserting themselves, the school has really trained the children in habits of disorder.

Investigation has shown that "the very young child cannot sit motionless more than thirty seconds, nor children from five to ten years for more than one minute and a half."[1] The tendencies to manipulation and vocalization are likewise spontaneous and insistent. These facts must be taken into account by the church school. In its program for the younger children variety is an essential quality. Provision for drill, story-telling, worship, handwork, and other elements, will give the child a measure of freedom of movement. It is necessary also that there be plenty of opportunity for the child to tell and to do. This work, however, will not be merely for the sake of activity, for there are other values to be considered. Nevertheless the enterprises and projects, the drill and the singing, the conversation and the discussion, the processes which allow the children to be active participants instead of merely passive recipients, are all valuable ways of providing direction for the tendencies to general physical activity.

2. THE TENDENCY TO FIGHT—

The teacher who has through-the-week contacts with his class, especially if it is a class of boys, will sooner or later have to face situations among his pupils created by the instinct of pugnacity. Even the restraining influence of the teacher's presence with a group of boys on a hike or outing will not prevent the appearance of this tendency in behavior. At a Sunday school class picnic, for example, there was the beginning of a fight when one of the boys found the water-jug empty and believed a classmate had emptied it "for a joke."

But pugnacity in some form will be recognized by the observant teacher not only out-of-doors. The

---

[1]Quoted from Curtis in *Psychology of Childhood*, Norsworthy and Whitley, p. 46.

classroom will provide its cases also and the tendency will be easily distinguished even in small children in the home. The instinct to fight is really one of the most obvious of the original tendencies. Of course it very soon becomes modified by the approvals and disapprovals of society, but its strength is indicated by the fact that it so frequently appears, even in somewhat primitive form, despite the disapproval with which it is commonly met.

The stimulus which calls forth this tendency seems generally to be the obstruction of some pleasing activity, especially of some other instinctive activity. Let a mother take a toy away from a child, a boy snatch a paper or a hat away from a classmate, or a teacher quickly seize the arm of an unruly pupil, and the instinct is likely to be aroused. The interference, however, may be caused not only by persons but by things, as when a man violently kicks the chair over which he has stumbled in the dark. And the response may be varied including such acts as screaming and kicking in the young child, fist-fighting in the boy, and boisterous, highly animated protestation in the class group whose activities have been interfered with by some untactful superintendent.

The tendency to fight is a most valuable part of the original equipment of man. It lies at the root of his struggles for freedom, his conquering of obstacles, and his fighting for high and worthy principles—

> "For the right against the wrong,
> For the weak against the strong,
> For the poor who've waited long
> And the age that is to be."

Society must modify the instinct to fight but it will do itself irreparable injury if it seeks only to suppress it. The church school teacher will have many opportunities to guide this tendency and to suggest substitute responses, both in the actual situations that will arise in the life of the class-group and in the imagined situations suggested by the lesson story.

Legitimate expressions of this tendency as in fighting for a cause, may well find a place in the program of the church school, for strength of character is scarcely possible without a measure of "fighting spirit." This tendency is closely related to the instinct of self-assertion the uses of which are discussed in a later section.

3. THE TENDENCY TO ENGAGE IN SEX BEHAVIOR—

The sex instinct is thought by some psychologists to be the strongest of all native tendencies. Whether this point of view is correct or not, it is certainly true that a great deal of human behavior after the first dozen years of life, is motivated by considerations of sex. Any tendency that has such a fundamental place in life is a matter of concern to the teacher.

Sex behavior that is clearly distinguishable as such, does not appear until relatively late in the development of the normal individual. It becomes prominent during the adolescent years and continues throughout maturity. Most careful observers are agreed, however, that the sex instinct begins to play a part in life as early as the eighth or ninth year and some psychologists of the more extreme schools, maintain that its influence in some form is traceable from the earliest years of infancy.

The particular responses involved in sex behavior *after puberty has been reached* are satisfaction in the presence of the opposite sex, display, the various activities involved in mating and courtship and, as the culmination of them all, the act of sexual union. Many of the specific activities which make up these responses are, of course, the result of training and, because of the late maturing of the instinct, it is quite impossible to distinguish clearly between the learned and the unlearned elements. The presence of members of the opposite sex is normally the stimulus for this tendency. "The sex characters of the one sex," says McDougall, "are the natural keys that unlock the door of the instinct in the other sex"[2]

The sex problem and the teacher.—Despite the importance of the tendency to sex behavior, it has always been difficult to secure for it frank and unbiassed consideration. The strength of the instinct, the necessary postponement of marriage in our complex civilization, and the overstimulation of sex interest by motion-picture, stage and magazine, cause a disproportionate place to be given to matters pertaining to sex in the lives of youth. Add to this situation the unwholesome attitude of many adults for whom sex signifies that which is gross and unmentionable, and the educational problem is apparent. As in the case of almost any other instinct, abnormal development or inadequate control of this tendency may, and often does, lead to gross indecencies. But the instinct itself is of inestimable value to society.

[2]*Outline of Psychology*, p. 159.

Not only does the existence of the race depend upon it, but it makes possible much of the happiness of life and finds its highest expression in the establishment of the Christian home.

The proper attitude of the church school teacher toward the sex tendencies, can be but briefly suggested here. The teacher of almost any group of children or young people would do well to have some dependable knowledge of sex matters, especially as to the development of the instinct and the unnatural expressions of it. Problems may arise at any time, if the teacher is on intimate terms with his pupils, where such knowledge will be invaluable. A church school leader of a group of early adolescent boys while out on a "hike," found the lads to be extremely curious to know some fundamental facts about sex, and wholly without any satisfactory sources of information. On consulting with the parents of some of the group, the teacher was requested to "talk to the boys" since they felt themselves unable to do so.

But it is not just because the teacher will have to meet these special problems that his attitude in this matter is important. The regular work of the church school should, sometimes directly and often indirectly, help the developing child and adolescent toward a wholesome view of sex. And if that is to take place the teacher's own attitude must be wholesome. Moreover the program of the church school for adolescents must provide for the normal exercise, under salutary conditions, of many of the sex tendencies. An adequate social room where young people of both sexes may mingle freely, is an essential factor.

4. THE TENDENCY TO ENGAGE IN PARENTAL BEHAVIOR—
The tendency to engage in parental behavior is involved in much human conduct of the more altruistic sort. It might almost be said to be the instinctive basis of Christian service, since the love and protection of the weak or dependent is a central motive in many benevolent enterprises. One of the most significant things the church school teacher can do is to stimulate and strengthen this tendency, to widen its field, and to guide its expression into wholesome channels.

The parental or "motherly instinct," while it is perhaps strongest in a mother who has borne children, is present in males and is observable in some form, even in very young children. Normal human beings of all ages are responsive to the cries and gurgles of the baby. They respond with smiles, attention, fondling, feeding, kindliness, sympathy, and acts of protection. Some of these responses easily become attached not merely to the human infant, but to the dependent, the needy or the weak, among persons of all ages, or among animals. The interest of children in babies, in dolls and in pets is rooted in this instinct.

The value of the parental tendency to the teacher and to society in general is obvious. McDougall says that it is "Nature's brightest and most beautiful invention . . . . the only truly altruistic element in Nature," and "the mother of both intellect and morality."[3] Its place and value in our civilization is evidenced by many of the most humane institutions

---

[3] McDougall, *Outline of Psychology*, p. 130-1. J. W. Luce and Co., Boston. Used by permission.

of society and of the church which have brought succor and comfort to the aged, the homeless, the sick, and the dependent of all kinds. The "tender emotion," the kindliness and sympathy, which accompany this tendency, are among the highest of human traits and, properly directed, may lead to the kind of love which is the core of Christian character.

As in the case of each of the other instincts this tendency requires direction and training. It is possible for it to shrivel into sickly sentimentalism or to develop into a strong and genuine social passion, according to the direction given to it by the processes of education. The wise Christian teacher will recognize this fact and will seek to engage his pupils in enterprises of Christian service which appeal to the parental instinct, and will not be satisfied to let the sympathy and kindliness of the child merely fritter away in sentimental expressions of pity. One of the most important phases of the task of the Christian educator is, as Shaver well says, "to stimulate habits of thinking as to why and how there may be more 'intelligent, active good will' in the world, to build into the nervous structure of the individual and into the accustomed ways of mankind yet undiscovered types of loving service."[4] A party for the unfortunate, a neighborly act for the shut-in, a song service for the aged, or the establishing of a recreational center for the children of the community are activities which will help to direct in a wholesome way the "tendency to engage in parental behavior."

[4]Shaver, *The Project Principle in Religious Education*, p. 42. University of Chicago Press. Used by permission.

5. THE TENDENCY TO SEEK THE COMPANY OF OTHERS—
Among the social instincts, which are so significant
for the development of Christian character, is the
tendency to seek the company of others, or the
gregarious instinct. This tendency is apparent even
in babyhood. It is evidenced by the satisfaction of the
infant in the mere presence of others and in his dissatisfied crying at being left alone. In later childhood
and early adolescence it takes the form of the desire
for associates of one's own age and its prominence
at this period has led some writers to speak loosely
of a "gang instinct." And in adult life, while many
other factors also impel men and women to seek
group associations, there can be little doubt that the
gregarious impulse lies at the root of much of our
social grouping, the satisfaction of city life and the
popularity of clubs, societies, and fraternities.

There is good reason to believe that this tendency,
which for convenience has been called gregariousness,
goes much further than the seeking of the mere presence of others. Woodworth suggests that the impulse
is not completely satisfied until there is *participation*
in what the group is doing.[5] And the behavior of
children often seems to indicate that this desire to
have a part in the activity of the group has its instinctive roots. When the impulse is inhibited the
child perhaps remains dissatisfied and lonely even in
the presence of his fellows. Fear, or some other
impulse, keeps him from "getting into the game."
In such cases there is obvious satisfaction when,
through sympathetic approach or merely by being

[5]*Psychology*, p. 147.

left alone, the inhibitions are finally overcome and the child gets "into the swing" of the group activity.

This fact should mean much to the church school teacher. In his effort to make his class a miniature Christian society in which there is co-operation and the sharing of experience, nature is not against him. There are native tendencies that are his allies. And if the group is engaged in doing things that are of interest to the pupils, these impulses will often aid him in securing the kind of co-operative behavior he desires.

The pupil is, of course, equipped with other tendencies besides those which lead him to find satisfaction in working with the group. And these often make co-operation difficult. Yet of all the lessons of life perhaps none is more important than that men learn how to live and work together. Upon their success in learning this lesson the future of society depends. And a beginning may be made in learning it in the group life of childhood and youth. The leader of almost any class or club will have many opportunities to teach co-operation and in this work he will be greatly helped by the pupil's desire to share in what the group is doing. Moreover the gregarious tendency will also make more easy the development of group loyalties which, if properly balanced by a wide social sympathy, may lay the foundation for a higher loyalty to the kingdom of God.

Sympathy, suggestion, and imitation.—Closely related to gregariousness are several other tendencies which must here be given brief consideration because of their place in the development of character. In his life in the group the individual tends to feel, to think, and to do as those about him feel, think and do. To these tendencies McDougall has given the names "sympathy," "suggestion," and "imitation." The terms do not mean, however, precisely what is meant by them in common speech.

Sympathy refers to "a sympathetic induction of emotion,"[6] and is a kind of reflex imitation by which the feelings of, say, the child are affected by the emotional attitudes of the group. Most of us have noted the difference in our feelings on coming into the midst of a group of mourners and on entering a group of merry-makers. It is not necessary that we understand all of the reasons for the sorrow or for the happiness of the company. The emotional tone seems to have a sort of contagion about it. Our feelings soon harmonize with those of the group.

Suggestion is the tendency to accept the views of the group without any "logically adequate grounds" for their acceptance. It is, of course, extremely valuable in education although it has certain inherent dangers. How easily the political and religious views of the parents become merely re-echoed in the lives of the children unless they are broken into by rational considerations, or by the "suggestions" of more influential groups than the family.

Imitation has commonly been thought of as an instinctive impulse to do almost anything and everything that others have been observed doing. In recent years, however, this view has received much criticism. There is, of course, an instinctive basis for the tendency "to do as others do," but there is

---

[6]McDougall, *An Introduction to Social Psychology*, p. 94.

probably much more of learning in the imitative acts of children and young people than the views of some psychologists have admitted. The little girl, for example, does not dress her doll because the instinct of imitation impels her to do what she sees her mother doing, but because she has learned to dress her doll and has found doll-play satisfying to herself. Imitation is nevertheless of tremendous value in education for it greatly enriches the child's experience and shortens the process of learning. Children learn to imitate and then, through imitative acts, gain experience in many important activities of life.

All of these tendencies—sympathy, suggestion, and imitation—may help or hinder the church school teacher in the attainment of his goals, according to the character of the environment in which the pupil lives. And since the church school has the pupil for such a small proportion of his time, it is doubly important that its every influence be wholesome. The whole life of the school must be such as to stimulate feelings of happy fellowship and reverent good will, its suggestions must be worthy, and its activities must be of a kind that the child may well imitate.

The gregarious instinct, then, lies at the root of man's associative life and because of the related tendencies of sympathy, suggestion and imitation, he tends to grow into the likeness of those with whom he associates.

6. THE TENDENCY TO BE ASSERTIVE—

The church school teacher will constantly have to deal with the tendency in his pupils toward self-assertion and mastery. If this instinct is not rightly guided in the life of the individual it may lead to a character that is egotistical, overbearing and blatantly self-assertive or, on the other hand, it may produce a personality that is meekly submissive, thoughtlessly obedient and altogether lacking in initiative and self-reliance. "Of all the native tendencies," says Woodworth, "this is the one most frequently aroused, since there is scarcely a moment of waking (or dreaming) life when it is not more or less in action."[7]

This tendency may be thought of as including such responses as overcoming obstructions, resistance of domination, rivalry and positive domination of things or persons. It appears very early in life and is the basis of such worthy traits as determination and persistency. A child of five was playing with a typewriter making row upon row of letters. When about a third of the way down the page she said to her father, "My, I am tired, but I am going to make a whole page just like you do." She persisted in her work, with intermittent sighs, until the page was filled with black letters and then, pushing it aside, said with evident satisfaction, "There, I did it." There was value in the experience even though the product was a page of meaningless letters.

The tendency may be observed in a thousand situations in life—in the child who objects to doing what he is told, in the boy who is not satisfied until he has made his sand castle stay in position, in the young leader who somehow gets his playmates to play the games he wants, in the youth who deliberately flies in the face of convention, in the team that fights till the last minute of play to overcome its

[7]*Psychology*, p. 161.

traditional rival, and in the Alpine climber who, asked why he risks his life in the effort to climb Everest, replies, "Just because it is there."

The school of the past was guilty of gross injustice to the child in its effort constantly to crush his self-assertiveness unless it happened to express itself in certain very limited forms of school work. The modern school, recognizing that initiative and self-reliance are essentials of strong character, seeks to give greater place in its program to the child's tendencies to be assertive. Whenever possible pupil initiative is called into play and the satisfaction that accompanies mastery of a thing is made use of in getting the child to "beat" his own record.

The church school must provide for the proper exercise of this tendency. It is a most valuable ally of the teacher and too often the only form in which it is appealed to is in the unwholesome rivalry of a membership contest with some other group of pupils. The wise teacher will find many opportunities to use and to direct the instinct of assertiveness. Pupils will be encouraged to take part in class discussion and to suggest things for the class to do, their views will be given a sympathetic hearing although they may be very inadequate, the children will be given reasonable recognition for worthy achievement, and they will be constantly encouraged to improve their past record either as individuals or as groups. In the period of adolescence leadership will be recognized and will be given responsibilities, and independence of thought will be welcomed. By these and other means the teacher will provide for wholesome, and guard against unwholesome, expressions of self-assertion. There is no place in Christian character for the conceit and arrogance that come from the wrong development of this tendency. On the other hand its thwarting may produce such abnormalities as sullenness, shame, and excessive envy and jealousy.

7. THE TENDENCY TO BE SUBMISSIVE—

The complementary tendency to that of self-assertion and mastery is what has been called "the instinct of submission." There seems to be a native tendency not only to resist and to dominate persons and things but also, under certain circumstances, to surrender and to submit to them and to find a genuine satisfaction in so doing. Of course for this to be true the submission must be voluntary. A forced surrender is irritating rather than satisfying and is really thwarted self-assertion. Cases of obstinacy among children attract attention because of the problems which they raise. The adult is apt to forget, at such times, that the child is throughout the greater part of his activity thoroughly tractable and that much of his learning depends upon this quality in him. The tendency to submission is to be traced in a child's yielding to the control of older persons, in the deference of a youth to the leader of his gang, in the student's feeling of dependence before the superior knowledge of the scholar, and perhaps in the religious experience of a Newman as, after years of struggle, he submits to the authority of the Church of Rome.

Submissiveness is by no means a trait to be despised although some writers on the subject of leadership would seem to suggest that, at least among those young people who are to be leaders, it should have no place. But the best leaders are, as a rule, good followers also and the over self-assertive individual is an impossible sort of person for any co-operative enterprise.

The tendency to be submissive, together with the emotion of humility that accompanies it, is an important instinctive root of the religious attitude. It is involved in an obedient spirit and, along with other tendencies, makes possible such religious attitudes as awe and reverence. One of the greatest of modern thinkers upon religion (Schleiermacher) has shown that close to the heart of it is the feeling of "absolute dependence." And while we can scarcely limit the essence of religion to this one element, perhaps all genuinely religious persons will agree that the sense of dependence is an essential aspect of the religious experience.

Closely related to this tendency is *the impulse to trust* which may be considered the correlate of the parental instinct. Trustfulness has its instinctive roots and few responses are more essential to the Christian attitude. Long ago the Master Teacher called attention to this trait of childhood and told his grown-up disciples that, in this respect, they must become like children if they would enter the kingdom of God. Reverent teaching about God, provision for worship "under conditions that are controlled by an educative purpose"[8] and a wholesome atmosphere that inspires confidence, will do much toward rightly guiding the tendency of the child to be submissive and trustful.

---

[8]Weigle and Tweedy, *Training the Devotional Life,* p. 63.

8. THE TENDENCY TO AVOID OR SEEK TO ESCAPE—

In the early part of life, whether due wholly to original nature or in part to training, man comes to be afraid of many things that are not worthy objects of fear. He may also be unafraid in situations that are fraught with danger. To bring about changes in the fears of the growing child—to rationalize and moralize them—is, then, one of the important functions of education and is a legitimate objective for the teacher in the church school.

The tendency to flight has as its most characteristic responses shrinking or hiding from the object arousing the instinct, crying, clinging to another person or running away. It is especially difficult here to determine what elements are really instinctive and what are due to training. One investigator who studied carefully the fears of young children became convinced that the child is not instinctively afraid of cats, rabbits, rats, the dark, and the like, but that the only two important original stimuli to fear are sudden loss of support and sudden noise.[9] In addition to these stimuli McDougall includes among the "keys to the gates of fear" the sudden movement of a large object, the danger cry of others, bodily pain and the mysterious or uncanny.[10] Whatever the conditions are that originally arouse the tendency to escape, the responses of fear become noticeable very early in the life of the child. A nine-months-old girl whose parents had been careful to avoid suggesting fear in any way to the child, screamed frantically at the approach of a large black dog and on a number of

---

[9] Watson, *Psychology from the Standpoint of a Behaviorist,* p. 199.

[10] *Outline of Psychology,* p. 152.

different occasions reacted similarly at the sudden approach of a cat or even a chicken. The fear of the dark may not be a native reaction but it is at least a very common one which children generally have to learn to overcome. And a child's religion may help him in gaining this victory. A boy of six was overheard saying to his younger brother in the dark bedroom, "Why don't you do what I do when I am afraid?" "What do you do?" inquired the four-year-old. "I say what I learned in Sunday school," came the reply, " 'In Thee O Lord, do I put my trust.' Then I am all right."

Seeking to escape punishment is another form of the avoiding reactions that have an instinctive basis and in this tendency is to be found the explanation of many of the lies of childhood. But fear and the impulse to escape are not characteristics of childhood only. They persist throughout life. The average adult seeks to escape from such experiences as the censure of his fellows, the knowledge of unpleasant and disconcerting facts and, to use an illustration of Professor Thorndike, from the scorn of "untipped waiters, cabmen and barbers."

Education, and especially religious education, should help the individual to rationalize his fears. The teacher must endeavor to make the child fear the lie more than the punishment; to bring the timid enquirer to fear self-deception rather than the knowledge of disconcerting facts; and to cause men everywhere more strongly to fear the disapproval of God than the censure of the crowd. To assist the pupil in such a development is one of the tasks of the church school teacher who must seek not to eliminate fear but to enlighten and redirect it. And in doing this the religious faith of the pupil may be a most significant factor. The conviction that "this is my Father's world" will do much to remove terror. It will do so because it inspires love and love purges fear of its unworthy elements. On the other hand, love and fear, together with humility, are blended in the more complex emotion of reverence which is an essential element in any high and worthy religious attitude. A recent and most thoughtful study of religious experience finds its psychological root to be a sense of awe-inspiring, yet fascinating mystery.[11] In religious awe the instinct of fear reaches its highest and most refined expression.

9. THE TENDENCY TO EXPLORE OR TO BE CURIOUS—

The impulse to escape runs counter, at times, to another tendency, namely that of exploration. The "mysterious" for example, may stimulate the curiosity of the investigator while at the same time putting him on his guard and bringing to a state of readiness the neurones involved in flight. Anyone who has attempted to investigate a strange sound on a dark night will have experienced these conflicting impulses and will feel, no doubt, that both of them have an instinctive basis.

The tendency to explore is closely related to manipulation, fighting and other native behavior but it involves something more than these tendencies. There is an instinctive satisfaction not merely in handling things, but in investigating them, finding out what is in them, tasting them, smelling them,

---

[11] *The Idea of the Holy,* Rudolf Otto.

rattling them and exploring their every nook and corner. Novel and unfamiliar things tend to arouse curiosity and since "the world is so full of a number of things" the young child has much to be curious about. As he grows older and becomes able to make use of language his explorations may be carried on by means of reading or by the questioning of adults. The persistency of the child in asking "Why?" and "How?" has become embarrassing to many a parent although it is a most valuable part of the native equipment of the individual.

One of the severest criticisms that can be made against the formal school is that it has too often thwarted, rather than stimulated, the natural curiosity of the child. The boy who is constantly making investigations and asking questions in his informal play- and home-life has in many cases had the channels of learning choked by the formalism of the school. At a parent-teachers meeting in a small town the teacher of one of the grades complained that the children were constantly "prying into things that were none of their business" and asked the parents to help her curb their curiosity. A wiser teacher would have sought to guide the exploring tendencies of the children into more worthy activities. The better schools of today strive to give the largest possible recognition to the interests of the pupils.

The value for the teacher of this tendency to explore can scarcely be overestimated. It is not the only instinctive basis of learning but it has in it "the germ of seeking for knowledge" and it tends to make learning satisfying in itself. The teacher of religion no less than any other, must recognize this fact. If he is wise he will welcome the pupil's questions and will meet them with the best truth he knows. To ignore them or to give answers that are merely evasive will but cause the pupil to seek his information elsewhere or else to feel that, in religion, questions are not to be asked. And even very young children may enquire concerning matters that are really profound and that call for the most careful consideration.

The church school teacher who enters into the life of his pupils during the week will be able many times to guide and to satisfy their tendency to exploration. On hikes and picnics there will be questions concerning nature, the processes of life, and many other matters in which he will be able to help the young people toward satisfactory answers. And, in many cases, the same enquiring attitude will be encountered in the classroom. At times the teacher will answer the questions himself. At other times he will guide the pupils to the sources of information. Thus by the use of Bibles and reference books and through investigations into church and community affairs, he will appeal to the desire to know so as to produce an intelligent and informed religious attitude.

10. THE TENDENCY TO SEEK THE APPROVAL OF OTHERS—

All learning, and especially that involved in moral and religious training, depends in a large measure upon the tendency to seek the approval of others. And this tendency is no doubt a part of the original nature of man. The fact that the pupil by nature finds satisfaction and happiness in smiles, approving looks and praise, and is irritated and displeased by

scowls of disapproval places in the hands of the
teacher and of society a most powerful means of
controlling the behavior of the developing child. Of
course, the presence of tendencies which lead in other
directions may make the right kind of appeal to this
instinct somewhat difficult, but few original tendencies are more important in the development of
moral personality than the desire for approval.[12]
Especially in the early years of childhood is the use
of commendation a legitimate and necessary means
of securing right conduct and while the developing
personality should become increasingly free from dependence upon mere praise, there are some natures
that wither under criticism but become very efficient
with reasonable approval.

A great deal of human conduct has its instinctive
roots in this tendency to seek the approval of others.
The little child whose tricks are laughed at and therefore approved, despite half-hearted words of disapproval; the seven-year-old girl who hides her spelling
paper from her parents because she failed to "get
a hundred"; the boy who prepares his Sunday school
lesson with great care because of his admiration of
the teacher; the youth who is restrained from immoral conduct by the thought of a disapproving society or who is impelled to some risk in order to
please "the gang"; the politician who fails to stand
for his principles because of his desire to remain in
the political ring—in these and in a host of similar
situations faced daily by people of all ages, the desire
for approval is a dominant factor.

---

[12]See the discussion of the different levels of conduct in
chapter vii.

It is the business of the church school, both by its formal teaching and by its whole organized life, to give a discriminating approval to the right kinds of responses, that is, to those that point in the direction of Christian character. If wrongly directed the impulse to seek approval may produce the stalwart defender of traditionalism, the slave of fashion, and the pander to the crowds. On the other hand, much of what society "approves" is not mere convention but is due to the moral experience of the race or to the insight of its prophets and seers—a fact that is being strangely overlooked by some of the advocates of the new morality. The foundation of any genuinely moral life must be laid in the approval of the family, the school, the church, and the community. With the acquiring of knowledge, the broadening of experience, and the deepening of insight, a higher approval will be sought and the growth of the Christian may continue until even the cry of the multitude for his blood cannot deter him from his purpose because of the inner approval of the voice of God.

QUESTIONS—

1. What attitude should the teacher take toward the question of boys' fights?
2. What instincts, by acting counter to the fighting tendency, tend to hold it in check?
3. Does your Church school program make adequate provision for the normal and wholesome expression of the gregarious and sex tendencies of the pupils? How is such provision made?
4. Why is the parental instinct of special significance in religious education?
5. How do sympathy suggestion and imitation tend to mould the child into the likeness of the group in which he lives? Give specific illustrations of the operation of these tendencies.
6. Why does the list of original tendencies given in the text not include a "religious instinct"?

7. Which of the instincts seem to you to be most directly concerned in behavior that is distinctly religious?
8. What evidences of fear have you observed in children? Do you think the fear response was instinctive or learned? Why?
9. Do Church school teachers, as you have observed them, encourage or discourage the questions of enquiring minds?
10. Is the desire to secure the approval of the teacher a sound motive for the child's doing an assigned task?

REPORTS AND INVESTIGATIONS—

1. Bring to class a number of cases of behavior that was largely instinctive, which you have yourself observed in children, young people, or adults.
2. Make a list of instances, either from observation or from reading, showing how native tendencies have helped or have hindered the work of the teacher.
3. Indicate which of the instinctive tendencies are most directly involved in: (a) The worship service, (b) the recreational program, (c) the membership "contest," (d) the missionary offering, (e) the promotion of pupils, (f) the Senior Department Social, (g) the discussion group, (h) the class lecture.
4. Compare the lists of instincts given in several of the books referred to at the close of the chapter. Upon which tendencies is there the most general agreement?

REFERENCES—

Betts and Hawthorne, Method in Teaching Religion, chap. ii. Abingdon Press.

Coe, George A., A Social Theory of Religious Education, chap. x. Scribners.

Gates, Arthur I., Psychology for Students of Education, chap. vii. Macmillan.

McDougall, William, An Introduction to Social Psychology, chaps. iii and iv. J. W. Luce & Co.

—, Outline of Psychology, chap. v. Scribners.

Thorndike, Edward L., The Original Nature of Man, chaps. iii and v-xiii. Teachers' College.

Woodworth, Robert S., Psychology, chap. viii. Henry Holt.

CHAPTER IV

INDIVIDUAL DIFFERENCES

Why and How Do Pupils Differ From One Another?

In chapters two and three consideration has been given to those basic human tendencies which are common to all pupils. You are concerned about these tendencies as a teacher because they are, in a sense, the raw material with which you work. Every member of your class possesses them and the changes which you are seeking to make in your pupils are largely dependent upon them. You will have observed, however, that no two of your class-members are quite alike even in their instinctive behavior. The tendency to seek the company of others, for example, seems excessively strong in one boy while another perhaps lives largely to himself. And in many other traits your pupils, although they may be of the same age and of the same sex, show marked differences. Some of the points of dissimilarity are of course quite obvious. Others may easily be overlooked. As you think over the names of the members of your class and call to mind the personality of each pupil, you will be able, no doubt, to note differences in height, weight, color of hair and eyes, vigor, quickness of movement, interest, talkativeness, responsiveness to approval or disapproval, and in many other traits. Such variations in the traits possessed by different individuals are referred to by psychologists as "individual differences."

Your work as a church school teacher is largely with the individual. The more intimate your knowledge, the more sympathetic your understanding of each member of your class group, the greater will be the likelihood of your making the kind of changes in their lives which the efficient teacher of religion desires to make. It will be evident then that effective teaching calls for a knowledge and understanding of "individual differences," of the nature and extent of them, and of their causes.

Even a casual observer of human life would quickly note that many differences among individuals are due to different teaching and training. But the study of the variations in human traits makes it very plain that many of them are due not to environment but to inherited equipment, to original nature. Not only are black-haired parents likely to have black-haired children, but the same sort of thing is true of other more subtle traits which are of greater importance to the teacher, although they are perhaps more difficult to trace.

The treatment of individual differences which is taken up in this chapter is in one sense, therefore, a continuation of the discussion of original nature. In the last two chapters consideration was given to those tendencies possessed by all individuals, at least in a degree, and which therefore tend to make all people alike. The present chapter deals with those tendencies, capacities, or traits largely although not wholly due to original nature, which tend to make people differ from one another.

The questions to be asked are: (1) In what respects do pupils differ from one another? (2) To what extent do they differ? (3) Why must special attention be given to the exceptional child? (4) What are the causes of the differences among individuals? And (5) What should be the attitude of the teacher toward individual differences?

IN WHAT RESPECTS DO PUPILS DIFFER FROM ONE ANOTHER?—

No two pupils are precisely alike. There are very noticeable differences among children of the same parents and even the so-called "identical twins" show pretty clearly that they are not identical. All normal children play, but they differ very greatly in the vigor with which they "get into the game." The instinct of pugnacity is part of the original equipment of every individual, yet there are boys who seldom fight and others who are "always fighting." Growth is a universal characteristic of healthy children, but no two children grow at exactly the same rate, nor with the same evenness of development. Every normal person has two thumbs but criminologists have long made use of the fact that the thumb markings of the individual differ from those of every other.

Pupils differ from one another, then, in a large number of traits and almost any group of children will illustrate these differences. In a single grade of the public school, or of the church school, there will be found children of varying height, weight, volume of body, color of hair, color of eyes, attractiveness of face, and the like. And these children will differ likewise in traits less easily observed. A group of seventh- and eighth-grade children, for example, were found by Chambers to show marked differences in handgrip, cancellation of a's from a page of print, addition of figures, spelling, making associations, memory of things heard and memory of things seen.[1] The use of various kinds of intelligence and educational tests has, in recent years, brought a much clearer recognition of such variations in the performance of children, and the more careful measurement of physical traits has shown the differences to extend even to such things as heartbeat and speed of digestion.

The church school teacher is, however, more especially concerned about the "individual differences" which need to be recognized in dealing with the religious development of children. Yet it is quite impossible to separate these traits entirely from others. Religious growth would seem to be at least largely dependent upon such factors as learning ability, intelligence, memory and sociability, and in these traits children show marked differences. An interesting question, although one that cannot be answered with certainty at the present stage of experimentation, is whether there are the same kinds of differences among

---

[1]*Journal of Educational Psychology*, Vol. I, pp. 61-75, quoted by Inglis, *Principles of Secondary Education*, p. 76.

children in inborn moral and religious capacity. It would seem likely that there are large original differences in these traits as in others.

To what extent do pupils differ from one another?—

The importance for the teacher of the differences between individuals largely depends upon the degree of the unlikeness. Two pupils may differ from each other in intelligence but the difference may be so slight that, for all practical purposes, the children may be treated alike. On the other hand, the differences may be so great that to treat the children in the same manner would be quite unfair to them and would make impossible the attainment of the teacher's real objective. If individual differences are slight, they may be ignored. If they are considerable, they must be recognized.

The measurement of these differences is therefore a matter of very great importance. It is one of the most fruitful phases of modern educational science. Not until ways were devised for measuring the various traits was it possible to understand the extent to which pupils differ from one another. Of course thoughtful teachers had always observed that one pupil was perhaps quick in responding to questions, that another was slow, and that still another seemed altogether unable to grasp the meaning of the question. But there was no adequate appreciation of the nature and extent of the unlikeness in any reasonably large group of children.

Differences among individuals with respect to some traits have now been investigated pretty thoroughly. Tests have been worked out so that the performance of pupils in school studies and in certain other activities can be noted and the degrees of difference can be measured. Studies have been made of large numbers of children and these have shown very clearly that, in any trait measured, there are large differences between the extreme cases. They have shown also that among any fairly large group of people differences as to intelligence, arithmetical ability, height in inches, or any other trait, will be distributed in a

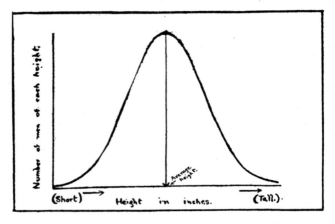

Curve showing normal distribution of height in a large unselected group of men.

fairly regular manner. Perhaps about sixty per cent of the group will differ from one another only slightly, thirty per cent will differ quite considerably, and ten per cent will show very marked differences.

Differences shown by the distribution curve.—Such facts as these are usually made clear by portraying them in diagrammatic form. The study of any sufficiently large group of men selected at random would reveal differences in height which would be represented by the normal distribution curve.

The significance of this curve will readily be understood. The larger number of men, it will be noted, are grouped about the average height and the number of cases decreases according to the distance away from the average either in the direction of shortness or in the direction of tallness. The number of cases falling below the average is equal to that above it. The extreme differences in height are shown by the ends of the curve.

A similar distribution to the one just considered would be found if almost any other trait were measured instead of height. For example, Terman found that the intelligence quotients of 905 unselected children ranged all the way from about 60 (feeblemindedness) to 140 (near genius). One third of the children, however, fell between 96 and 105.[2]

As illustrations of the extent to which individuals differ from one another, differences in height and in intelligence have been used. The same kind of variation would of course be found if almost any other trait were measured, provided the number of people were sufficiently large and they did not constitute a "picked" group. Obviously if individuals were selected because of their possession of a particular trait the nature of the distribution would be altered. The group might then contain all tall people, or all short people, or all people of high intelligence. The range of differences which is portrayed in the normal distribution curve is dependent upon what is called a "random selection" of individuals.

---

[2]See Terman: *The Measurement of Intelligence,* p. 66.

If an investigator were to take say every fifth name in the city directory, or perhaps every third name on the public school roll, he would have a group that would be fairly typical of all the people of the city, or of all the pupils in the school.

The teacher's interest in individual differences.— The church school teacher is interested in the differences in intelligence among his pupils. If they are considerable he will need to recognize them in the treatment of the members of his class. But he is even more concerned about other traits such as co-operativeness, desire to do the right, friendliness, loyalty, self-control, faith, and the like. At the present time standard tests for the measurement of such traits are not available. It is not possible, therefore, to secure objective knowledge of the range of differences among individuals with respect to such qualities. There can be little doubt, however, that whether due to original nature or to training, the variability would be very similar to that of the traits which can be measured.

The practical question for the teacher to ask concerning any particular pupil is: Where, in the curve of distribution, does this boy or this girl belong? The position of the pupil as to some traits may be determined with a fair degree of accuracy. It may be possible for the teacher, for example, to learn from the public school the relative positions of his pupils as shown by tests of intelligence and of school achievement. But in many important matters the judgment of the teacher will have to be depended upon. Obviously if a pupil belongs near the upper end of the curve he is a very different sort of individual and will need to be treated differently from one who belongs at the lower end of the curve. Two boys in a Sunday school class may be inattentive and troublesome but that fact should not be interpreted to mean that both pupils should be treated alike. The teacher who will take the trouble to find out all he can about the boys may find that one is rather below normal in reading ability and the use of words, while the other, perhaps, is considerably above the average in this ability. The one may be inattentive because the oral work is too difficult for him, the other because it is too easy.[3] One may be helped most by giving him a larger part in handwork and class activities, the other by promoting him to another grade in the church school. In a similar manner the many other differences among the pupils in a given group will call for different kinds of treatment both in the work of the class and in the teacher's personal contacts with the pupils outside of the class period. The more consideration the teacher gives to the individual pupil, the more effective his teaching is likely to be.

WHY MUST SPECIAL ATTENTION BE GIVEN TO THE EXCEPTIONAL CHILD?—

The study of individual differences has called special attention to two classes of pupils, namely, those at each extreme of the curve of distribution. These pupils are, of course, the individuals having the trait being studied in an exceedingly high degree or, at the other extreme, those that are almost altogether lacking in it. They are the so-called "ex-

[3]See *Case Studies for Teachers of Religion*, Watson and Watson, p. 102-109.

ceptional children.'' The school is particularly concerned about differences in ''general intelligence''
and in ability to do school work. In these respects
the exceptional child may be either supernormal or
subnormal, that is, his ability may be far above the
average, or far below it. If the ability of the child
is so much above the average as to make him, say,
one in a hundred, he is a child of very superior intelligence. If he falls so far below the average as to
make him one in a hundred, he probably should be
considered feeble-minded. There is no marked break
between the different degrees of ability in a sufficiently large, unselected group of children. Abilities
will be found to be distributed according to the normal curve and to range all the way from perhaps
definite feeble-mindedness to what may be called
''near genius.'' The great majority of pupils of course
cluster about the average, but the children at the extremes of the curve deserve some special consideration.

The public school has come to realize in recent
years that it must make some provision in its work
for these two groups of exceptional children. The
more progressive school programs make it possible
for the children of rather unusual ability either to
progress at a faster rate than the other children, or
to widen the scope of their training by following a
broader and richer course of study. Similarly the
group of children whose ability is so limited as to
make it impossible for them to be benefited by ordinary school work are being trained in special schools
with a different curriculum and different methods of
teaching. In many cases highly trained teachers who
have made a thorough study of the needs of the sub-

normal child are employed to teach the children in this group.

The church as well as the school must recognize its responsibility toward exceptional groups. And it must never forget that young people who possess exceptional ability may become either the most valuable or the most dangerous citizens. They may come to occupy the places of moral and spiritual leadership in our civilization, or they may swell the number of ingenious criminals or brilliant but corrupt politicians who are a constant source of the ill-health of society. The outcome will be determined largely by the kind of education given to these "leaders in the making." Their value to society will depend upon their sense of moral responsibility and their spiritual discernment. And these qualities of life will be best developed by a genuinely religious education. The church, therefore, must share with the public school the responsibility for training children and young people of exceptional ability. Such training will involve, among other things, provision for these young people to participate in the affairs of the church, a leadership training program that will discover and develop their special abilities, and a sympathetic response at all times to their enquiring attitude of mind and their youthful impatience of mere convention.

WHAT ARE THE CAUSES OF THE DIFFERENCES AMONG INDIVIDUALS?—

The teacher's concern about the differences among his pupils is, of course, not limited to the exceptional children. The members of any class group will be benefited by a more individual treatment and a clearer recognition of their points of dissimilarity.

And any adequate understanding of the problem of differences involves a knowledge of their causes. Some of the variations are changeable by education and some of them are not; some are due to hereditary factors and others to environmental influences. Although it is quite impossible to separate the contribution of the various factors that constitute the make-up of the individual, it is clear that some of the traits in which people differ are due to their sex, others to the race to which they belong, others to their particular family inheritance, others to their age or maturity, and still others to the many environmental influences that have played upon them from the beginning of life. The causes of individual differences may thus be classified as sex, race, family, maturity, and environment.

1. *Differences due to sex.*—The church school has recognized sex differences by its organization of "boys" and "girls" classes. And society has always spoken of some traits as being "boyish" and others "girlish." In recent years, however, psychologists have become interested in the question as to just what traits are really due to sex and not to the different treatment given to boys and to girls from their earliest years. They have also attempted to find out, by the experimental method, how great are the differences between the sexes.

One of the earlier studies of sex differences was that of Dr. H. B. Thompson[4] who gave a variety of tests to a group of men and women students in the University of Chicago. The tests measured, among other things, motor ability, skin and muscle sensitive-

---

[4]*Educational Psychology*, Thorndike, Vol. III, pp. 171-180.

ness, hearing, vision, memory, ingenuity, and the ability to give general, literary and scientific information. The experiment showed some small variations in particular traits but, on the whole, indicated that there was no marked difference between the sexes. Other experiments have pointed in the same general direction. In some of them the attempt has been made to rate boys and girls in traits which can scarcely be measured objectively. The results of these and other tests have suggested that boys are more athletic, more self-assertive, duller in conscience, and slightly superior in such subjects as geometry, physics and chemistry; and that girls are more emotional, more unselfish, and slightly superior in memory and in such subjects as languages and literature.

A common view, supported by such authorities as Thorndike, is that men are more variable than women. If this view is correct it would mean that in any large unselected group of men and women, or perhaps of boys and girls, the males would tend to be at the extremes of the distribution curve with respect to any given trait and the females would show a greater tendency to group about the average. There seems to be considerable evidence that this is the case, although the view is by no means clearly established so far, at least, as such a trait as intelligence is concerned.

It is becoming increasingly clear that the native differences between the sexes are much less than has been thought to be the case in the past. Even some of the traits which have been considered peculiarly "feminine" or "masculine" are probably due, in a large measure, to the training given by society rather than to original nature. From the earliest years society brings all its force to bear upon the girl in order to bring her actions into harmony with what girls are "supposed to do." The boy is similarly trained to do the things proper for boys. Their native equipment may be much more alike than the final product would seem to suggest. In appealing to the interests of his pupils, however, the teacher will be compelled to give consideration to the differences between boys and girls whether they are due to nature or to training.

After discussing a number of experiments in the field of sex differences, Thorndike summarizes the results in the following statement "Sex is the cause of only a small fraction of the differences between individuals. The differences of men from men and of women from women are nearly as great as the differences between men and women."[5]

Sex differences and the school.—The program of the church school, as a rule, gives little recognition to sex differences until the child has gone beyond middle childhood. In later childhood the sexes are usually separated for class work, although this division should probably be considered of less importance than age grouping when the numbers are too small to permit of both age and sex classification. During the period of adolescence, sex differentiation has been very largely practiced.

Probably no rigid rule can be laid down regarding the separation of the sexes in the church school. That too much weight may have been given to sex group-

[5]*Educational Psychology,* Vol. III, p. 205. Teachers College, N. Y.

ing in the past is suggested by the trend of the experimental studies of sex differences, and by the fact that modern educational theory seeks to make the life of the school as much like normal life outside of the school as possible. There seems to be good reason for the separation of the sexes during the early years of the adolescent period. Above this level, however, the class groupings should, no doubt, be somewhat flexible. Obviously where there are very different interests, there should be separate groups for study and investigation. But differences in interests will, as time goes on, be less and less determined merely by considerations of sex. Youths and maidens must live their lives together in the larger world. Except where peculiar problems are involved, they should learn to live together, on a Christian level, in the activities of the church school. And as they grow toward maturity, an adequate church program will call them both—men and women—into a partnership of service.

2. *Differences due to race.*—Among the individual differences which the teacher may have to consider are those that are due to remote ancestry or race. In the more homogeneous communities the problem of racial differences may be negligible. In some situations, however, the observant teacher may find himself compelled to study and to give recognition to the racial characteristics of his pupils.

The scientific study of differences between races has been exceedingly difficult. It has been impossible to secure for testing purposes a small group of people who were truly representative of a race. Various comparisons between negro and white children have been made on the basis of tests by Mayo, Pyle, and others and on the whole the white children have shown superiority in school work. The difficulty of securing true racial representatives is, however, well illustrated by the fact that in the Army Tests the negroes of one section of the country were very superior to those of another locality.

Numerous other tests have been given by experimentors in an effort to measure racial differences, but there is as yet little scientific knowledge of the importance, or of the amount, of unlikeness due to race.

3. *Differences due to family inheritance.*—The most obvious cause of individual differences, apart from training, is family inheritance. The fact that children resemble their parents and thus tend to differ from children of other families, is a matter of common observation. It is generally taken for granted that tall parents will have tall children, that there are family resemblances in face, walk, build, and manner which may be recognized in children of the same parents, and that the offspring of parents who are possessed of exceptional ability will likewise be above the average in ability. Of course there are individual cases which do not seem to be in harmony with these general observations and these exceptions are sometimes confusing to the casual observer. A short man may be the son of tall parents, a mother who is highly talented in the fine arts may bear a child who has no ear for music, and a child of the manse may have little or no interest in things religious. Such cases as these are, however, more or less exceptional. They show clearly the complexity of the factors that contribute to the hereditary equipment of man.

To determine how far family resemblances are due to original nature, and how far they are the result of the particular kind of training provided by the family is not a simple matter. Nevertheless some traits are clearly due to inheritance. The particular contour of the face which makes a boy look like his father, the color of hair and eyes, and other physical traits, cannot be attributed to the influence of training. Thorndike gives some interesting figures to show the importance of family inheritance with respect to such a trait as deafness. A person who is born deaf will be found to have brothers or sisters who are deaf in 245 cases out of 1000, whereas among "a thousand brothers or sisters of hearing individuals, the number of deaf persons is certainly less than one, probably much less."[6]

What the teacher is concerned about knowing, however, is whether mental and moral traits, and perhaps even religious capacity, are as greatly influenced by family inheritance as are these physical traits. It must be understood that, so far as we know, what is inherited is always physical. It is the physical basis of mental ability or of moral control that is heritable. Everything that is handed on from one generation to the next, so far as biological heredity is concerned, is in the germ cells which unite to form the new individual at the time of conception. Furthermore the transmission is not, in the most precise sense, from parent to child, but from the germ cells of the parent to the child. The view that is most widely held by psychologists and biologists is that this "germ plasm" is transmitted from

[6]*Educational Psychology*, Thorndike, Vol. III, p. 234.

generation to generation practically uninfluenced by the changes in the body of the parent which has served as a home, and as a means of transmission, for the germ cells. A father who has developed large biceps does not thereby have muscular children, a mother who through constant practice has become an expert pianist does not transmit to her children any of the facility in handling the keys that has been gained by practice, and parents who have zealously observed religious practices and ceremonies do not, because of that fact, beget children with increased propensities toward the religious life.[7]

This view calls attention to the importance of family inheritance as a cause of individual differences. It must be remembered, however, that in the union of two germ cells there is possible an almost infinite variety of combinations of the factors determining the various traits.

Mental and moral inheritance.—How far, then, are mental and moral traits to be traced to family inheritance? A number of interesting studies have been carried on in an effort to answer this question. One of the earliest of these studies was made by Francis Galton, the famous English scientist of the last century. Galton found that about a thousand English men of genius—judges, statesmen, scientists, poets, and the like—had more than half that number of eminent relatives, whereas the number of eminent

---

[7] It is not meant, of course, that the life and conduct of the parents have no influence upon the next generation. The influence is indeed great, but it is to be considered as a factor which modifies original nature after birth, and not as a determiner of what that original nature shall be. That is determined by the hereditary strains represented in the germ cells of the parents, and these are in the main unaffected by what the parents do.

relatives among a thousand men of average ability would be less than five.[8] On the basis of this and other studies of heredity Galton declared that one-half of the individual's inheritance came from his two parents, one-fourth from his four grandparents, one-eighth from his eight great-grandparents, and so on, the contribution of each generation decreasing in proportion to its distance from the individual under consideration.

Another well-known study of heredity made by Frederick Adams Woods showed that among certain of the royal families of Europe intellectual and moral attainment clearly "ran in families."[9]

The far-reaching influence of "bad heredity" is shown by the studies of the Jukes and the Kallikak families.[10] In the first of these investigations the progeny of Max Jukes, a mental defective who lived near New York City about the middle of the eighteenth century, were traced through several generations. The line was exceedingly fruitful in mental defectives, paupers, criminals, harlots, epileptics, and drunkards.

Descendents of Martin Kallikak have been traced in two lines, one through his wife who was a normal woman of good ancestry, the other through an illicit union with a feeble-minded girl. In the almost five hundred descendents of the first union there were no cases of feeble-mindedness, while of the progeny of the feeble-minded girl, four hundred and eighty in num-

[8]*Heredity Genius,* Francis Galton—quoted in *Educational Psychology,* Thorndike, Vol. III, p. 236. The exact numbers were 977 and 535.

[9]*Mental and Moral Heredity in Royalty,* Woods, p. 286.

[10]*Heredity in Relation to Eugenics,* C. B. Davenport, *The Jukes,* R. L. Dugdale, *The Kallikak Family,* H. H. Goddard.

ber, almost a third were feeble-minded and many others were less than mediocre and of low moral calibre. There were also a large number of cases of criminality.

It will be understood that in many of these cases it is difficult, in fact impossible, to exclude the influence of environment and training. However, moral delinquency is so often associated with feeble-mindedness and other obviously hereditary traits that the significance of inheritance, at least in "the lower extreme of morals," is clear enough.

Although it is not possible to state what proportion of the mental and moral equipment of the individual is to be attributed to near ancestry, there can be little doubt that the contribution of this factor is very considerable. The teacher who is genuinely interested in his pupils and who is really seeking to guide their moral and religious development will not infrequently be helped in understanding them by some knowledge of their family inheritance.

4. *Differences due to maturity.*—Strictly speaking, individual differences that are due to maturity would be those variations among pupils, in any trait, that are solely the result of different degrees of progress toward full growth. A child of six, for example, differs from the same child at four years of age not just because he has had two more years of training but also because of the inner growth of his body and mind. Practically, however, it is impossible to separate the influence of training from that of maturity. A group of thirteen-year-old children will differ from a group of nine-year-olds partly because they have had four more years of training, partly

because they have had four more years of growth (which would have gone on even without the training, provided only life had been sustained) and partly because they are a group of different children. The nine-year-old group four years later will not be the same as the thirteen-year-old group is now, even though, at that time, they will have had the same number of years of growth and of training.

The teacher is interested in differences due to maturity, from a practical point of view. He knows that as he observes them, they are not free from the influence of other factors such as training, but that they are nevertheless important. The grading scheme in most church schools, and the divisions into departments, are largely based upon them. The mistake has been made, however, of assuming that the mere chronological age of the pupil is an accurate indication of his degree of maturity in body or in mind.

No fixed stages of growth.—It has been too generally assumed, also, that there are definite, more or less rigidly fixed stages in the development of the individual, each stage having its own peculiar characteristics and its rigid age limits. This view of the way the pupil grows, at least any extreme form of it, has largely been given up by psychologists today for two reasons: (1) The bulk of the evidence suggests that mental traits do not develop one after the other in stages, but that, in a general way, they develop side by side. There is not a stage when the powers of sense perception are developing, then a period when memory develops, and still later a time when reasoning comes into play. These processes rather "develop gradually, continuously, and in a relative degree concomitantly.''[11]   (2) In the second place the great individual variations in capacity and rate of growth make impossible the division of the pupil's development into clearly defined stages. A pupil who, on the basis of age, would be said to be in one ''stage'' of development may actually be found to possess many of the characteristics of another period. A child of seven years may for example, show ability equal to that of the average child of nine. A girl of twelve may be as mature physically as another girl of fourteen. ''It is by no means difficult,'' according to Thorndike, ''to find seven-year-olds who can do intellectual work at which one in twenty seventeen-year-olds would fail.''[12]

A rough indication of the nature of the differences due to maturity is given by a comparison of the average performances of the child for each year of age. The average child of three for example can repeat six to seven syllables, the four-year-old can repeat twelve to thirteen, and the six-year-old sixteen to eighteen. The average child of five can define such words as chair, horse, folk, doll, pencil and table ''in terms of use,'' while the eight-year-old defines at least some words in terms ''superior to use,'' i.e. by description, classification, and so forth.[13]

There are many traits, however, for which there

---

[11]Inglis, *Principles of Secondary Education*, p. 40.

[12]*Educational Psychology*, Vol. III, p. 280.

[13]Terman, *The Measurement of Intelligence*, pp. 149, 160, 167, 221.

Note.—For children of medium height the average girl of six is 45 inches tall and weighs 45 pounds, at nine she has a height of 52 inches and weighs 64 pounds, and at twelve the figures are 58 inches and 86 pounds. Boys in the same class (medium) have a height of 46 inches, weight 48 pounds, at six; 52 inches and 64 pounds at nine and 58 inches and 85 pounds at twelve.—Baldwin-Wood. Weight-Height-Age table. *The Child, His Nature and His Needs*, M. V. O'Shea, Editor, p. 24-5.

are no adequate measures and in the development of which progress toward maturity cannot be accurately traced.

It would be of very great value for the church school teacher if he could know what might be expected of the average child at the various age levels, in moral control and achievement in the religious life. But very little accurate information is available as to what differences in maturity mean in the moral and religious realm. The question as to how Christian a nine-year-old or a thirteen-year-old can really be is thought-provoking but very few facts are available to help the teacher in answering it. It must always be remembered, also, that the teacher does not deal with the theoretical "average child," but with particular individuals who may belong anywhere in the curve of distribution.

The large divisions of life.—In a broad, general way, differences due to maturity may be seen by viewing the characteristics of the large divisions of human life. The three periods into which the life of the individual most naturally falls are childhood, adolescence, and adulthood. The particular year of age which divides one period from another differs with individuals. Childhood, however, extends from physical birth to the "birth of the procreative powers"; adolescence from the maturing of the sex functions to the "full maturity of all the powers"; and adulthood from the attainment of maturity until the end of life. Childhood is a period of growth and acquisition when the foundations of life in habits and attitudes are laid. Over sixty per cent of the weight and over eighty per cent of the height are attained before the close of this period. Adolescence is also marked by growth—especially of those powers that are connected directly or indirectly with sex maturing. It is a period of adjustment, of the "deepening" of thought and feeling, and of increased development of self-consciousness and of social consciousness. Adulthood means that maturity has been attained. There is little further physical growth and the mind now "has all the kinds of power it is to have." "The leading characteristic here," says Tracy, "is the consolidation, and use of power, with approximate fixity and finality in habits, opinions, tastes, preferences, and ways of looking at things. The capacity for steady and prolonged effort, for unremitting pursuit of one object and purpose, under the guidance of ideas that have become a secure possession, should now be fully achieved."[14]

5. *Differences due to environment.*—The four factors which have been so far considered as causes of individual differences are all phases of heredity. Sex, racial traits, family characteristics and the possibilities of growth, have their basis in the germ plasm. But in the discussion of each of these sources of individual differences, it is difficult to eliminate the influence of training. Environment is thus the other

[14]*Psychology of Adolescence,* p. 20. The Macmillan Co., N. Y. Used by permission.

Note.—Each of these periods may be subdivided according to various changes in growth and in environmental conditions. The divisions on the basis of which the church school is organized are as follows: *Childhood* (1-11 years) includes Infancy 1-3, Early childhood 4-5, Middle childhood 6-8, and Later childhood 9-11. *Adolescence* (12-23) includes Early adolescence 12-14, Middle adolescence 15-17 and Later adolescence 18-23. *Adulthood* (24-d.) includes Early Manhood or Womanhood 24-40, Middle Age 40-60, Older Manhood or Womanhood 60-70, and Advanced Age 70-d. For a discussion of the characteristics of these periods see the specialization units of the Standard Leadership Training Curriculum.

large factor which, together with heredity, contributes to individuality. It includes all the influences of the pupil's surroundings, physical or spiritual, the country in which he lives, the people with whom he associates, the books he reads, the pictures he sees, the school and church he attends, the instruction and training that he receives.

The question as to which factor—heredity or environment—contributes most to the life of the individual is an age-old controversy. For the most part it is a futile one. The contribution of heredity is useless without an environment to stimulate it and to provide it with the means of growth. On the other hand the most favorable environment and the best of training cannot stimulate the individual to do that which requires more ability than he possesses.

The whole educational enterprise is based upon a conviction of the effectiveness of environment in changing human nature. And if the facts given in the discussion of family inheritance suggest a pessimistic view of the potency of training, it should be remembered that while heredity sets the limits of the individual's achievement, few, if any, persons ever reach their limit. If, on the other hand, environment seems to occupy too large a place in making the individual, it will be well to recall that most people determine, in a measure at least, what their environment shall be, what associates they shall have, what books they shall read, what institutions shall command their loyalty and devotion.

The teacher of religion should keep clearly in mind the fact that although the amount of power possessed by any individual may be determined by inheritance, the direction in which that power shall be used is largely a matter of training. It is said that of the thousands of waifs rescued from the streets by Dr. Barnado and educated in his Homes, the records show only about two per cent to have failed to "make good." Of course poverty is not necessarily an indication of poor heredity, but the figures are nevertheless suggestive. The conclusion of Thorndike is pertinent in this connection. "Morality," he says, "is more susceptible than intellect to environmental influence. Moral traits are more often matters of the direction of capacities and the creation of desires and aversions. Over them then, education has greater sway, though school education, because of the peculiar narrowness of the life of the schoolroom, has so far done little for any save the semi-intellectual virtues."[15]

The church school must seek to free itself from the narrowness to which Thorndike refers. It must accept the task of developing character by means of a broader education in the religious life. The remaining chapters of this book deal very largely with environment as a factor in the moulding of character. They are concerned about showing that training can give direction to life, that original nature can be changed, that Christian personality can be developed.

WHAT SHOULD BE THE ATTITUDE OF THE TEACHER TOWARD INDIVIDUAL DIFFERENCES?—

The wise teacher will seek to understand each individual pupil. In his thinking he will not try to fit the child into this or that "type," for he will

[15]*Educational Psychology*, Vol. III, p. 314. Teachers' College, N. Y.

know that there are almost as many types as there are children. He will rather gather what information he can that will throw light upon the extent of the individual differences among his pupils and the causes of them. With respect to particular pupils he will ask such questions as: What traits does he possess which call for my special attention and study? How far does he differ from other members of the class in these traits? Is he helped or hindered in the development of Christian personality by reason of them? How far are they to be traced to family or other inheritance? How far are they the result of training? What do they require of me as a teacher of religion who is seeking to guide this pupil into the Christian way of life?

It is hardly necessary to say that the teacher's attitude must be sympathetic. His obligations extend to the slow as well as to the quick, to the impulsive as well as to the thoughtful, to the practical and matter-of-fact child as well as the more idealistic, to the pupil of very limited endowment as well as to the richly endowed. In the fine words of another, the teacher needs "an eternal optimism regarding the possibilities of human nature,"[16] and he must seek to instil into each individual "the conviction that there are some special services which, on account of inborn differences or peculiar environmental circumstances, he, and he alone can render."[17]

QUESTIONS—

    1. Why must the teacher never lose sight of the individual pupil? What is the relation of this emphasis upon the individual to the fact that education is a social process?

---

[16]Chapman and Counts, *Principles of Education*, p. 186.
[17]Ibid. p. 190.

2. How do you account for the fact that the significance of individual differences has, in recent years, been much more clearly recognized than formerly?

3. What is the Intelligence Quotient? Of what importance is an understanding of this measure to the teacher of religion?

4. Have you known any instances of young people of exceptional ability being lost to the church? What was the reason? How might the break have been avoided?

5. In what departments (or classes) in your church school are the pupils separated according to sex? Why is this separation made?

6. In what way does the program of the church school provide for differences that are due to age or maturity? Is this provision adequate in your own church school?

7. What is the trend of the evidence concerning racial differences in intelligence? Does it have any significance for religious education?

8. How would you explain biologically (a) strong likenesses between father and son, and (b) marked differences between father and son?

9. Why do psychologists no longer divide life into rigidly fixed stages?

10. What evidence can you give of the effectiveness of environment in changing human nature? What do you think of the statement of Thorndike that "morality is more susceptible than intellect to environmental influence"?

REPORTS AND INVESTIGATIONS—

1. If you are in close touch with a church school class (or some other group of children or young people) find out, if possible, the intelligence rating of the members of the group. Perhaps the information can be secured from the public school. If the pupils were ranked on the basis of quality of their church school work, what differences would there be in their relative positions in the class? How do you account for the differences? (If it is not possible to make this investigation, find out whether the pupils who do the best work in the church school are also among the best students in the public school.)

2. Consider some of your acquaintances as to their possession of the following traits: (a) Intelligence, (b) co-operativeness, (c) appreciation of beauty, (d) honesty, (e) interest in the Kingdom of God. Indicate where in the curve of distribution you would judge each person to belong with respect to each of these

traits by grading them on a five-point scale as follows: Very low, low, medium, high, very high. Have several members of the Training Class rate the same persons and compare the results. Discuss the significance of the differences among individuals in the traits studied.

3. Make a note of differences which you have observed in the behavior of pupils in the church school and which you consider to be due to (a) sex, (b) family inheritance, (c) age, and (d) environment.

4. Report on differences revealed by tests that have been given in your church school. (Graded lesson tests, Bible knowledge tests, etc.) Perhaps you could give a simple Bible knowledge test to a group of pupils and could report the results.

5. Read and prepare a report on chapters v and vi of *The Measurement of Intelligence* by Terman.

REFERENCES—

Chapman and Counts, Principles of Education, chap. xi. Houghton Mifflin.

Gates, Arthur I., Psychology for Students of Education, chaps. i, xv and xvi. Macmillan.

Norsworthy and Whitley, Psychology of Childhood, chaps. i, xv and xvi. Macmillan.

O'Shea, M. V. (Editor)—The Child: His Nature and His Needs, chaps. xiii-xiv. The Children's Foundation.

Terman, Lewis M., The Measurement of Intelligence, chaps. v-vi. Houghton Mifflin.

Thorndike, Edward L., Educational Psychology, Vol. III, chaps. vii and ix-xiii. Teachers' College.

Weigle, Luther A., The Pupil and the Teacher, chaps. iii-vii. Doran.

CHAPTER V

LEARNING AND HABIT FORMATION

How Are Changes Made in Original Nature?
The Simpler Forms of Learning

"What we are at maturity," says Pyle, "depends upon the modifications that have been wrought upon original nature. Bringing about these modifications constitutes our education and education is important to the extent that these modifications are important."[1]

The three most basic questions for which the teacher must find answers are, therefore: (1) What is the nature of man's original equipment? (2) What changes must be made in it? And (3) How can these changes be brought about? The preceding chapters have dealt chiefly with the first of these questions. Here and there the second has been touched upon, but it is not within the scope of this book to discuss it in detail. To do so would open up the whole field of the philosophy of education and of life itself. Nevertheless certain basic assumptions as to the modifications which must be made in original nature underlie all that is said upon the various topics considered in this study. They were stated in general terms in chapter one and some of the desirable changes were suggested more specifically in chapter three. It is assumed throughout this discussion that the objectives of the church school teacher are changes that look in the direction of a growing Christian personality and the progressive realization of a Christian social order.

The question which now presses for an answer is, therefore: How are desirable changes to be made in original nature? And the two chapters on "Learning and Habit Formation" seek to answer this question. In the present chapter the topics to be considered are: (1) Why may society not trust the undirected original impulses? (2) How are the earliest changes in original nature brought about? (3) How are changes effected through ideas?

[1] *The Psychology of Learning,* p. 14.

WHY MAY SOCIETY NOT TRUST THE UNDIRECTED ORIG-
INAL IMPULSES ?—

The major activities of human life have a basis in
original nature. The native tendencies lead to physical activity, food seeking, fighting to overcome opposition, the avoidance of danger, association together
in groups, satisfaction in the approval of others,
mating and sex behaviour, and the parental care of
the immature.

In one form or another, and with varying emphasis, the suggestion has often been made that
society should simply trust these native tendencies.
It has been contended that to interfere with the
"natural" expression of original impulses is artificial
and is detrimental to the welfare of the child and of
society. This point of view in one form was elevated
into an educational doctrine by G. Stanley Hall and
his followers. By the doctrine of catharsis it was
maintained that the individual should give expression
to all of the instinctive tendencies of childhood, and
that by so doing he would eliminate many of the
unworthy impulses as he passed on to the higher
stages in his development. Even selfishness, greed,
lying and cheating were to be allowed their natural
expression in the earliest years in order that later on,
in the period of adolescence, generosity and altruism
might "spring up naturally."[2]

This view of "nature's infallibility" has been
given many theoretical formulations, the most
thoughtful and thorough being that of Rousseau.

[2]See quotations from a number of representatives of this
point of view in Thorndike, *Educational Psychology*, Vol. I, pp.
271-7.

But it has never been completely carried out in practice. One reason for this failure is the simple fact that the child cannot be left to himself and live. The native tendencies of the human infant are not adequate to sustain life. In this respect man differs from many of the lower forms of life. The baby chick can pretty well take care of itself from the day it is hatched. It can run, scratch, peck, eat and drink. It can be taken from its mother and, provided only that food is not too difficult to find, it can develop more or less normally. The chick does not have to learn how to make these responses. The original tendencies which it possesses are sufficiently definite and fixed to equip it for the simple activities of its life.

Original tendencies not adequate for life.—The young child, however, is almost helpless at birth, and is quite dependent upon society for many years for the care, protection, guidance and provision which are necessary to maintain even a merely physical existence. The original nature of the child is looser and less rigidly organized than that of the chick and is thus more susceptible to the influences of learning. This difference in the fixity of the instincts at the different levels of life is illustrated by Weigle. "Instinct," he says, "leads the bee to build a honeycomb, and provides for both material and pattern; it leads the bird to build a nest, and the beaver a dam, with less specific direction; it impels the child to constructive play, but what and how the child shall build, it does not determine."[3] The looser or-

---

[3] *Talks to Sunday School Teachers,* p. 20.

ganization of the original nature of the child makes necessary a longer period of infancy—a longer period during which its actions can be more or less determined by others, and in which modifications or original responses may be learned. This extended infancy of human beings is of the greatest educational importance. It means that, since the instincts do not provide for the necessary activities of life, habit, intelligence and reason are called into play. The chick is fairly well equipped for its simple existence by nature, but to fit the child for life requires both nature and nurture.

Even the extreme advocates of freedom in education would, of course, have to admit the necessity of such direction of the child's activities as is necessary to sustain life. The parental instincts of the older generation might be trusted to provide this direction, however, and beyond it the native impulses might largely be given free expression. But the original tendencies of the child are not adequate to equip for the complex life of modern society. They would serve much better in the simple social group of uncivilized man. Men who would be stirred to combat by a slighting remark are often quite indifferent to a great social wrong. The child who fears the thunder may pick up a live electric wire, and the lad who seeks the company of others may associate with a group that will corrupt his morals. A slight injury to a child will call forth profuse expressions of pity from a parent who perhaps is a bitter opponent of a law that would guard the welfare of all children. And anything unusual in his neighbour's affairs will often arouse the curiosity of the sensation seeker who is altogether apathetic regarding the secrets of the Universe.

It is clear, then, that society cannot trust the un-directed original impulses. Some of these tendencies it must eliminate, others it must cultivate, still others it must modify and redirect. For while modern edu-cation gives a large place to considerations of freedom and immediate interest, it cannot be content with a mere *laissez faire* attitude toward original nature. It must recognize that "true life is full of purpose, and ever has its eye fixed on some worthy goal only to be reached after much struggle and strenuous en-deavour."[4] It must accept the task of bringing about changes in original nature, and it must guide those changes in the direction of a worthy goal.

How are the earliest changes in original nature brought about?—

Changes in the original nature of the pupil are brought about through experience, and experience involves learning and habit formation. The best ap-proach to the study of how these changes are made is through an analysis of learning in its simplest form, the kind of learning that takes place from the earliest years of life.

A young baby is lying in a bed wriggling its arms and legs. These movements are instinctive. They are due to the original tendencies to general physical activity and have their basis in certain "connections" established by nature in the nervous system. In the midst of these random movements the child's hand comes in contact with a bright object which it grasps. In addition to the feel of the object which perhaps

---

[4] J. Welton, *What Do We Mean by Education?* p. 105.

is satisfying, there is a pleasing rattling noise. This simple experience has really wrought a change in the original nature of the baby. Hereafter the neurones concerned in the particular responses of grasping and rattling the object will be "preferred" over the others which lead merely to general activity. The baby may not at first be able to control the arm muscles sufficiently to grasp the object deliberately, but each time it happens upon the rattle and enjoys the experience, the neurones involved become more and more permeable, that is, a habit becomes more firmly established. In time the child will be able to direct its grasp straight to the object and to repeat the experience as often as it desires to do so. The baby with this habit established is a changed individual. He has learned something which has added to the enjoyment of life and which has perhaps given him more control over his movements.

But a very different kind of experience might also come to this child. Perhaps one day, while he is crawling on the floor, he sees another object which attracts his attention. This time it is a bright piece of nickel on a heating stove. As he touches the object he finds that it is hot and quickly withdraws his hand. The experience is distinctly unpleasant. Instead of a feeling of satisfaction he is displeased and pained. And once again a change has been wrought in his original nature. It may take several such experiences before the child learns not to touch the stove. But even this one will tend to make the response less likely than it would otherwise be. For the neurones involved will have become less permeable because of the unpleasantness of the experience. In time, because he has had several burns, or his hand has been slapped, or in some other way disapproval has been expressed by his elders, the habit of avoiding the hot stove will have become established. And the child will thereby have learned something more of life.

The laws of learning.—These simple experiences of a young child illustrate two of the most basic and important laws of learning which are operative not only in infancy but throughout life. They are known as (1) the law of exercise and (2) the law of effect, and they may be stated simply in terms of situation and response.[5]

The law of exercise states that, other things being equal, exercise strengthens the bond between situation and response. This law involves also another principle, namely that, other things being equal, lack of exercise weakens the bond between situation and response.

The law of effect states that a satisfying effect tends to strengthen, and a dissatisfying effect tends to weaken, the bond between situation and response.

The experiences of the young child already referred to show clearly the operation of these laws. In the first case the bond between the situation sight-of-bright-object-lying-within-reach and the response grasping-and-rattling-the-object was strengthened both by exercise and by reason of the resulting satisfaction. In the second instance the bond between the situation sight-of-attractive-nickel-plate-on-stove and the response reaching-for-and-touching-the-plate was weakened because of the discomfort and dissatisfaction which resulted from its exercise.

[5] If necessary, read over again the discussion in chapter two of "stimulus," "response" and "connection."

There are certain factors and conditions which modify the influence of exercise and effect, but these laws are basic considerations in all learning. It should be understood that dissatisfaction does not necessarily mean pain. In fact a response that is, at least mildly, painful may at times be inherently satisfying, because it achieves the end desired by the individual. Moreover, even an instinctive response may under some conditions really be annoying. It may be so because the response has been forced when the neurones involved were not "ready" to act. This fact and others closely related to it, are sometimes put into the form of a third law of learning namely the law of readiness which has already been stated in chapter two.

A vast amount of human learning, especially in the earlier years of life, is of the simple habit-forming type that has been used to illustrate the laws of exercise and effect. Beginning with mere random movements or purely instinctive responses, the individual is soon rewarded or punished either by the natural consequences of his acts, or by the actions of his elders, so that simple habits are formed and one response tends to be made rather than another. These simple habits form the basis of more complex ones. The unco-ordinated movements of hand and arm lead to the reaching and grasping responses; grasping the rattle develops certain muscular habits which may be used in handling a spoon; some of these habits will later make possible the holding of a pencil, and still later, together with others, they will lead to the necessary movements involved in scribbling, in making crude drawings, in sketching, and in the skillful touches of the master artist upon the canvas.

One of the most important facts for the teacher to note in this brief description of habit formation, is that all of the learning is dependent upon the activity of the individual. If the baby had not been active it would not have touched the rattle, if it had not grasped the rattle it would not have learned the nature of the object nor have had the satisfaction of handling and rattling it. The principle that "the child is active in learning" seems clear enough in these simpler forms of learning. It is just as true, however, of the higher, more subtle types, and the teacher does well to keep it in mind always.

In the beginning the activity of the individual is the gift of nature. "The little human animal is born going." As has been pointed out in earlier chapters, he possesses original tendencies to action which are the basis of the teacher's work. Almost from birth, however, the stimulus of the environment and the operation of the laws of exercise and effect bring about the modification of original nature. Changes of one kind or another are made. If the parent or the teacher would guide these changes, he must use the laws of learning. As an aid to the teacher, therefore, Thorndike draws from these laws the practical pedagogical principle: "Exercise and reward desirable functions, prevent or punish undesirable connections."[6]

Learning a new response.—The thoughtful reader may have noticed what perhaps seems a rather serious omission from this discussion of the nature of learn-

---

[6]*Educational Psychology*, Vol. II, p. 20.

ing. In the instances given the active response was one that was connected with the stimulus by original nature. The child grasped the rattle, or reached for the nickel-plate on the stove, because of the inborn connections in the nervous system that lead to the responses of general physical activity or of manipulation. But how is it possible, one may ask, for a new and different response to be connected with this stimulus? How, for example, does the child learn to respond to the sight of the nickel-plate by moving away from it?

To understand how new reactions are learned it is necessary to call to mind the fact that all situations are complex. They involve not one but a great many "connections" between different aspects of the total situation and particular responses. In the words of the psychologist a situation involves many stimulus-response bonds. Two sets of these bonds are clearly operative in the situation of the child and the stove. One set connects the sight of the nickel-plate with the response reaching-for-and-touching-it, the other connects the sensation of pain aroused by touching the hot stove with the avoiding reactions. As has been pointed out, the dissatisfaction accompanying the first of these responses would result in a weakening of the bonds involved, while the exercise of the second would strengthen the avoiding reactions. Moreover the close association of these two sets of connections makes possible the attaching of the response of "moving away" to the original stimulus, so that the child may form the habit of moving away at the sight of the nickel plate.

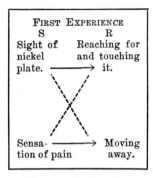
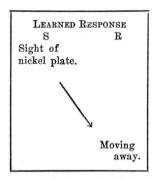

Diagram showing how a new response is learned.—At first two stimuli (sight of nickel plate and sensation of pain) were necessary to secure the response (moving away), but after several experiences with the hot stove the sight of the nickel plate alone became a sufficient stimulus to secure the avoidance reaction. (Adapted from Gates.)

But the two, or more, sets of connections need not pull in opposite directions as was the case in the illustration just used. Each of two simultaneous stimuli may call forth its own response. The responses may be different but their close association makes possible the attachment of either reaction to either stimulus. An illustration may be taken from the classroom. A teacher indicates a point on the map of Palestine and secures the response of attention on the part of the pupils to the location of a city. At the same time the teacher says, "Jerusalem," and the pupils respond by saying, "Jerusalem." By exercising both of the bonds involved in this situation the teacher will soon be able to secure the response "Jerusalem" merely by pointing to the location of the city on the map.

Pointing to the map will then have become a sufficient stimulus to arouse the response "Jerusalem'' whereas at first it required the two stimuli to secure the desired response.

If the teacher sees that the newly-formed bond is ''exercised'' and ''rewarded'' it will soon become firmly established and the pupils will have formed the habit of saying ''Jerusalem'' when the correct point is indicated on the map or, in other words, they will have learned the location of Jerusalem.

It will be seen that this discussion of learning new responses has not moved very far from the simple laws of exercise and effect. The other factor has been the association together of two or more stimuli and responses. Thus Gates generalizes, ''By means of association and exercise any reaction which the organism can make may be attached to any stimulus to which the organism is sensitive.''[7]

Exercise and effect operate throughout life.—The question at the beginning of this section was, How are the earliest changes in original nature brought about? The experiences of the young child in learning to play with a rattle and to move away from a hot stove served to show that original nature is changed by the activity of the individual, by the stimulation of the environment, and by the strengthening of bonds through exercise and satisfying results, and the weakening of bonds through disuse and dissatisfaction. Learning to locate Jerusalem on the map involved more elaborate systems of connections, but it was essentially the same kind of learning as in the other cases, namely, learning of the simple habit-forming type. As a matter of fact not only are the earliest changes in original nature made in this

---

[7] *Psychology for Students of Education,* p. 222.

way, but throughout life a large part of human learning is of this character. The stimulus is a perception of objects actually present to the senses, or of relationships, the response is a muscular movement and the particular habits learned are largely the results of exercise and effect.

Of course, as the child grows older, there is less and less of uncertainty in his responses, because he has learned to control them better. By the time he enters school, according to Pyle, ''he has practically mastered most of the responses that will ever be required of him.''[8] There is also more conscious attention to the particular reactions to be learned, and observation of others makes possible more accurate and useful responses. Moreover the kind of satisfactions that are effective become more refined and subtle. But learning that is essentially of this simpler sort is found in all periods of life. It is seen in the activity of the infant who becomes able to handle his spoon or fork, in the child who learns to write, in the youth who by constant practice gains skill in the use of the typewriter or in driving an automobile, and in the golf enthusiast who, by much trial and many errors, learns how to ''make it in par.'' This type of learning is also involved in many of the activities in which the church school teacher is especially interested. It enters into the process by which the pupil learns to find Bible references, to memorize passages of Scripture, to cooperate in the games, to participate in the worship services, and to do unselfish and helpful deeds. It is involved likewise in his learning to be inattentive, to be irreverent, to be unco-operative, and

---

[8] *Psychology of Learning*, p. 8.

to act selfishly. Which set of habits the pupil shall have will depend upon what bonds have been exercised with satisfaction.

How are changes effected through ideas?—

The changes in original nature that have been considered thus far have been changes in muscular reactions, that is, changes in objective behavior. These modifications are of course very important. Many activities of the Christian life should early be established as habits.

But it must be apparent that there is a good deal of learning which at least seems to be very different from that of the simple habit-forming type. There is the whole realm suggested by the word "knowledge," the learning by means of ideas or, as the psychologist calls it, "ideational learning." How are changes brought about in this realm?

One of the reasons why ideational learning seems to be different from habit-formation is that it does not appear to involve a muscular response. The stimulus is perhaps the spoken word of the teacher, but the response may be an idea in the mind of the pupil. This idea may then become a stimulus which calls forth, as a response, another idea. In fact, the day-dreamer may sit perfectly still in his chair while a whole chain of ideas flit through his mind. Much learning, then, consists of the gaining of ideas and the teacher needs to understand what ideas are, and how they are acquired.

From the practical point of view an idea is "the awareness of any thing, event, or fact when it is not present to the senses."[9] An object lies upon the table

---

[9]Gates, *Psychology for Students of Education*, p. 298.

before my eyes. I *perceive* that it is a book. Later
on I call the book to mind although it is not present
to the senses, i.e., I have an idea of the book. In
this case my idea is of the particular book that had
been lying on the table. But by similar processes
of recall, and through many experiences of different
kinds of books, my idea of *a book* has been built up.
Ideas, then, arise out of experience. They are, in a
sense, "bits of revived experience"[10] and they are
made richer and more meaningful by the broadening
contacts of the growing person. The little child, as
yet unable to read, whose knowledge of books is confined to the old-fashioned family photo album has a
very limited and inadequate idea of what a book is.
The word will mean to him merely the ponderous
volume of strange looking pictures that is sometimes
given to him for a plaything. For the book lover,
however, the word is filled with all the rich content
that his wide reading and his many prized volumes
give to it.

Ideas dependent upon experience.—This dependence of ideas upon experience is a fact of first importance to the teacher. Teaching may be almost
valueless if it involves ideas with the elements of
which the child has had no first hand dealing. All
knowledge perhaps does not come through the senses,
but the basis of all knowledge is actual sensory experience. It would be quite impossible to convey an
accurate idea of the perfume of the rose to one who
had never enjoyed the fragrance of flowers, or to
describe a prairie sunset to a man born blind. Like
wise it is impossible for the teacher effectively to

---

[10]Pyle, *Psychology of Learning*, p. 92.

teach young children by the use of ideas for which,
either because of their immaturity, or because of some
deficiency in the surroundings and conditions of
their lives, they have no adequate basis in experience.
The words which the teacher uses in a lesson mean to
the child not what the dictionary gives as their meaning, but they have whatever significance the child's
own experience gives to them. The word love can
hardly yield a Christian sense to one who knows it
only as a name for the mawkish sentiment which too
often gains the center of interest in the novel of the
screen. Nor can the "fatherhood of God" be much
more than a meaningless phrase to him who knows
no father but a cruel and unthinking one who is his
own.

It is necessary that in the early years of life the
child be given a rich sensory experience, that he be
encouraged to touch, taste, feel, see, and hear many
of the objects in the world round about him. As
time goes on his widening contacts with the world
will give him a foundation in experience for the
understanding of words and the building up of ideas.
It is especially important in religious education that
the needs of the young child in this respect be met
and that the life of the church and of the home provide children with the experiential basis for Christian teaching.

Not only are the basic elements of all ideas to be
traced to experience, but it is by means of their
connection in experience that ideas are linked together in the mind and thus gain new meaning.
"What is experienced together in perception," says

Pyle, "comes back together as ideas."[11]   Knowledge may be thought of as organized systems of connected ideas and the gaining of knowledge, or ideational learning, as a process of linking ideas together.   The division between learning of the habit-forming type, and ideational learning is thus seen to be largely artificial.   There are habits of thought as well as muscular habits, and ideas are connected to their stimuli in much the same way as are active responses. In fact, the thinking involved in connecting ideas is an active response as truly as is any overt action.

Learning as connecting.—Ideational learning takes place as soon as the child is able to recall objects not present to the senses, and it is, of course, closely related to learning of the simple habit-forming type. The child who has played with the rattle may think of the toy when it is not actually before him.   His experiences with the hot nickel plate will give him some idea, even if a very inadequate one, of the stove.   These experiences, too, may be connected with certain words and the child's store of knowledge may thus be increased.   If, after perhaps several burns, he approaches the stove again and the parent cries— "No! No! Hot! Hot!" the word "hot" may be linked with the avoiding response and may come to serve as an adequate stimulus to arouse it.   A parent may hold up a book before a young child and at the same time say, "Book."   The word is thus connected with the object because the two are experienced together.   After sufficient exercise of the bonds involved, not only will holding up the object call forth the response "Book" from the child, but the spoken

[11]*Psychology of Learning*, p. 93.

word will bring the idea of the book to the child's mind. Later, when the child goes to school, the teacher may show him a card on which the word "BOOK" is printed. At the same time she will say "book" and again the child's store of knowledge will be increased as he connects both the spoken word, and the idea of a book, with the printed letters. A simple and practical view of the nature of learning is therefore that "learning is connecting." And this is true of many of the more complex processes as well as of the simple ones.

The task of the church school teacher involves much more than the imparting of information. This fact has been emphasized throughout the preceding chapters. But instruction, in its narrower sense, is nevertheless an important part of the teacher's work. There will be much of this simple sort of connecting to be done. Names will need to be associated with places, ideas with actions, Bible passages with book and chapter, hymns with authors, names with people, and people with achievements and ideas of character. And, at times, it will not be easy to prevent wrong connections from being made. The child may come to look upon Sunday as "the day the funny-paper comes." He may link up with Jesus the idea of a mild and rather effeminate oriental; or he may associate religion merely with certain practices of the church school. What is needed, in such cases, is that a large number of other connections be established that will enrich the meaning and significance of the child's "ideas." It is especially important that the child shall meet with religion in his home, in his week-day activities, in his school, in his visits to the homes of others, in his reading, in his conversation with other children, and even in his play, in order that it may come to be associated with every phase of his life.

Factors of advantage in recall.—But a problem has no doubt suggested itself to the reader. Almost any idea that may be present in the mind at one time, has no doubt been connected in past experience with a large number of different ideas and percepts. Yet of all these different associations only one pair of connected ideas comes to the mind at the same instant. What is it that determines which idea is recalled?

I think, for example, of Jericho, a word which has been connected in my past experience with many incidents in Bible story and in other situations. I have read of the fall of the city before Joshua, of a certain man who "was going down from Jerusalem to Jericho" and who "fell among robbers," of a blind man who "sat begging by the wayside nigh unto Jericho," and of many other incidents connected with this city. I have heard a lecturer on the Holy Land describe Jericho, have seen pictures of it, and have many times found the name on a map of Bible lands. In addition to these associations, I have come across the name several times in reading that remarkable story of modern Palestine, *Revolt in the Desert.*

Which of the many possible ideas will come to my mind in response to the stimulus word "Jericho" will depend upon "the most pervious neural path at the moment."[12]   And the most previous neural path will depend upon certain factors which Woodworth calls "factors of advantage in recall." They are in

---

[12]Pyle, *Psychology of Learning*, p. 94.

reality but aspects of the laws of exercise and of effect, but they should perhaps be considered here from a somewhat different point of view from that of the earlier discussion. If some one of the responses has been connected with the word "Jericho" much more frequently than any of the others, that is the one which is most likely to occur now. The fact that I have so recently been reading *Revolt in the Desert* may, however, outweigh the other factor and cause the word to suggest the names of Allenby and Lawrence. There are still other possibilities. A rather vivid experience may have connected "Jericho" with a view of the city which now comes to my mind. Or my interest in geography may have given a particular bent to all of my thinking so that the first association that the word makes is with the location of the city on the map.

The first three of these "factors of advantage" will be readily understood. It is clear that the frequency with which a connection has been made, and its recency and intensity, are factors the relative strengths of which determine to a large extent what particular response shall be made. But the fourth factor, the present state of the mind, or the mental set, perhaps requires further discussion. It is, in some respects, the most important factor of all, for it has a directive function. The *purposes* of the pupil give a bent to all of his thinking.

The importance of "mental set."—The mental set of the pupil may be either a temporary or a more or less permanent attitude. A temporary set is a bent given to the mind by the particular purpose the individual is pursuing at the moment. If that purpose is to find certain passages in the Bible, the stimulus "John 3:16" spoken by the teacher will arouse a very different response from that which would be made if the purpose were to recite passages from memory. If the mind set has been given by a series of lessons in Old Testament history, the word Saul will suggest the first King of the United Kingdom, but if the lessons have been on "The Early Church," the name will bring to mind immediately, Saul of Tarsus.

The response which the individual makes is also influenced by his more permanent attitudes. These predispositions are due to such factors as his interests and aversions, his ambitions and loyalties, his particular brand of patriotism or of religious or racial prejudice. They color almost all of his thought and action.

The mental set or attitude functions in two ways. It helps to determine (1) which bonds shall act, and (2) which results shall satisfy.[13] It is obvious that a pupil whose background and training have developed in him strong racial prejudices will respond to a situation involving racial relationships in one way, while one who, having been brought up in a different atmosphere possesses a more brotherly attitude, will respond in quite another way. With these pupils, not only will different bonds act, but the results which bring satisfaction will also differ. In the case of the first child, the satisfying response may be the suggestion that the member of the "inferior" race should be taught to "know his place,"

---

[13]*Educational Psychology*, Thorndike, Vol. II, p. 51.

whereas the obvious implications of this response may make it quite distasteful to the pupil of more sympathetic disposition.

The same kind of thing is true in the simpler processes of learning. One pupil will be satisfied with a very mediocre performance in the recitation, handwork, dramatization, and so forth, while another —with a different set—may register strong dissatisfaction and may wish to try again. Moreover the same person after a period of training may be thoroughly dissatisfied with a response which earlier was quite acceptable to him. It will be apparent, therefore, that one of the important functions of education is the development of worthy attitudes. "A large part of the theory of education," says Thorndike, considers the problem of getting the pupil "permanently disposed to respond to the subject matter of instruction by zeal, open-mindedness, scientific method, and the like, and temporarily disposed to extract the most value from the particular situation of a given lesson."[14] And the church school teacher even more than the general educator, must seek to bring about proper attitudes on the part of his pupils, for religious education is so largely concerned about the development of enthusiasms, interests, loyalties and appreciations. The way in which attitudes are built up will be discussed in the next chapter.

QUESTIONS—
1. What criticism would you make of the doctrine of catharsis from the educational point of view?
2. What is the significance of the fact that the period of infancy is so much longer in the case of human beings than it is among the lower animals?

[14]Thorndike. *The Psychology of Learning,* p. 26, Teachers' College, N. Y. Used by permission.

3. Do you agree with the statement that, "the original tendencies of the child are not adequate to equip for the complex life of modern society"? Give the reasons for your position.

4. Can you think of any situations in which pain might be satisfying?

5. Where, in the program of your church school, are the laws of exercise and of effect being used in an efficient and wholesome manner?

6. How do you connect the names of new acquaintances with their faces? Why do you fail to remember the names of some of them?

7. A three-year old child said: "I am going to Sunday school where God the Father gives us breakfast food." What explanation of this response can you make in terms of the connection of ideas?

8. What are the four "factors of advantage in recall"? Give some illustrations from your own experience of the way in which they operate.

9. Why are pupils in the church school often satisfied with a very poor performance in recitation while in the public school they perhaps demand much more of themselves?

10. Learning is made more effective where there is definiteness of objective and a knowledge of results. How can these conditions be secured in the church school?

REPORTS AND INVESTIGATIONS—

1. Hold an attractive object within reach of a baby who is less than six months old. Note carefully what happens. Is the child able to direct its grasp straight to the object? Try the experiment several times. Is there any evidence of the operation of the laws of learning? Why? Why not?

2. Suggest six specific ways in which the law of exercise may be used in the work of the church school teacher (or of the parent). Suggest also six ways of using the *law of effect*. Prepare a diagram, similar to that in the text, illustrating what takes place in learning the "location of Jerusalem" as described in this chapter.

3. Examine some of the church school lesson material intended for Beginners or for Primary children. Note any words which seem to you to be too difficult for young children. On what basis do you judge the suitability of the words?

4. Ask a number of young children the meaning of some of the following words: river, ocean, mountain, snow, swine, turtle, sheep, pavement, synagogue, Sunday, Sabbath, worship. Note how the answers differ according to the age and experience of the children.

5. If you have made use of tests in a church school class, or have known of classes where they have been used, report on any improvement in the work of the pupils that resulted from the use of the tests. How do you account for the improvement?

REFERENCES—

Betts and Hawthorne, Method in Teaching Religion, chaps. iv and v. Abingdon.

Chapman and Counts, Principles of Education, chaps. vi, vii. Houghton Mifflin.

Gates, Arthur I., Psychology for Students of Education, chaps. x-xiii to page 305. Macmillan.

Norsworthy and Whitley, Psychology of Childhood, chap. xi. Macmillan.

Pyle, William H., The Psychology of Learning, chaps. i-v and vi to page 96. Warwick and York.

Thorndike, Edward L., The Psychology of Learning, chaps. i-iii. Teachers' College.

Woodworth, Robert S., Psychology, chaps. xiii and xvi. Henry Holt.

CHAPTER VI

LEARNING AND HABIT FORMATION
(Continued)

How Are Changes Made in Original Nature? (The Higher Forms of Learning)

It has been insisted upon from the beginning of this book that education is primarily the "production and prevention of changes" in the lives of the pupils. That being the case, no more important problem can be faced by the teacher than the question discussed in the last chapter—How are changes made in original nature?

For the most part only the more elemental forms of learning have thus far been considered, and it is necessary to devote another chapter to the basic problem of how the original nature of the pupil may be modified. Although the distinction between the various types of learning is not to be rigidly drawn, there are differences which the teacher needs to understand. And while much of his work calls for efficiency in guiding the pupil in the formation of habits and the connecting of ideas, he needs to understand, even more clearly, other complex phases of the learning process. To some of these consideration will now be given. In the present chapter attention is directed to the following questions: (1) How are changes effected through abstract thinking? (2) How are changes effected through reasoning? (3) How are changes effected through indirect learning? (4) How may the learning process be viewed as a whole?

How are changes effected through abstract thinking?—

The kinds of learning that were discussed in the preceding chapter involved merely the establishing of muscular habits and the linking together of ideas. And ideas were defined as the awareness of things, events, or facts not present to the senses.

It will no doubt be apparent to the reader that much of man's thinking and learning cannot be fully accounted for in these simple terms. The gaining of knowledge is not merely a matter of adding one idea to another and establishing a connection between them. And ideas are frequently not the awareness of particular things at all. Man may have ideas of such abstractions as truth, beauty, or goodness. How, then, are changes brought about in the realm of abstract ideas? How far can these changes, as well as those involved in the simpler forms of ideational learning, be explained in terms of the exercising of certain bonds or connections?

At the beginning of this discussion the fact must be made clear that young children do not think in abstract terms. For the first dozen years of life the great bulk of the pupil's thinking deals with the concrete and particular, and the appreciation of abstract ideas develops but slowly toward the close of this period. For the little child, selfishness may mean unwillingness to allow a playmate to hold a prized doll; to be kind may mean to take flowers to a sick person; to be honest, to bring back the correct change from the store. It is only after some years of experience with concrete "things" that the wider meaning of abstract terms can be understood. Even an eleven-year-old asked by Miss Whitely to explain what "pity" means, said, "She lost her pocketbook; it was a pity."

"An average child of three or four," according to Gates, "can correctly perceive a large number of objects such as a key, knife, watch, pencil, various animals, fruits, and so on, but he is usually five before he understands correctly heavy or light. He is six before he has abstract notions of right and left. Not until past eight does he realize the meaning of, or take much interest in, abstract differences, such as the difference between a fly and a butterfly, or an egg and a stone. Not until twelve is the child able to define such abstract words as pity, charity, revenge, justice. Previous to this year, the average child may have been taught to express pity and to act charitably, but the idea has not been thoroughly abstracted. He may, too, have been taught verbal definitions of some of these terms without really having the idea in abstract form."[1]

Abstract ideas built upon concrete experiences.— Abstract ideas are, then, built up out of concrete experiences and the way in which this development takes place must be briefly considered. The connections between ideas which have been associated together are not, if the matter may be put somewhat crudely, between the whole of one idea and the whole of another, but they are linkages between certain parts or aspects of the ideas. The pupil, for example, may associate the name of a man with the kind of clothes he wears, he may connect snow with "whiteness," or religion with church-going. To refer again to the illustration of the child and the hot stove, the sensation of pain may be connected with the brightness of the nickel-plate, with the blackness of the stove, or even with the position of the stove in the room. The child may thus come to avoid either bright or black objects, or he may keep away from the corner of the room where the unpleasant experience came to

---

[1]Gates, *Psychology for Students of Education,* pp. 306-7. The Macmillan Co., N. Y. Used by permission.

him. Moreover, he may connect the word "hot" with any one of these reactions. The reason for his behaving in this manner is that he has not been able to separate the element of "hotness" from the total situation. Only gradually and after many and varied experiences will he learn to understand the abstract word. And the process by which this knowledge will be gained may be traced through three stages. (1) Because the child feels the heat and sees the stove at the same time he will perhaps connect the idea "hot" with the stove. (2) After a time, however, he will have had the sensation of heat in connection with many different objects—a steam pipe, a teakettle, an electric bulb, and the like. In these experiences the bonds between the feeling and the idea of heat will be strengthened by exercise. The different kinds of situations, however, will prevent the idea from being too firmly connected with any particular object. (3) Finally when the child has had experience with both hot and cold stoves, pipes, or other objects, "hotness" will be so completely disassociated from all irrelevant elements that the child will have a clear idea of it and will be able to think of it apart from any particular situation.

In some such manner as this all abstract ideas are formed. And although the process seems at first to be very different from that of the simpler associational learning, the difference is largely in the fact that, in the acquiring of abstract ideas, the connections are formed between the finer, more subtle elements of the situations involved.

A very practical consideration for the teacher grows out of these facts. He can scarcely be too careful about the use of abstract terms in the teaching of children. A glib recital by the child of such words as sin, salvation, righteousness and faith can by no means be taken to indicate that he really grasps the ideas for which the words stand. Before he can fully understand an abstraction like "faith," for example, the pupil must face many situations containing the element of faith in such form that his attention is directed toward it. This learning must be done also under many different conditions so that the other elements will vary while the faith element remains constant, and thus the idea will not be connected merely with some particular situation. The child will perhaps be led to know something of the faith of a dog in its master, of a boy in his "Dad," of a sick person in his physician, of a learner in his teacher, and of a depositor in his banker. Even then the idea will not be thoroughly abstracted until faith has been seen in contrast to doubt and lack of trust.

It will be clear, then, that the teaching of children must be chiefly in concrete terms. Definitions and abstract doctrinal formulations should come relatively late in the process if they are to be genuinely helpful. Otherwise they will lead to superficiality. A child's religion cannot be judged by the freedom with which he uses theological words and phrases. He can without much difficulty be taught to repeat adult expressions which, because they have no basis in his experience, are little more than empty words to him. In this way, all too often, the child is robbed of the feeling of reality which should accompany the ex-

pressions of religion. A group of four- and five-year-
old children were heard on one occasion singing lus-
tily before an adult audience:

> "I was sinking deep in sin
>   Far from the blissful shore
> Very deeply stained within,
>   Sinking to rise no more. . . ."

One cannot but wonder what was being done to the
child's sense of genuineness in religious utterance
by this exercise.

The transfer of training.—There is a problem of
learning upon which considerable light is thrown by
an understanding of the process of abstraction. Brief
mention of it must be made here. It is the problem
as to how far a response learned in one situation
will transfer to another and different situation. A
great deal of educational discussion has centered in
this question of the transfer of training because it
is one of the points of marked difference between the
older and the newer conceptions of education. The
excessive emphasis upon ancient languages and mathematics in the older view was due largely to the belief that habits of application, of sound thinking, of
accurate observation, of memorization, and the like,
would carry over from these subjects to others, and
to the various activities of life outside the school.
Psychological study and experiment during the past
decade or two has shown that any extreme view of
the amount of transfer must be given up. Practice
in memorizing Latin declensions does not necessarily
improve the pupil's ability to memorize poetry. Special school training in neatness in arithmetic does not

necessarily make the pupil neat in his school work as a whole or in his habits at home.

The question of transfer is still, to some extent, an open one. There is need for much more experimentation in this field. But the general trend of the evidence now available is clear enough. The amount of transfer is much less than has commonly been supposed and it varies greatly according to certain known conditions of learning. The most favorable condition is that in which there is a conscious effort to secure the transfer, and where the pupils possess high intelligence and ability to generalize upon their experience. The reason for this is made clear by the fact already touched upon in the discussion of how abstract ideas are built up. It is obvious that it requires both intelligence and the power of abstraction to see the connection between, say, honesty in the use of money and honesty in school-work; or between a courageous response to an Old Testament battle situation and courage to do the Christian thing today in a critical and unfriendly environment. Yet the possibility that the habits and attitudes learned in one of these situations will carry over to the other is largely dependent upon such connections being seen and understood.

Shall the church school teacher expect the training given to his pupils in Bible story situations, or in classroom situations, to carry over to the playground, the home, and, later on, the business world or the world of politics? This transfer is likely to take place only as definite applications are made to a variety of situations and as the pupils become able to see the "common elements" in them and to make their own generalizations. As the pupils gain this ability they build up abstract ideas of courage, honesty, loyalty, dependability, and the like, and these may, in a manner to be described in later chapters, became effective ideals that will control conduct even in new situations. For young children, however, it is clear that teaching must be very concrete and must seek to equip for the actual situations that the children face from day to day.

How are changes effected through reasoning?—

Learning, even in the narrower intellectual sense, involves much more than the acquiring of ideas, the gaining of information. Although education has, in the past, too largely centered its attention upon the transmission of knowledge, men have always recognized a difference between knowledge and wisdom. They have understood that it is one thing for a man to be able to recite innumerable facts, and quite another thing for him to have the ability to "think things through." And while there are vast differences in the way in which men use their powers of reflection, these powers constitute a most important part of human equipment. Human beings learn not only by establishing motor reactions, or habits, and not merely by connecting or by abstracting ideas. They learn also by reasoning. And many of the most significant changes that are wrought in the individual result from the development of reflective thought. How these changes are brought about must now be considered.

What reasoning is.—What reasoning is may perhaps best be seen by examining some typical situations in which it is exercised. These situations will involve the facing of problems; for reasoning and problem solving may be considered as almost synonymous terms. Confronted with a difficulty most mature persons will, at least to some extent, try to reason their way out. Their method of attack will differ, in important respects, from that of one of the lower animals placed in similar circumstances. Consider, for example, the differences between the behavior of a young child in whom reflective thought is relatively undeveloped, when faced with a puzzling situation, and that of a thoughtful adult. Perhaps a mechanical toy has suddenly refused to operate. Such a thing has never before happened and the child is perplexed. He pulls and pushes, thumps and shakes and then pulls again. Possibly he jars something loose and the toy works once more. But he does not know exactly what he has done, and should the situation arise again, he would go through the same performance even if, this time, the trouble was caused by an unwound spring. His method of attack is that known as "trial-and-error." If the problem were faced often enough he would perhaps "hit upon" the solution once in a while and would gradually learn how to start the toy again, at least in some cases.

Suppose, however, the child fails to achieve the desired result and, with tears in his eyes, brings the toy to his father. The adult may at first shake it and pull at its various parts, but soon he ceases these "random movements" and thinks. Perhaps the toy is unwound. The key is turned a few times, but without results. Then there must be something broken, or perhaps bent. Turning the object in his

hand the father finds the bent part and straightens
it. The toy now works as well as ever.

In three important respects this behavior of the
adult differs from that of the child. (1) There is
a more careful examination of the object with attention directed toward certain parts of it instead
of vaguely at the whole. (2) There is a calling upon
past experience when similar situations have been
faced, for suggested solutions. (3) There is the
formulation and testing out of hypotheses. One of
these hypotheses—"the toy is unwound" proved to
be incorrect; the other "there must be something
bent" was found to be true and it led to the solution
of the problem.

The situation used in this illustration is, of course,
a very simple one. Yet it will be found to be quite
typical of those which involve much more complex
processes. And the three points of difference between
the behavior of the adult and that of the young child
are really the marks which distinguish reasoning from
other forms of learning.

Reasoning as mental exploration.—Of course the
problem may be one that does not call for an actual
motor response. The "trying out" may be done with
the mind instead of with the fingers. Thus, in the apt
phrasing of Woodworth, reasoning is said to be "the
process of *mental*, as distinguished from *motor* exploration."[2] And it will not be difficult to discover
elements of similarity between even its more complex
and subtle forms and the procedure of the man with
the mechanical toy. The steps which have been outlined, if they are not thought of in too rigid a man-

---

[2]*Psychology: A Study of Mental Life*, p. 462.

ner, will be found to characterize most adult thinking under circumstances where merely habitual responses will not suffice.[3] There is always an element of novelty about situations that stimulate reasoning. There is a measure of truth in the statement that man does not really think until he is "up against it."

It would be an error, however, to suppose that reflective thought is entirely different from other forms of learning. Even the most brilliant reasoning is dependent upon past connections. The "flow of ideas" which is evoked by a new, or partially new situation will be in accord with the principles of association discussed in the last chapter. The richer one's experience in dealing with related problems, the freer will be the flow of ideas; the more training one has had in looking for significant details, the more fruitful will be the clues that suggest themselves. To the experienced automobile mechanic whose car suddenly stops on the highway, many ideas are immediately suggested. To the novice in a similar situation perhaps the only idea that comes is: "I must be out of gas." This dependence of reasoning upon ideas, upon experience and knowledge, points to the fallacy in some uses that are made of the discussion method of teaching. It is of little value for a class group to discuss matters about which they do not have a sufficient background of knowledge. To do so but leads to superficiality, inefficiency, and even false reasoning.

How new ideas arise.—There is one aspect of reflective thought which cannot be explained merely on the basis of past connections although it is by no

---

[3] Read the illustration of reasoning in the church school on p. 131 of this book. Distinguish the three steps in this case.

means independent of them. After one has been wrestling with a problem for some time there may flash into the mind a new idea which perhaps contains the solution of the difficulty. How does this new idea arise? I have been thinking over the question: How old is John? I recall the fact that James is four years older than John. I remember also that Mary, who has just passed her tenth birthday is two years younger than James. And although I may never before have known John's age I now "see" that he is eight years old. I have learned something new by reasoning upon facts already known to me.

The process by which such "new ideas" arise is really a kind of "perception that is not sense perception."[4] It is what is usually called an inference and is perhaps best thought of as a response to the common elements of several ideas held in the mind at the same time. A somewhat similar response was described in showing that abstract ideas are acquired by responding to certain common features of many different situations. The syllogism provides another simple illustration.

> All men are mortal.
> John Brown is a man.
> Therefore John Brown is mortal.

By holding together in the mind the idea of the mortality of human beings and of the humanity of John Brown, one perceives that the man in question must be mortal.

---

[4] Woodworth, *Psychology*, p. 422.

The greater the complexity of the problem upon which one is reasoning the larger is the number of facts which must be put together, and the finer and more subtle are the relations which must be perceived, if the solution is to be reached. Yet the process by which hypotheses suggest themselves, and inferences are made, is essentially the same as in the simpler cases. The man who is reasoning about intricate matters may have to arrange and rearrange the ideas in his mind many times before he "sees" the elements which provide him with a fruitful hypothesis. He may also, because relations are not "seen" clearly, follow many false clues. But if he has a sufficient motive and sufficient fertility of mind, he will try out in imagination one hypothesis after another until the satisfactory solution has been found. And when the "key idea" comes to him it may seem so obvious that he will wonder why he did not "see it" long before. There are facts and principles of science which, if they are pointed out to him, may be grasped by the schoolboy today and yet, only a few decades ago, men of genius and of high scientific training could not see them.

Factors upon which reasoning depends.—Given a sufficient motive, successful reasoning depends upon three factors: the free flow of ideas; the fertility of the mind in providing hypotheses; and the proper mental set—a purposeful, attentive, and critical attitude.

1. The first of these factors simply means that as already pointed out, efficient reasoning is dependent upon the possession of an adequate body of information about the field in which the reasoning is to be

done. If the pupils in the church school are to find the Christian solution of a moral problem they must not only have a knowledge of Christian principles, but they must have connected those principles in their past experience with many situations having points of similarity to the one under consideration. Otherwise the necessary ideas are not likely to suggest themselves.

2. The fertility of the mind is largely a gift of nature. It is, no doubt, a function of intelligence and there are vast differences among individuals in the degree to which they possess it. There is something incalculable about the way "insights" come to the mind. They cannot be forced. They either occur to the reasoner or they do not. Training may add to the pupil's store of knowledge, or it may improve his method of attack, but it can do little toward the improvement of this important quality of his mind.

3. The third factor, however, like the first is susceptible of improvement by training. Reasoning is purposive thinking. And the purpose—to bring about the solution of the problem—is really a mental set which directs, to a large degree, the flow of ideas and determines the responses that will satisfy and those that will be rejected. Much, therefore, depends upon the attitude of the learner. Is he capable of sustained attention? Has he learned to keep the main problem constantly before him? Has his training made him observant of all significant details? Above all is he severely critical of his inferences and conclusions, testing them in every way possible before finally accepting them? For the person who reasons effectively these questions can be answered in

the affirmative. And they suggest traits which training may do much to develop. The improvement of reasoning, however, will not be brought about by special courses in "the art of thinking." It will result from practice in the solving of problems under the skilful guidance of a sympathetic and understanding leader. The way to learn to reason is by reasoning. But democratic guidance is necessary because of the many pitfalls that lurk along the way.

The reasoning of children.—A word must be said about the reasoning of children. The doctrine that childhood is an unreflective period and that reasoning develops more or less suddenly with the dawn of adolescence, has had a considerable influence upon the pedagogy of the past. A closer study of the behavior of children has, however, revealed the fallacy in this doctrine. Children do reason. And their thinking has many of the same characteristics as that of adults. But the process often appears different because of the limitations due to their immaturity. Norsworthy and Whitley, in their illuminating discussion of reasoning in children,[5] point out that there are three main differences between the thinking of the child and that of the adult. (1) *Children think less than do adults* both because they have less need to think, and because their thinking is generally discouraged by the adult members of society. All too often problems are moved out of their way and their attempts at reasoning are ridiculed because they appear strange from the adult point of view. (2) *The thinking of children is less accurate than that of adults.* But this is due to their immaturity. Their supply of

---
[5]*Psychology of Childhood*, pp. 169-184.

facts is very limited, their information is inaccurate, their power of sustained attention is relatively undeveloped and they do not have the necessary experience to enable them to take a critical attitude toward their problems or toward the conclusions which they reach. (3) *The data used by children in their thinking is that which arises out of their own interests.* They reason about apparently trivial matters, about their play and their childhood fancies. But the unimportance of the material does not make the process valueless. The three-year-old boy who was afraid that the camp fire, since it was not in the grate, might run away, and the little girl who asked her mother why she was "washing the soap," were thinking in their own way. It is with just such data that the reasoning of the young child will be concerned.

The reasoning ability of children normally develops with the years. The problems which they are able to solve gradually increase in difficulty. There is no sudden change at the beginning of adolescence and maturity is reached somewhere in the middle teens. Thus the youth of sixteen can reason, in fields where he possesses the facts, about as well as the average adult, the limitations of his thinking being due chiefly to his lack of experience. Adults, however, differ very widely in their powers of reflective thought. They range all the way from the man who cannot solve correctly the problem: "If two pencils cost five cents, how many pencils can you buy for fifty cents?" to the philosopher who seeks the solution of the ultimate problem of the universe.

Reasoning in the church school.—The teaching of the church school may, if it will, do much to encourage reflection. It may frequently confront its pupils with problems, whether of thought or of conduct, that call for solutions in terms of Christian ideals; it may help them to think of all the pertinent facts which may contribute toward the right outcome; it may encourage them to face unflinchingly the Christian implications of their thoughts and acts, and it may seek to provide opportunity for them to carry out their conclusions and to accept responsibility for them. Suppose, for example, that a class of young people has been discussing the question: Can we live according to Jesus' ideal of love in the world today? For many class-periods they have sought answers to the various sub-problems involved in the larger issue. What is Jesus' ideal of love? Is it practicable to follow it? What are the relations of life in which it would be most difficult to apply it? What might be the result of its application in these situations? What are the possible attitudes to take toward this whole problem? Which one shall we adopt as our own? In attempting to answer these questions the young people have studied many passages of the New Testament, prominent among them being Matthew 5:38-48; John 13:34-35; Ephesians 4:31; 1 Corinthians 13; Luke 10:25-37; and Matthew 25:31-46. They have also called to mind many present day situations in business, church, and race relationships, where the principle of love has been followed, and also where it has been flagrantly violated. They have decided that there are but three possible attitudes which may be taken toward the main problem. (1) That the ideal is wrong and therefore, of course, is not to be followed. (2) That the ideal is right but is not to be practiced since it was meant to be applied only in an ideal world. (3) That the ideal is right and is to be practiced today. After much discussion they are ready to vote and they place themselves on record in the words: "That it is the sense of this group that as Christians we can and should practice Jesus' ideal of love in the world today, whatever the consequences."

Such a procedure will stimulate much more thinking on the part of the young people than the more formal methods of teaching. And it is much more likely to bear fruit in life. In the course of the discussion many local situations, which call for the practice of love will arise. The best outcome of all, and the one without which the learning process is incomplete, will be attained when the young people, as a group as well as individually, put into practice the things about which they have been talking, and act in a Christlike way toward that foreign family, toward the young people of a less-favored social group, in that important business transaction, and in other concrete situations in their lives during the week.

Thinking, reasoning, problem-solving, accepting responsibility for one's conclusions—these things make for genuineness in religion as in other realms. Where they are encouraged, the pupil's beliefs and convictions come to be not just what he has been told, but what he has seen for himself. And his religion is something very different from that of the man, described by William James, whose "religion has been made for him by others, communicated to him by tradition, determined to fixed forms by imitation, and retained by habit.''[6] He has a better understanding of the truths which have been taught him, a finer appreciation of their meaning for life, and a firmer grip upon them as guides to conduct and as incentives to Christian living.

How are changes effected through indirect learning?—

Attention has thus far been directed toward the question of how the pupil learns particular things. The discussion, it is hoped, has thrown some light upon the way in which a habit is formed, or a certain bit of knowledge is gained, or the solution of a particular problem is brought about. But no one of these things takes place as an isolated process. The pupil is never engaged merely in establishing a habit, in memorizing, or in reasoning. Throughout all, he is living. In any one class period he learns not only the thing which has, or is supposed to have, the center of the stage. Many learnings are going on at the same time. And the teacher who is interested in more than simply teaching the lesson text, cannot but be vitally concerned about the other matters which the pupil is learning indirectly; about the attitudes and interests he is building up, and the ideas of well-being or distress, of zeal or boredom, of enjoyment or antipathy, that come to him during the recitation period.

"Simultaneous learnings" in the church school.— A concrete situation will perhaps make clearer what

---

[6]*Varieties of Religious Experience*, p. 6.

is meant by these "simultaneous learnings."[7]   The topic for the day in a certain class of Junior boys is: "Hezekiah Rebels Against Sennacherib," a lesson based upon parts of the eighteenth and nineteenth chapters of the Book of Second Kings.   The teacher has spent considerable time in studying the historical and geographical details of the story and is trying to make plain the rather intricate political relationship involved in it.   But it is a large undertaking for one brief lesson period.   The pupils have trouble in reading the many strange sounding words, Hezekiah, Zechariah, Asherah, Lachish, Rabsaris, Elia,-kim, Sennacherib, and the like.   They listen to what the teacher says but many wayward thoughts flit through their minds: I wish my parents did not make me come to Sunday school; I wonder what "sackcloth" looks like and what the "Asherath" were that Hezekiah cut down; I don't like this teacher—he is "too religious"; I wish I could reach Tom with my foot—he needs a "jolt"; I hope the bell rings soon—it must be about time for it.   These and many other similar ideas occur to the boys as the story proceeds.   When it is finished, the majority of the pupils feel relieved.   They have, in varying degrees, appropriated the main facts of the lesson—at least they know that Sennacherib was a proud heathen king, that Hezekiah was a good man, and that 185,-000 of the Assyrians were slain.   But the lesson has been endured rather than enjoyed, so far as most

---

[7]The expression is one that is used by W. H. Kilpatrick whose "Foundations of Method" contains a suggestive discussion of indirect learning.   Kilpatrick uses the terms associate and concomitant learning for two different phases of the process.   Many of the ideas which follow are taken from his treatment of the subject.

of the boys are concerned. Perhaps Tom is an exception. He had a little better grasp of the story than the others and the spectacular Assyrian rather caught his fancy. He felt something of the glory of the "cohorts . . . . gleaming with purple and gold" despite the tragic ending of the enterprise.

In the class period just described, the boys probably learned many things besides the lesson which was assigned for the day. Or at least they would do so if they had several such lesson periods. The teacher had intended that the pupils should learn some facts of Old Testament history. He had really hoped also that the lesson would "strengthen love of the right and hatred of the wrong." But as he walked home that day he was very doubtful about his success in attaining the latter objective and he comforted himself with the thought that the boys seemed to "get some of the facts anyway."

A critical observer of the class, however, might well ask some searching questions. Are the pupils learning to dislike Sunday school? Are they coming to think of the Bible as a rather dry book of history? Do they feel that the class is a poor place to find out things they really want to know? Is there being developed in them an attitude of disrespect for the teacher and perhaps for the church? Will Tom's response to the splendor of the Assyrian army tinge his whole life of feeling with a sensitiveness toward the glory of battle? The observer would, no doubt, find himself compelled to answer many of these questions affirmatively. It would be clear to him that while the pupils were learning some facts of Old Testament history, they were also being taught many wrong attitudes which might color their whole outlook on life.

The process by which these things that are not directly aimed at in a given lesson are learned is what has been designated indirect learning. Such learning is indirect so far as the pupils are concerned although the wise teacher will always give it much consideration. He will do so because he knows that the attitudes which are built up in this way may be wholesome rather than harmful, and that they may, if properly guided, contribute much toward the attainment of the objectives of religious education.

Marginal and focal responses.—Indirect learning is not any less dependent upon the laws of exercise and of effect than the other forms of learning which have been considered. If the pupils learn to dislike the Bible it is because certain responses of hostility or aversion have been made in connection with it and have brought some sort of satisfaction to the pupils. If, on the other hand, they are developing an attitude of reverence in the worship services it is because they are finding satisfaction in responses of respect and devotion. The difference between direct and indirect learning, however, is that in the latter the responses are largely marginal rather than focal, that is, they are matters that are not directly in the center, but are in the margin of consciousness. At any one time the thing to which the pupil gives direct attention may be thought of as being at the focus of consciousness. But there are many stimuli of which he is perhaps vaguely conscious: the pressure of his arm upon the desk, the presence of other pupils about him, the temperature of the room, the pictures on the wall, the sound of a passing automobile. These things are in the margin of the pupil's field of attention. But attention shifts easily and an unusual sound, or sight, or an alluring train of thought suggested by something the teacher says, may bring any of these marginal stimulations to the center of consciousness. Moreover what is now at the focus of attention may very quickly pass to the margin.

Both the focal and the marginal responses of the pupil are important although the latter are too often ignored. In the class that has been described the pupils learned many unwholesome attitudes because, while they were engaged in memorizing, or in listening to the teacher, or in reading the lesson text, they were making numerous marginal responses involving feelings of discomfort and dissatisfaction. And these responses were more or less satisfying to them, for it is not contradictory to say that one may find satisfaction in being dissatisfied. But under more wholesome conditions the marginal responses would be very different. There would be a sense of happiness in the task, a feeling of respect for the teacher, a desire, perhaps, to be more thorough in learning, a silent resolve to "know more of this," or to carry the lesson into everyday life. And such responses would not only increase the amount of direct learning; they would tend to build up attitudes of appreciation and loyalty toward the Bible, the teacher, the class and the church.

How the right kind of marginal responses can be secured is thus an important question for the teacher.

Yet these responses because they are so numerous, so complex and subtle, may appear to him to be quite beyond his control. They are all a part of the teaching and learning process, however, and the teacher must to a large degree be held responsible for this indirect learning of his pupils.

Conditions of sound indirect learning.—It is not possible, of course, for the teacher to have in mind and to plan for each of the attendant learnings that may go on during the lesson period. There are, however certain conditions of learning which favor the right kind of marginal responses, and tend toward the development of the more desirable attitudes. This kind of indirect learning is most likely to take place first, when the environmental conditions under which the pupils work are pleasing as well as wholesome; and second, when the pupils enter enthusiastically into activities and enterprises which they feel to have genuine worth.

1. Many factors enter into the wholesome surroundings which stimulate satisfactory marginal responses. According to Kilpatrick the most "immediately impelling" of them are the tone and manner of the teacher, and the observed responses of the other children.[8] If the teacher has a pleasant voice and a sympathetic and understanding manner, and if the members of the class respond readily and with evident satisfaction in the discussion of the topic, the situation is favorable to wholesome indirect learning. But there are very many contributing factors: the sense of successful achievement as the work of the class moves forward, the beauty and significance of the pictures

[8] *Foundations of Method*, p. 120.

on the wall, the attractiveness of the room, the appropriateness of the music, the methodical manner of taking care of routine matters—these and a host of other items have their quiet but important influence upon the pupils. Nor must it be forgotten that, among the important marginal stimulations, are such factors as the teacher's through-the-week contacts with his pupils and even the general attitude of the church toward its children.

2. The second condition that is conducive to the development of right attitudes involves engaging the pupils, as far as possible, in purposeful activities. If the teacher would secure the desired results from indirect learning, he must use a teaching technique that stresses "activities, enterprises, experiences which enlist the heart and soul of childhood and youth." For "when children work successfully at purposeful activities which challenge their powers, they almost certainly build favorable attitudes toward everything that entered helpfully into the success."[9]

It is not within the scope of this book to discuss teaching methods as such. And the securing of wholesome indirect learning is more largely a matter of the spirit of the classroom—or of the teaching situation wherever it may occur—than it is of the particular techniques used by the teacher. If due consideration is to be given to the development of attitudes, however, a larger place must be made in the work of the church school for pupil-activities. These activities may include a great variety of undertakings but the essential thing is that they engage the pupil in actively pursuing some worthy end that ap-

---

[9]Kilpatrick, *Foundations of Method*, pp. 129, 134.

peals to him. At times they will be predominantly
mental activities, as in discussion and investigation;
again they will be largely manual, as in handwork;
and at still other times they will involve such enterprises as giving a party for some foreign children,
planning a worship program for the department, or
carrying on a "Go-to-Church" campaign.

The place of self-chosen pupil activity.—It will be
clear that this principle means giving much more consideration than has been thought wise in the past, to
the desires, the likes and dislikes, and the choices of
the pupils. The activities will be such as make a
genuine appeal to the children or young people, and,
as far as possible, they will be self-chosen. Mere external coercion usually leads to very questionable outcomes because it means conflicting mind-sets. One
set is given by the necessity of doing what is demanded; another by the real desire of the pupil.
And, because of the conflict, the learning is not very
effective and unwholesome attitudes are developed.
Where there is a singleness of purpose the results,
both of direct and of indirect learning, are likely
to be much better than in cases of coercion, and they
will make a larger contribution to the growth of
the learner.

The emphasis upon pupil-activity should not, of
course, he interpreted to mean that there is no place
for external coercion in the learning process. Situations arise where a measure of compulsion has to
be used. But if the proper relationship exists between teacher and learner—whether in the home or
in the school—they will be much less frequent than
is commonly supposed. And in such situations co-

ercion should always be used with care and understanding, since the amount of genuine learning which
it may be expected to secure is largely determined
by the ability of the learner on the one hand, and
by the strength or the weakness of his resentment
against constraint on the other.

The value of the right kind of indirect learning
in religious education can scarcely be overestimated.
The wise teacher of religion knows that the development of appreciations, interests, and loyalties, is a
most important part of his teaching work. And many
such attitudes are built up by means of the marginal
responses of the pupils in the church school. The
contribution that is made by indirect learning to personality and character is thus far-reaching and of
vast significance. Despite the good intentions of the
teacher it is quite possible for his manner of conducting the class to defeat his purpose. It may even
mould the disposition of the pupil in the direction
of irreligion and of hostility toward the Bible and
the church. Under wise guidance, however, indirect learning will result in more wholesome attitudes.
It will lead the pupil to find lasting satisfaction in
the enterprises of the church; it will, at its best, give
him a keen and abiding interest in the Christian life
and in all that relates to the cause of Christ in the
world.

How may the learning process be viewed as a
whole?—

This chapter and the preceding one have described
how changes are brought about in original nature.
For convenience in study the process was divided into
five different phases each of which was considered

separately. Attention was first directed to learning of the simple habit forming type, or (1) Animal learning as it is sometimes called because it is the kind of thing that takes place even among animals. It was seen, however, that the young child soon becomes capable of another kind of learning in which ideas are used; and the simplest form of ideational learning was described in chapter five. This phase of the learning process, since it involves little more than the connecting of ideas, is often referred to as (2) Associational learning. The present chapter began with an account of the way abstract ideas are acquired, and then took up the discussion of reasoning or reflective thought. These two higher forms of the process of bringing about changes are called by Thorndike: (3) Analytic learning, and (4) Selective learning.[10] Finally the changes that result from the marginal responses of the pupil were discussed under the heading of (5) Indirect learning.

This fivefold division of learning is necessary for purposes of study but the reader should not interpret it to mean that there are five different processes involved. It would be much more correct to think of each division as but a different aspect of the same process. Learning is done by the pupil and not merely by his muscles, or by his nerves, or by any faculties of memory or reasoning. The pupil functions as a unit. The learning process is one. It is quite possible for the five kinds of learning to go on at the same time. In the formation of a habit, such as is involved for example in the playing of a bar of music on the violin, a child will not only

[10]*Educational Psychology*, Vol. II, p. 17.

make certain muscular responses, but will associate ideas, use abstraction and reasoning, and at least begin to build up certain attitudes, perhaps of appreciation and interest. Moreover, the highest type of abstract thinking may be conditioned by physical factors and often involves muscular reactions.

The changes that are brought about in the pupil are, therefore, not independent of each other. They cannot be made after the manner in which a carpenter alters a building, changing first one room and then another. They are wrought out, rather, as vital processes in the life of a single active, growing person. Throughout all of these changes, and largely by means of them, the pupil comes to have a certain kind of personality. He becomes some sort of person. He lives some kind of life. The remaining chapters of this book will discuss more specifically how the growth of the pupil may be guided so as to make probable the attainment of Christian personality; so as to lead toward the manner of life which meets all situations ''in the spirit and way of Christ.'' The reader should be clear, at this point, that the nature of the pupil's learning is essentially the same whether the changes are brought about in the home, the school, or the church. The pupil learns by thinking, feeling, doing, experiencing —in a word, by living. The process of education is always some kind of living; the outcome is always some manner of person.

QUESTIONS—

1. How does the pupil acquire abstract ideas? Explain the process by showing how the word salvation may come to have meaning for him.

2. In what respects does adult behavior in the face of a puzzling situation differ from that of the very young child?

3. How do "new ideas" arise in the mind?

4. What do you do when you are confronted with a problem and no ideas that suggest a possible solution come to you? Give instances.

5. In what sense is correct reasoning always dependent upon information? Give several illustrations of reasoning that was faulty because the facts were not known.

6. How does the reasoning of children differ from that of adults?

7. Why is reflective thinking a peculiar need of Protestantism? Do the teaching methods used in your church encourage reasoning? How?

8. How may compelling a child to go to church defeat the very purpose the parent has in mind in insisting upon church attendance?

9. Do you agree with the view that wholesome educational guidance involves giving "much more consideration than has been thought wise in the past to the desires, the likes and dislikes, and the choices of the pupils"? How would you answer the objections to this position?

10. Why is it more correct to think of the types of learning as five aspects of a single process rather than as five different processes?

REPORTS AND INVESTIGATIONS—

1. Ask a number of children, nine to twelve years of age, the meaning of such words as, kindness, selfishness, pity, sin, salvation, justice, righteousness, faith. Note carefully the answers. How far do the children seem to have a clear understanding of the abstract word?

2. Give some illustrations of children's reasoning. Where the reasoning is faulty explain what has taken place.

3. Describe one or more cases that have come under your observation where the members of a church school group (in the classroom or out of it) have made a serious effort to think through to a Christian solution a problem that confronted them. Evaluate the experience.

4. Examine some of the lesson material in use in your church school especially in the Young People's Division. Do the topics, questions, and suggestions lend themselves to a treatment that will stimulate the pupil's thinking? Give a number of specific references in support of your answer.

5. Make a detailed list of the conditions that are favorable to the right kind of indirect learning. Observe a church

school class in session and test it by your list. What attitudes would you say were being developed in the pupils by the work of the class?

REFERENCES—

Chapman and Counts, Principles of Education, chap. viii. Houghton Mifflin.

Gates, Arthur I., Psychology for Students of Education, chap. xiii from page 305—chap. xv. Macmillan.

Kilpatrick, William H., Foundations of Method. Especially chaps. i and vi-ix. Macmillan.

Pyle, William H., The Psychology of Learning, pp. 96-112. Warwick and York.

Thorndike, Edward L., The Psychology of Learning, chap. iv. Teachers' College.

Woodworth, Robert S., Psychology, chap. xviii. Henry Holt.

CHAPTER VII

PERSONALITY

How Does Personality Emerge?

The chief interest of the teacher centers in persons. In the course of his teaching he may have to give a great deal of attention to materials and processes, but his interest in these things depends upon their contribution to the personality of his pupils. In the preceding chapters there has been little mention of personality as such. Yet much that has been said has borne directly upon its development. The discussion of original nature and of the different kinds of learning has called attention to many of the factors that tend to make the pupil what he is. Thus far, however, the emphasis has been upon particular processes and these, for convenience in study, have been considered separately.

There is a need that the teacher study the development of personality from a somewhat broader point of view. In addition to a knowledge of the matters treated in chapters five and six, he should understand how the individual is moulded by his social environment and, at the same time, how the self develops, and the choices which the pupil makes as a morally responsible being determine so largely what he becomes. It is to considerations of this kind that the remainder of the book is devoted. In the present chapter the questions to be faced are: (1) What is the meaning of personality? (2) Upon what factors is personality dependent? and (3) How is personality conditioned by the developing idea of the self?

WHAT IS THE MEANING OF PERSONALITY?—

Personality is a word of varied meaning. It is thought of in so many different senses that, if a good substitute could be found, a different term should perhaps be used to describe the developing life of the pupil. But there is no substitute for this really meaningful word. It is too fitting and suggestive to be discarded, and it cannot wisely be avoided in thinking of the objective of religious education; for "no lesser term can be found to express the richness and fullness of the abilities and possibilities to be found in persons."[1] The sense in which the word is to be used must, however, be made clear.

In loose speech and in popular writing personality is often referred to as if it were a kind of psychic force by means of which the salesman may overcome the resistance of his customer, or the leader bring the multitude into harmony with his will. It is frequently said, also, that the success of the good teacher is due to his "possession" of personality, while the lack of this necessary qualification is given as the reason for the failure of the teacher who is inefficient. On the other hand, an attractive appearance, a clear eye, and a glib tongue, may be sufficient endowment for a man to be described as a "forceful personality." And the term is even applied, at times, to one who is made conspicuous among his fellows merely because of his eccentricities.

Such uses of the word are erroneous or are at least inadequate, although they call attention to certain qualities—appearance, individuality, influence—which can scarcely be ignored in thinking of its meaning. But every individual who has developed normally, has some kind of personality whether it is strong or weak, repulsive or fascinating; and the mere possession of a few striking traits does not justify an extravagant use of the term. *Personality is what the individual is as a whole.* It is "one's whole self, in its weakness as well as in its strength, in its moods as

---

[1] C. E. Rugh, *Religious Education*, Vol. **XXI**, p. 607.

well as in its principles, in its dispositions as well as in its will, in its relations to the whole of its surroundings.''[2] In a broad sense, therefore, education has to do with *the whole pupil* '' in all his activities, in all his relations, in all his aspirations.''[3] His personality is the total way in which he thinks, feels and acts. It includes his disposition and temperament, his presence and demeanor, and especially his character. It is all that he is—the product of forces both within and without himself.

But effective personality, whether good or bad, is something of an achievement. The term can scarcely be applied to the pupil until at least a measure of ''wholeness'' has been attained. And while it was said in the last chapter that the individual functions as a unit, there is a sense in which this is not true at first. Unity has to be achieved. How the pupil comes to act as a whole, as a more or less unified self, is, therefore, a basic question for the teacher. For the child, at first, is little more than a bundle of impulses or an aggregate of many uncoordinated situation response bonds. He is only potentially a person. In time, however, his habits, ideas, feelings, sentiments, and aspirations, become linked up together into a whole. His behavior is consistent. The teacher knows about the way he will act in at least the more common situations. Thus the pupil attains unity. He becomes this or that sort of a person. He has a personality that is considered attractive or repulsive, or one that is, perhaps, thought of rather indifferently. The present chapter seeks to analyze some of the factors that contribute to ''the individual

²Welton, *What Do We Mean by Education?* p. 85.
³Ibid. p. 89.

in the making,'' and to outline the process by which personality emerges. It should be noted, however, that the central interest of the church school teacher is not simply in the growth of personality but in the development of *a certain kind of high and worthy personality*. The church school wants the pupil to become a moral and religious person. And it desires for him that his morality and religion may develop in harmony with the Christian ideal. Its objective, in a word, is Christian personality. Nevertheless, the guidance of Christian growth requires an understanding of the development of personality at its lower, as well as at its higher levels. Thus attention must first be directed to the earlier stages of the process by which selfhood is attained.

UPON WHAT FACTORS IS PERSONALITY DEPENDENT?—

Of one thing the student of human nature soon becomes aware: no simple analysis of personality is possible. Among the pupils of a single class there may be found the slow and the quick, the cheerful and the gloomy, the talkative and the quiet, the persistent and the easily discouraged, the attractive and the unlovely, the consistent and the unstable, the generous and the selfish. And any serious effort to understand just why this or that pupil has come to be the kind of person he is, will immediately raise far-reaching questions about physical and mental endowment, previous training, environmental influences, and about the deeper philosophical problem of the self. It is quite impossible for the psychologist of today to provide a complete analysis and description of the factors that enter into personality. Only a beginning has been made in this field of investigation. Some of the elements are more clearly understood than others, however, and all that is known of them is of concern to anyone who is interested in human nature. It is possible here merely to suggest in a general way the main factors which give to the pupil his own particular personality. They are bodily constitution; instincts and capacities; environment and training; and the self, or self-organizing principle of the mind.

1. *Bodily constitution.*—Psychological research has revealed the fact that many of the traits to which the term temperament is commonly applied have their basis in certain conditions of the bodily organs —especially the glands—and in the constitution of the nervous system. Some kinds of quickness and of slowness are no doubt due to differences in nervous structure, and the temperament of the bright or of the gloomy child may be traced, at least in part, to bodily factors. Physical health and a proper working of the organs of the body favor an objective attitude of mind and a cheerful disposition.

The ductless glands.—In recent years very great interest has centered upon the study of the ductless or endocrine glands, some of the more important of which are the thyroid, the pituitary, the pineal and the adrenals. It has become clear that many temperamental differences among children and adults may be traced to these organs of internal secretion. In fact, books of a high order have been written to show that the glands are the most potent factors in personality. The author of one such book states as his main thesis: ''That the whole life of man is controlled primarily by his internal secretions.''[4]   And another writer declares: ''We know now that the size and shape of a person's body, the quality of his mind, his personal characteristics—his 'personality' —all are dependent upon a group of minute structures in the body known as endocrine glands.''[5]

This extreme view of the dominance of man by his internal secretions will not be acceptable to the teacher, but, in rejecting it, he will do well to keep in mind some of the more important facts concerning the glands.   For while there is still much to be learned about their functions, the importance of their contribution to the growth of the individual and to his general outlook on life cannot be questioned.   To take but a single illustration: deficiency in the secretions of the thyroid gland is known to have a very serious effect upon the development of the child.   In such cases the brain becomes sluggish, the features are heavy, growth is stunted, the skin is dry and hairless, and the sex organs are poorly developed. On the other hand excessive thyroid activity has the opposite effect and may lead to a condition of animation ''verging on maniacal excitement.''   Very remarkable results have been brought about by feeding thyroid extract to persons deficient in this secretion. In some cases it is possible by such treatment to restore, to a considerable degree, physical and mental vigor. There can be little doubt that many of the other glands, also, profoundly affect the well-being of man and that together they have much to do in determining his temperament. The significance of this fact is seen when it is realized that temperament gives almost a constant bias to the mental development and activity of the individual. "The child natively endowed with a cheerful temperament will be receptive to bright influences, his thoughts will tend to dwell on the future in pleased anticipation, optimistic ideas will easily find a foothold in his mind, while gloomy, pessimistic ideas will gain no permanent influence over him in spite of being intellectually grasped. And with the child of gloomy temperament all this will be reversed. In this way temperament determines our outlook on life, our cast of thought and lines of action."[6]

2. *Instincts and capacities.*—The contribution of the instincts and capacities to personality has already been discussed at length in chapters two, three and four. Some particular aspects of it must now be given further consideration. The instincts, no doubt, vary in strength with different individuals and thus many of the traits that distinguish one person from another, may be due to this kind of dissimilarity in native endowment. It would seem, for example, that the more aggressive type of personality might at least be partially explained by the strength of the instinct of pugnacity or of self-assertion. Most of the "individual differences" discussed in chapter four were seen to be due to variations in original nature having their sources in family and racial inheritance and these differences were not merely in instinctive tendencies but in those higher capacities and special aptitudes which contribute so much that is distinctive to the individual.

[6]McDougall, *An Introduction to Social Psychology,* p. 123. J. W. Luce, Publisher. Used by permission.

The thwarting of impulses.—But there is a very different way in which the instincts may become a determining factor in personality. Instead of their being given wholesome expression these tendencies may be *repressed.* And the thwarting of native impulses not infrequently leads to aberrations of thought and conduct. The way in which repression occurs, and its effect upon human conduct, are matters of very great importance to the serious student of human nature. The limitations of space, however, and the complexity of the subject, make quite impossible any adequate discussion of them here. Only a few of the more significant facts can be mentioned.

There are many reasons why all of man's native impulses cannot be given expression. (1) In the first place, they themselves are sometimes conflicting. The tendency to self-assertion may run counter to that of submission; the impulse to flight may conflict with curiosity; the sex instinct may clash with the desire for social approval. (2) In the second place these impulses may be out of harmony with acquired habits of thought or action and with ideals. The fighting instinct may impel toward conduct that is contrary to one's ideal of good behavior. And this kind of conflict may occur also between the systems of ideas, emotions, and active tendencies that are built up in the course of the individual's development. These sentiments or complexes may themselves conflict. A situation may arise which will cause a clash between a man's patriotism and his religious ideals, or between his "golf complex" and his ideal of persistence at his task. (3) A third reason for the thwarting of many human tendencies is that the environment at any particular time may prevent their expression. A pupil of mediocre ability may find it quite impossible to satisfy in a normal way his impulse to self-assertion if he is placed in a group of "superior" students. The tendency to seek the company of others may be thwarted by a forced separation from friends, or by inability to make friends of those with whom one is compelled to associate.

The thwarting of impulses may be serious or unimportant according to the strength of the impulse and the ability of the person concerned to make satisfactory adjustments. In this ability, as in all other respects, there are large individual differences. And although it is only in extreme cases that thwarting leads to abnormal behavior, an understanding of what happens in extreme cases throws much light upon certain aspects of the thought and conduct of normal persons. When basic impulses are continuously denied expression, some kind of substitution is made, either consciously or unconsciously, by the individual, and satisfaction is found in the new response.

Substitute satisfactions for thwarted impulses.—
1. One of the easiest ways out of the difficulty and one to which almost every person has resorted at one time or another, is to fall back upon the imagination. If the boy cannot be the leader of the gang in fact, he can imagine himself to be "the Pirate King" and really enjoy the day dream. The adolescent girl who is unattractive and unpopular may find satisfaction in imaginary adventures as a princess with many suitors. On the other hand, a lad who feels that he has been rather badly treated by parents or teacher

may brood over his hard lot and imagine himself seized by bandits and carried away to some mountain fastness, while newspaper headlines proclaim to the world the fact that he is missing, and those who have mistreated him search in vain for him.

Daydreaming of this kind does little harm provided the individual does not form the habit of dealing with difficult situations by withdrawing into the unreal world of the imagination and refusing to face the facts. Where this response has become habitual there can be no strong personality. In extreme cases the condition may become pathological and lead to a form of insanity.

2. But there are other ways of dealing with thwarted desires. If an impulse cannot be gratified, one may find reasons why it should not be gratified, and the fictitious reasons may give him a measure of satisfaction. Or if a certain impulse is indulged, despite the promptings of another more worthy one, the tension may be relieved by the process that is known as rationalization, by finding reasons to justify the act to oneself so that it has the appearance of being rational instead of impulsive. Whatever the facts may be, the grapes which cannot be reached are said to be sour. The pupil who cannot surpass another in the attainment of some desired end may decide that the object is not worth striving for, and may even take toward his ''opponent'' an attitude of dislike which he will justify on entirely different grounds. The teacher who leaves his lesson-preparation to go to a ''movie'' finds that he is badly in need of a little recreation. The team that does not win in the contest discovers—perhaps after the game is over—

that there was unfairness on the part of the officials. The youth who gives way to some unworthy impulse attributes his conduct to the influence of his companions. This kind of rationalization which seeks to evade responsibility by projecting the cause of failure beyond oneself is what the psychologist calls projection.

3. Another kind of bent which may be given to the personality by reason of the thwarting of impulses is that known as compensatory behavior. Compensation refers to the tendency to make up for deficiency in one direction by an effort to excel in a different one. Such "substitute responses" may be thoroughly wholesome. The student who could never gain recognition on the athletic field may well throw himself into the work of the discussion club and make a place on the debate team. But compensation may go to extremes and, where the whole situation is not frankly faced by the individual, it may result in peculiar mannerisms or even abnormal behavior. A man of impure mind may denounce impurity in others with puritanical vigor. A speaker whose thought is meagre may, perhaps quite unconsciously, try to make up for the deficiency by loudness of voice. A youth of sensitive nature may assume a rough and boisterous external manner. A Christian of weak faith, who is fearful of losing what faith he has, may affirm his beliefs with an exaggerated certitude.

The superiority of some forms of compensation over others is well pointed out by Gates: "If the maternal instinct is thwarted, better than idle daydreaming, or novel reading, or a pessimistic view of life, or 'sour-grapes,' or a cheery indifference of the Pollyanna type, better than some silly or harmful compensatory activity, would be the substitution of some social, religious, or educational work."[7] In a similar way other impulses which cannot be given normal expression may find an outlet through wholesome substitute activities.

4. Conflicting impulses may lead the individual to still another kind of attempted adjustment that works against the growth of effective personality. A man who is a church member and a politician may, under certain circumstances, find the activities expected of him in these two capacities to be quite out of harmony with each other. As a result of his Christian training he is impelled toward conduct that is in harmony with the Christian ideal. Because of his desire to gain political power he has many impulses to act in ways not in accord with the Christian standard. He may solve the problem by banishing his political activities from his mind when he is thinking "religiously," and by forgetting his religious principles when he is engaged in the enterprise of politics. Of course he will not succeed in making an absolute breach between these two areas of his life. There may, at times, be qualms of conscience because the separation is not complete. Nevertheless if one who knew this man only as a politician were to read an account of his religious activities, it might be difficult for the reader to understand that the item referred to the person known to him.

The method of segregation is a dangerous and altogether unsatisfactory way of dealing with conflicting impulses. In its milder forms, however, it is quite

---

[7] *Psychology for Students of Education,* p. 199.

common. And wherever it occurs it indicates a personality that has not attained unity. In pathological cases it may result in complete dissociation. A system of thoughts, feelings, and acts, may be so split off from that which is looked upon as the individual's normal self as to bring about the condition known as double-personality. A single body, in a sense, houses two "persons" each of whom thinks, feels, and acts independently of the other. This phenomenon is, of course, only rarely found, but it indicates the unwholesome trend of the process of dissociation.

The thwarting of imperative desires will lead the individual to make some kind of accommodation. The common feature of almost all these types of adjustment is the effort to secure some kind of indirect satisfaction of the thwarted impulses. Such efforts may be relatively harmless; they may give a peculiar bias to the personality of the normal individual; or they may lead to abnormal behavior and the disintegration of the self. The outcome will depend in part upon the nervous constitution of the person concerned, and in part upon the way in which he deals with his impulses. Repression tends toward unwholesome adjustments. Impulses that are repressed, that are inhibited, refused recognition, and banished from the mind, may lead to nervous disturbances having varying degrees of seriousness. *A frank recognition of the impulses, a facing of all the facts, and a conscious redirection of activity toward some worthy end, will be much more likely to result in genuine self-control and effective personality.*

3. *Environment and training.*—That environment and training contribute much to personality is per-

haps a commonplace. This book would not have been written but for the conviction that education can bring about changes in original nature and can so direct the development of the individual as to make possible the attainment of Christian personality. And it is clear enough that what the individual is, he is in part because of his home, his friends, his books, his games, his school, his church, his community, his nation, his "day and generation." The church school teacher who would understand his pupils must seek to know as much as possible of their home surroundings, of their through-the-week activities, of their school and community contacts, and of other aspects of their environment which tend to mould character and personality.

It is important to note, however, that environment is a matter of special importance in the early years of life. At this time control of conduct is almost wholly external. The forces of the child's world are at work moulding him in this direction or in that. In the course of his development he gains more of inward control and in time he becomes a morally responsible being. But in early infancy the child is the product of his original nature plus the stimulus and direction, conscious and unconscious, of those who make up his world. Horace Bushnell perceived this truth with vividness and expressed it in his inimitable way when he said that the child during these years "is still within the matrix of the parental life."[8] The infant is not fully born. What he is, is determined by forces outside himself.

The importance of the early years.—It is for this

---

[8] *Christian Nurture,* 1916 edition, p. 19.

reason that the beginning years are of crucial importance in the development of personality. They contribute much to what shall be. In them the foundations are laid. Long ago no less a voice than Plato's declared: ''The beginning is the most important part of a thing, especially a young and tender thing.''[9] And many other observers of human nature have followed the most famous of the Ancient Philosophers. Bushnell used to say that: ''more as a general fact is done, or lost by neglect of doing, on a child's immortality, in the first three years of life, than in all his years of discipline afterwards.''[10] And a noted psychologist of today points out the significance of early infancy by declaring: ''There is no time in life more important for psychological development than that between the ages of three and four.''[11] The reasons for the importance of the pre-school age in the development of personality are stated by Hadfield to be: (1) the impressionability of the child; (2) the inadequacy of his adaptation to the world in which he lives (3) his tendency to form, during these years, a general attitude toward life; and (4)—perhaps the most important consideration of all—the fact that his *attitude toward himself* is largely determined by the treatment he receives at this time. The way in which this attitude toward the self affects personality must presently be considered.

4. *The self, or self-organizing principle of the mind.*—There is another factor upon which personality is dependent if the faith of men in their moral natures is sound. It is perhaps best referred to as

---

[9] *The Republic,* Book II ; 377.

[10] *Christian Nurture,* p. 211.

[11] J. A. Hadfield, *Psychology and Morals,* p. 53.

the self, of the self-organizing principle of the mind. The existence of this factor has been implied in many parts of the preceding discussion and it has been assumed throughout. Despite the skeptical attitude of many present-day thinkers, the rank and file of mankind, as well as many of the wisest of men, continue to believe that each individual has a real self, a core of being having continuity, which cannot be explained merely in terms of hereditary impulses and environmental stimuli. The self is by no means unaffected by these influences. It is not simple, but complex; not static, but growing; not organized, but an organizing principle. Yet there is that which is permanent and unitary about it, and its most essential quality is the power of rational self-determination which makes genuine moral conduct possible.

Any adequate treatment of selfhood would involve an excursion into the field of philosophy that would hardly be in keeping with the purpose of this book. The reality of the self is here assumed. It is a necessary postulate of any valid conception of moral personality. But the discussion of reality of any kind is the business of philosophy, rather than that of psychology. And the main emphasis throughout this study is upon the matters with which the psychologist, from his more empirical point of view, is concerned. A brief quotation from a philosopher, however, may serve to set these things in their proper relations. Says Leighton: "The materials of individuality are the congenital impulses of the organism. The patterns for the work to be done are the social types of conduct, thought, sentiment, character and trained capacity, which have been worked out by other socially creative selves in the history of human culture. The ultimate agent in the process of self-development or creation is the attentively selective, valuing, purposing, organizing mind of the individual."[12]

Some of the psychological aspects of developing selfhood are of vital concern to all those who would help the child toward the attainment of a wholesome and effective personality. Three phases of the process are of special importance: (1) The manner in which the idea of the self is built up—How the conception of the self is affected by educational influences, and how it in turn affects the total personality; (2) The way in which the individual attains the power of self-direction—How conduct comes to be controlled by self-chosen ideals and a genuine moral life is made possible; (3) The way in which the integration of personality is brought about—How the self attains a more perfect unity and brings all of the activity of the individual into harmony.

To the first of these three problems attention is now directed; the others will be considered in later chapters.

How is personality conditioned by the developing idea of the self?—

If the reader has any difficulty in connecting "the idea of the self" with the matters which he feels fall legitimately within the field of this discussion, let him recall how often the word *self* occurs in judgments about conduct, personality and character. A teacher is disappointed in the performance of a pupil

[12]*The Field of Philosophy*, p. 303.

and says: "He did not seem to be himself today."
A woman is distracted with grief and her friends
remark: "She is beside herself." One poet urges,
"To thine own self be true," and another calls upon
men to rise upon "the stepping-stones of their dead
selves to higher things." The moralist has much to
say about striving to realize the better self. And
there are no terms that are more common or more
significant in descriptions of character than those
which indicate an attitude toward the self—self-conceit, self-centeredness, self-confidence, self-sacrifice,
self-control, self-respect, and the like. The use of
these expressions in the speech of every day suggests
an important truth: One of the most significant
factors in the personality of any man is his attitude
toward himself, what he thinks about himself, how
he feels toward himself, and what he desires for himself.

The idea of the self begins to emerge in babyhood
and its development continues through adolescence.
In fact the conception one has of one's self never
ceases to be modified by experience, although it is
more or less stabilized by the time maturity is reached.
Some phases of the process by which it develops are
matters of real concern to one who would guide the
growth of the child's personality. They may be discussed conveniently under the headings: discovery,
adjustment, socialization, expansion, and idealization.

1. *The discovery of the self.*—At the beginning of
life the baby probably does not distinguish between
himself and the other objects in his world. He soon
discovers, however, that when he grasps the side of
his cot he has one sort of sensation and that when

he grasps his toes he experiences something different —really a sensation from the toes which are touched and from the hand which touches them. By means of many such experiences the baby's bodily self comes to be separated from the general environment, but it is some time before he becomes conscious of what might be called his social self. As he begins to use and to understand language, however, he is helped in the process of discovery. The word "baby" is found to have a special relation to his own experiences and in time "I" and "me" are understood as referring to his own desires. A young child, apparently a bit puzzled about the whole matter, used to say to his mother at bedtime: "Mama, cover my me." It is thus during the first three or four years of childhood that the conception of the social self begins to be built up. At first, according to McDougall, it is but a vague idea of a "being capable of feeling and effort."[13] Soon wish or will are the very core of it. It becomes quickened by the child's cry, "I want—," and by the necessary refusals of the adult members of society always to gratify his wishes. It is made more definite also by his imitation of others, with the new experience it brings and the limitations it makes clear. And the first impression of himself that the child receives may profoundly affect his personality. He may be spoiled either by too much or by too little attention from his elders. The more natural the situation is in which he comes to self-consciousness the more wholesome the results are likely to be. Hartshorne states the matter truthfully and with clarity. "Display before strangers," he says, "doing

[13] *Social Psychology*, p. 189.

tricks to make friends laugh, being the center of interest constantly for any cause at all, carries in its train a host of problems in the achievement of a normal personality that ought never to arise. Far better is it for the child to come into possession of himself through the normal processes of social living, in which adjustments to the group life are gradually made, and in which he is able to discover himself not as the cynosure of admiring eyes but as a member of a cooperating household working together for some recognized common interests.''[14]

2. *The adjustment of the self.*—In the give and take of life children have to make many adjustments to the other selves with whom they have contacts. They thus come to know themselves in some sort of relation to others. One child, however, finds that he has a proper place among persons whose actions are orderly, consistent, and sympathetic. Another is constantly puzzled by an inconsistent, chaotic and unfriendly environment. And the growing idea of the self will very readily reflect the character of the child's surroundings. What others think of him will often determine what he thinks of himself, a fact that reveals the danger in constant negative suggestion. One cannot but have a good deal of sympathy for the child who, after being constantly taunted by her parents for her misconduct, burst out: ''Oh, I know I am a naughty little girl; and I ought to be ashamed of myself; and I don't like God.''

In the early adjustments of the self there is a good deal of experimentation. The child, often with considerable shrewdness, will see how far he can go in

---

[14]*Childhood and Character,* pp. 14-15.

his disobedience without incurring punishment. If told to close the screen door, he may hold it open an inch or two to see what will happen. If asked to stop making a noise, he may continue his noise-making in a minor key carefully watching his elders to see what effect his conduct has upon them. He is experimenting to see where the line is to be drawn between the self and others. He is adventuring "on the borderland of ethics." His conduct is not yet moral but through the treatment he receives the foundations of his morality may be laid. And in that treatment there are few things more essential for his well-being than consistency and reasonableness. Moral chaos and a divided self are often the outcomes of an inconsistent and irrational environment.

3. *The socializing of the self.*—One of the most interesting phases of the individual's development is that which may be spoken of as the socializing of the self. The process has two aspects, both of which are exceedingly important in moral training: On the one hand, there is a growing sensitiveness to the opinions of others regarding the self; and on the other hand, a growing desire to share in the fellowship of the group. Thus the child tends to be moulded into the likeness of the society in which he lives as his conduct is directed in ways that are acceptable to it.

a) A degree of sensitiveness to the opinions of others regarding the self is, of course, very desirable. It is the basis of man's responsiveness to moral judgment as expressed in public opinion and is also an important factor in his becoming susceptible to the teachings of religion. He who is unaffected by the verdict of society upon his conduct is likely to be indifferent to the voice of God. It will be readily seen, however, that the overdevelopment of this tendency may produce a personality that is weak and unstable. The way in which a wholesome regard for the opinions of others is built up can be but briefly sketched here. McDougall, in his *Social Psychology,* shows that such an attitude is brought about by the normal development of the "self-regarding sentiment." If the tendencies to assertion and self-display, with their accompanying emotions, are allowed free rein, they are likely to result in the "pure pride" of the person who is incapable of being humbled, and who is indifferent to the moral censure of his fellows. If, however, the submissiveness of the child is called forth by a reasonable authority, and its emotions are blended with those of the self-assertive tendencies, there may be developed a wholesome self-respect and, at the same time, a capacity to profit "by example and by precept, by advice and exhortation, by moral approval or disapproval."[15]

b) The socializing of the self also results from the child's desire to share in the fellowship of the group. Even a baby will show signs of pleasure at being in the presence of other members of the family. But from about the fourth or fifth year there is an increasing desire to share in what others are doing and to find satisfaction in conduct that is pleasing to the group. In a salutary home life, or in a properly conducted church school group, this tendency may be a valuable aid in developing desirable social traits. That child is fortunate indeed whose early experiences

---

[15]*Social Psychology,* p. 202.

of fellowship come to him in the wholesome atmosphere of a genuinely Christian family.

The child's desire to do that which is pleasing to others—especially to those whom he loves—often results in admirable qualities of character. It is not to be despised as a motive of conduct in childhood although, of itself, it can scarcely lead to rugged moral personality. Many of the kindly acts of children grow out of the satisfaction which they feel in giving pleasure to their elders and these little services may lead on, sometimes almost imperceptibly, to conduct that is more truly unselfish. There is much that is of worth in the action of the little girl who helps her mother wash the dishes because she enjoys the mother's commendation, or in that of the boy who willingly cleans up the yard on the day his father is to return home, or who learns his memory work at Sunday school because he likes his teacher. These children may not be entirely forgetful of self, but their motives are as high as those of many of their elders ever become, and they are learning lessons of serviceableness which are invaluable. Nor is it always easy to say just where the line is to be drawn between this kind of conduct and that which is genuinely altruistic. A six year old girl seemed to sense the grief of a visiting friend who had recently suffered bereavement. "Mother," she said, "I want to do something for Marion." When the mother replied that she did not know what the child could do, the little girl filled a glass with water and took it to her bereaved friend. The motive of the child was perhaps not free from egoistic elements, but experiences like these make their contribution to the development of Christian personality. They are closely akin to the service of those to whom it shall be said: "I was thirsty and ye gave me to drink."

Self-assertion and submission.—By a training that provides for a proper balance between self-assertion and submission and for the proper encouragement of the individual's desire to bring pleasure to others and to share in the fellowship of the group, the child may come to possess a wholesome self-respect that is duly considerate of the rights and needs of his fellows. In this way he will be saved from such abnormalities as the self-conceit of the egotist, or the self-depreciation and false humility of the man of weak and vacillating personality.

Social behavior is common in childhood. It is not, as some of the older psychologists used to maintain, a peculiarly adolescent phenomenon. There is, however, a very marked development of the social self during the years of adolescence and both the susceptibility to public opinion and the desire for fellowship in the group take on new significance. The youth becomes keenly sensitive to the judgments of those of his own age upon himself and the group spirit is likely to be expressed in the loosely formed gang, or in the class, team, fraternity or club. There is a new sense of power. It is a supreme moment in the development of the self when the girl realizes for the first time that she is as beautiful as her mother, or the boy that he is as tall as his father. There is a new consciousness of sex. For good or ill the idea of the self is greatly affected by the consciousness that accompanies the maturing of the sexual powers, and the formation of wrong attitudes and unworthy habits at this time may warp the personality in the direction of reticence, self-consciousness, and unwholesome preoccupation with ideas and emotions that center in sex relationships. And there are new problems of adjustment.

The youth has again to "find himself," to become adjusted to a world which has grown larger and become more complex, and to learn how to take his place among his fellows in the more serious enterprises of life. Thus during adolescence the pupil's attitude toward himself becomes greatly modified.

Two other phases of the developing idea of the self must be given brief consideration. They may perhaps best be described in terms of expansion and idealization.

4. *The expansion of the self.*—The impulses and emotions that center in the self may be extended to others, and especially to social groups or to institutions. The parent may so identify himself with his child that he will react toward the child's treatment by others almost as if it were an experience of his own. The over-sensitiveness of some parents about the placing of their children in anything but the highest group in the school grade is not infrequently due to such an extension of "the self-regarding sentiment." In a similar manner the "booster" identifies himself with his town, the partizan with his political party, and the sectarian with his denominational group. Many men of very mediocre attainments find satisfaction and a sense of power and importance through identifying themselves with some organization that is numerically strong.

But this expansion of the self often leads to more

worthy outcomes. It is involved in a reasonable family pride, in devotion to one's college, in a wholesome church loyalty, and in a sane patriotism. In its more refined form it may result in the sacrificing of narrowly selfish interests for a genuine concern about the welfare of the group with which the self is identified. It will often be found to be an underlying motive of the pupil's interest in class or club, in department or school. And loyalties of this sort are not to be despised. The pupil should find satisfaction in speaking of "my class," "my school," or "my church." This kind of extension of "the self-regarding sentiment" to the group is perhaps a necessary step in the development of a wholesome idea of the self, as well as of worthy group loyalties.

5. *The idealization of the self.*—Even more important than the pupil's idea of his actual self is his idea of the self he would like to be. This ideal self is built up during the years of childhood and youth and it is the task of the teacher to contribute to it as much that is wholesomely Christian as his contacts with the pupil make possible. Few factors are of greater significance in determining the personality of the pupil than the character of the self he desires to be, the ideal self which he seeks to realize. One is reminded in this connection of the well-known story of the New York bank errand boy who returned to the officers of the bank the roll of bills he had found while sweeping. The distressing circumstances and poverty of his family added to his temptation to keep the money, but, after a struggle, the right course of action was decided upon. When asked by the banker why he had made such a decision, the boy replied,

"Sir, as long as I live I have to live with myself and I don't want to live with a thief." The story, whether true or imaginary, is a kind of parable of what takes place, sometimes quite consciously, at other times with the idea of the self only in the background of consciousness, as many of the moral decisions of the pupil are made.

The highest level of conduct has been reached when the moral decisions of the individual are in harmony with his own ideals. The manner in which the idealization of the self takes place, and progress is made from the lower to the higher levels of conduct, is a matter of sufficient importance to receive separate consideration. It will be taken up in the next chapter.

In the course of the pupil's development he builds up different ideas of the self in relation to the numerous and varied situations of life. The resulting conception may therefore contain many conflicting elements. As these are brought into harmony with the ideal-self, and the behavior of the individual gains greater consistency, personality, in its more specific sense, begins to emerge.

QUESTIONS—

1. Is there any necessary conflict between "Christian personality" and "social progress" as educational aims? Why? Why not?
2. What differences in temperament have you observed in the members of your church school class, or in any group of acquaintances? How far do you think these differences are to be explained by their physical basis?
3. Which of the substitute responses discussed in this chapter seem to you to be the least objectionable? What is the best way for the individual to deal with his conflicting impulses?

4. How would you account for the divided personality of the politician described in the text? In what way might a more adequate religious education have helped this man?

5. Do you agree with Bushnell's statement concerning the importance of the first three years of life in the development of personality? Why? Why not?

6. What is the self? Is the statement justifiable that the reality of the self is "a necessary postulate of any valid conception of moral personality"?

7. Why does wholesome personality require the proper balance between self-assertion and submission?

8. What kinds of modifications in the attitude toward the self may take place in the period of adolescence? Give some specific illustrations.

9. Have you known persons who resented, almost as a personal affront, any criticism of their city, or perhaps their denomination? What is the psychological explanation of such a response? Discuss its values and its dangers.

10. What do you think of the philosophy of the poet suggested by this verse?

> To thine own self be true,
> And it must follow, as the night the day,
> Thou canst not then be false to any man.
> *(Hamlet,* Act 1, Scene 3, line 78.)

Under what conditions is the statement true? When would it be untrue?

REPORTS AND INVESTIGATIONS—

1. Ask several people what personality means. Note the answers and be prepared to criticise them. If possible report on such a book as *The Glands Regulating Personality,* by Berman.

2. Give some instances from your own experience or observation of the thwarting of impulses and of the substitute responses that were made. Show how conflict and thwarting may lead to (*a*) responses in imagination, (*b*) rationalization, (*c*) compensation, (*d*) segregation or dissociation.

3. Prepare a list of questions that might be used in securing information from parents regarding the problems of adjustment of children or of adolescents. (For suggestions see Chave: *The Junior,* pages 164-168.) If possible, use this list to gather material for class discussion. What attitudes toward the self appear in the cases reported?

4. Recall instances that you have observed of children in the third or fourth year of life coming to a consciousness of self. Did they come to a knowledge of themselves in a wholesome manner as members of a "co-operating household"? Or were they constantly thrust into the center of attention and perhaps even encouraged to "show off" for the benefit of visiting friends?

5. Make a list of the things the teacher should know concerning the (a) home life, (b) the school or business life, and (c) the recreational life, of his pupils. Why must the church school be concerned about these matters?

REFERENCES—

Berman, Louis, The Glands Regulating Personality. Macmillan.

Chapman and Counts, Principles of Education, chap. ix. Houghton Mifflin.

Gates, Arthur I., Psychology for Students of Education, chap. ix. Macmillan.

Hadfield, J. A., Psychology and Morals, chaps. vii-ix. Robert M. McBride.

Hartshorne, Hugh, Childhood and Character, chaps. ii and iii. Pilgrim Press.

Leighton, Joseph H., The Field of Philosophy, chap. xxii. R. G. Adams.

McDougall, William, An Introduction to Social Psychology chap. vii. J. W. Luce and Co.

Woodworth, Robert S., Psychology, chap. xxi. Henry Holt

CHAPTER VIII

MORAL GROWTH

How is Personality Conditioned by Moral Growth?

For the church school teacher, the most important aspects of personality are those that have to do with the moral and religious life. The thoughtful teacher knows, of course, that morality and religion cannot be separated from the rest of experience but he knows also that they give to the whole of life a distinctive quality which he desires his pupils to possess. He is interested, therefore, in the question as to how personality is conditioned by moral growth and by religious experience. These are the topics treated in the next two chapters.

It will be seen that the discussion which follows is really a continuation of that begun in chapter seven. Personality, in the more restricted sense of the term, is not attained until there is a measure of moral control. Character and personality while they are not identical are, as will be shown presently, very closely related. Before these matters are considered, however, it is necessary to inquire as to: (1) What constitutes moral conduct? The other questions discussed in this chapter are: (2) How is progress made from the lower to the higher levels of conduct? (3) How is character related to personality?

WHAT CONSTITUTES MORAL CONDUCT?—

The man in the street has an easy answer to the question: What is moral conduct? To be moral is, for him, to act in ways that are approved by the group in which he lives. Certain acts are recognized by society as good. Other forms of conduct are bad. And the distinction between the two is so thoroughly imbedded in the traditions and customs of the group that few further questions need be asked.

But the more reflective person understands that

this practical attitude toward morality overlooks many significant facts which constitute grave problems. For society has not always approved the same things, and there are very marked variations in standards among different groups today. There have been societies in which lying was approved provided the liar was not detected in his untruthfulness. And it is only in recent times that duelling and slave-holding have been declared immoral even by civilized society. Furthermore there can be little doubt that many of the practices that receive the approval of society today will be banned as immoral by that better society of tomorrow "for which the clear in mind and the pure in heart are continually striving."[1]

Yet the objective standards of what is right or wrong must in the end be traced largely to society. Moral conduct is conduct that is in harmony with the good of the group. Men may differ in their conception of what is good, and they may be mistaken in their selection of means for the attainment of it, but that the welfare of society is the ultimate test of the good act perhaps few would deny. Christianity, as was suggested in the first chapter, does not change this conception of the end of moral endeavor, but raises the whole tone of it, and conceives of it in terms of the will of God. It does not mean by the good of society merely physical welfare, but the highest good of which man as a spiritual being is capable, or may become capable. Whatever else is embraced within this conception it would seem that it must include a *world-wide* society dominated by the "Christian spirit of Love." One real test of a

---

[1]Chapman and Counts: *Principles of Education*, p. 486.

moral act, from the Christian point of view, is therefore: Does it help create more love in the world?[2]

Moral conduct and self-direction.—But so far as the individual is concerned the moral quality of an act is not determined by its objective results alone. A child may do what is right simply because he cannot, under the circumstances, do anything else. Assuming that it is right for him to share his toys with his play-mate, he may act in this way only because he is compelled to do so by the insistence of the parent. Likewise he may do many things which, objectively considered, are wrong, because of impulses which as yet he is quite unable to control. Such conduct is, strictly speaking, neither moral nor immoral. It is unmoral. And some of the behavior even of adults must also be placed in this category. Men may engage in activities that work against the highest good of society because they lack the intelligence to discern the moral implications of their acts, or the knowledge necessary for the proper evaluation of them, or because they are so deficient in physical and psychical health that self-control is not possible. On the other hand right conduct may result merely from mechanical habit, or from physical or social compulsion. In all such cases the behavior of the individual must be considered unmoral. It is determined by forces external to his will. It lacks the essential quality of genuine moral conduct namely self-direction. A good practical definition of morality is that

---

[2] It is significant that this question is also one of the tests which Shaver applies to educational enterprises to determine whether or not the thing done is a project in *Christian* education.—Shaver; *The Project Principle in Religious Education,* p. 53.

it is the intelligent choosing of ideals and of ways of action that are in harmony with the good of society.

The basic elements in conduct that is wholesomely and thoroughly moral are therefore: (1) A knowledge of what is right; (2) A genuine desire to do it; and (3) the ability to put knowledge and desire into practice. This does not mean, it must be emphatically said, that these three phases of moral conduct are, or can be, cultivated separately, or that the order given is the order in which they should be emphasized in the education of the pupil. The training and discipline of the individual in early childhood may be an important factor in his ability to do what he later learns to be right. Nevertheless a fully developed moral life involves the three elements named. And it is both prepared for and attained by the establishing of habits, the gaining of knowledge, and the acquiring of ideals.

Moral conduct is thus largely dependent upon original nature and upon the educational influences which bring about changes in it. Many of the native tendencies impel toward conduct that is in harmony with the good of society but they are not sufficient in themselves. They have to be modified by learning. And the pupil learns to live the moral life, as he learns anything else, by thinking, feeling, doing, experiencing—by living. Although some particular aspects of moral development must presently be considered the process involved in guiding it is, in the main, the same as that described in chapters five and six. Moral habits and moral ideas are not essentially different from other habits and ideas. They are derived from the interaction of the individual with his environment especially in its personal and social aspects.

But since the essential quality of moral conduct is self-direction, the moral life develops not only from without but also from within. And it is both a growth and an attainment. It is dependent upon a certain physical and mental maturity and upon the development of self-consciousness and self-control. The degree to which freedom may be attained by children and young people at the different age levels is a matter about which there is little dependable knowledge. No one could give more than a mere opinion in answer to the question: How much self-control can the average ten-year-old boy be expected to show in a situation involving personal insult? It is clear, however, that freedom is gradually attained and that certain educational procedures hinder and others help the attainment of it.

Any kind of worthy social conduct that is chosen by the individual is, in a sense, moral. But even a good act may be chosen from unworthy motives. A man may choose to give alms or to pray in order to be seen of men; or he may choose to refrain from wrong doing only because he fears the punishment that will follow either in this life or in the life to come. *Conduct has not become moral in the highest sense, however, until it is chosen by the individual not because of these external considerations but because of ideals that are really his own.* The question as to how conduct rises to this level and ideals become part of the self, is, therefore, all important.

How is progress made from the lower to the higher levels of conduct?—

The stages by which the individual reaches the plane where his conduct is regulated in accord with ideals are set forth very convincingly by McDougall.[3] He distinguishes roughly four levels of conduct. (1) In the first of these, behavior is instinctive and is modified only by pains and pleasures incidentally experienced. (2) In the second, behavior is modified by rewards and punishments systematically administered by society. (3) On the third level conduct is controlled in the main by anticipation of the praise or blame of society. (4) And on the highest plane conduct is regulated by an ideal of what is right, regardless of the praise or blame of an immediate society.

Abundant illustrations of the first two types of behavior have been given in earlier chapters. They portrayed conduct that was externally controlled. The determining factors in the behavior of the child who learns not to touch the hot stove by being burned are, in a sense, outside of himself. This is true also of the infant who refrains from opening the ice-box, despite its attractive handle—and contents, because his hand has been slapped whenever the act was attempted.

There is a beginning of inward control, however, when conduct is directed not by actually experienced punishment or reward, praise or blame, but by the anticipation of the possible judgment of parent or society upon it. The growth of rugged moral personality requires that this motive be transcended.

[3] *Social Psychology*, p. 186.

Yet the conduct of many adults who live very respectable lives may seldom rise above it. The abject fear which keeps some men and women from running counter to the dictates of fashion reveals how strong the motive may become. Conduct is still on this plane when a youth is kept in the path of rectitude by thinking of what people would say if he departed from it, when a business man refrains from making a dishonest transaction merely because there is a law against it, or when the efficiency of a preacher or of a teacher is dependent upon the praise of those to whom he ministers.

The highest level of conduct.—But strong character requires a firmer foundation. If conduct is not to be turned this way or that by the winds of circumstance it must be grounded in convictions and ideals. Not until this stage has been reached is there inward control of behavior in the truest sense of the term. The approval that is now desired is not that of an immediate society but that of the individual's best self. This ideal self, however, is by no means wholly independent of society. It simply refuses to be dictated to by the group into which the man is thrown by the exigencies of time or place. It chooses rather to heed the judgment of the great and good of all time. "At this stage the drama is performed not before the limited spectators which crowd the house, but before an imaginary gallery peopled by the prophets, priests, and seers in whose ideal presence the individual has chosen to live. Not by arbitrary etiquette, by convention, and herd morality of 'his set,' but rather by those great precepts, admonitions and ideals—the distillate of the wisdom and heroism

of the ages—is his conduct shaped.''[4] The early
Christians were urged to live worthily before such
an ideal gallery by the writer of The Epistle to the
Hebrews. Having reviewed the triumphs of the
heroes of the faith the author appealed to the Christians to run a good race, since they were ''compassed
about by so great a cloud of witnesses.'' (Heb. 12:
1-2.) Courage and faithfulness in the face of persecution could not be maintained by pandering to the
wishes of an immediate society, but by thinking of
the revered saints and martyrs and by ''looking unto
Jesus the author and perfector of our faith.''

It will be apparent that it makes a vast difference
to the character of an individual just who are the
real or the ideal spectators before whom he chooses
to live his life. The young painter who is truly in
love with his art cares not for the fulsome praise
of men, but desires the approval of the master artist.
The scientist who is devoted to research is indifferent
to newspaper publicity, but is deeply concerned about
the pronouncement of competent judges upon his
work. The Christian who is striving earnestly to live
the higher life stands ready to face the abuse and
contumely of his fellows if he may have the approval
of Him who is the acknowledged master in the realm
of life and spirit.

In the course of the pupil's development ideals
may become detached from the concrete personalities
in connection with whom they have arisen. It is,
however, their original personal association and their
constant expression in behavior, that gives them their
warmth and driving power. The ideal of love may
be held as a theoretical principle by the most

---

[4]Chapman and Counts—*Principles of Education*, p. 129.

apathetic philosopher, but let it be inspired by the glowing personality of Jesus Christ, and be expressed in many loving acts, and it may lead to deeds of such heroic self-sacrifice that men cannot but recognize something divine in them. It was to such an ideal that Edith Cavell was true when, facing death at the hands of an enemy reputed to be ruthlessly cruel she said: "Patriotism is not enough; one must have no hatred, no bitterness."

Ideals cannot be forced upon the pupil. In a peculiar sense his ideals are his own, the results of his choices. Yet it is the task of the religious educator to help mould them and to heighten their quality. The growth of ideals and the way in which they become effective in life is a matter of sufficient importance to demand a more detailed treatment. A knowledge of what is good and ability to do it are not enough to secure good conduct. There must be the desire to do the right. And what the pupil desires depends upon the quality of his ideals.

Ideals and the moral sentiments.—The process by which ideals are built up begins with the development of the moral sentiments. As the term is used here, sentiments are systems of reactions, highly emotional in character, which center in some object or idea, so that meeting the object, or even recalling the idea, tends to arouse them. The responses involve impulses, feelings, desires, and aversions, that are, in the main, not innate but are derived from experience. The moral sentiments are simply such responses organized about some bit of moral conduct, some idea of a right or a wrong act, or some abstract moral idea such as justice or truth. The indignation aroused by an act of cruelty; respect for the aged; and love of fair-play, are typical moral sentiments.

Very early in life the individual begins to build up these systems of responses in harmony with those of the group in which he lives. The processes of sympathy, suggestion, and imitation cause his likes and dislikes to be moulded by society. He thus comes to approve the things that are most consistently approved by those about him, and to disapprove those things that are universally condemned. As he becomes able to distinguish the moral quality of acts, his emotional responses are linked to these moral qualities and thus, with the growth of the power of abstraction (see chapter six), he builds up the abstract moral sentiments. He comes to love justice, honesty, and mercy, or to hate laziness, cruelty or tyranny.

But the persons who make up the world of the pupil do not all have the same ideals. The growing child finds himself within an ever expanding society and, as his horizons widen, he is brought into contact with a great variety of moral codes. Which of these shall become incorporated into his moral sentiments will be determined, in a large measure, by the respective degrees in which they are embodied in persons whom he admires. For, "in the main, it is by sympathetic contagion and by suggestion from admired personalities that the child's moral sentiments are shaped."[5]

The influence of admired personalities.—The wise teacher—whether in home or school—will seek to bring before the pupil, in a manner that will make them appeal to him, those men and women in whose

[5]McDougall, *Outline of Psychology*, p. 436.

strength of character and nobility of life the essential Christian qualities are most clearly seen. Actual living persons with whom the pupil has immediate contact will perhaps wield the strongest influence over him. But "in modern societies this influence is exerted, not only through personal contact, but on a very large scale by literature; for, in so far as we learn to grasp in some degree the personality of an author and to admire him, the expressions of his abstract sentiments exert this personal influence upon us, more especially, of course, upon the young mind whose sentiments are not fully formed and crystallized."[6] If the teacher would help the pupil in the attainment of Christian ideals one of the things he must do is to kindle appreciation of Christian characters so that they "catch the imagination and move the feelings." This is an exceedingly difficult but altogether necessary part of the educational task. It is difficult not because such lives are lacking in attractiveness, but because there is so much in the civilization of today—in the moving-picture, the newspaper, the novel, and the accepted standards of community and national life—the pull of which is all in another direction. Yet only as the heroes of youth are men and women who, according to Christian standards, are worthy of emulation, can there be developed the kind of moral personality at which religious education aims. Almost all persons are ruled much more by their admirations than by purely intellectual processes and, while the educator must always seek to bring about a more rational control of conduct, he will not greatly affect character if he

---

[6]McDougall, *Social Psychology*, p. 229.

fails to realize the strength of the emotional dispositions and sentiments. Unless the pupil is made to
feel something of the glory of an Isaiah or a Paul,
a Francis or a Luther, a Livingstone or a Grenfell,
his knowledge of these world characters cannot be
expected to have much influence upon his life. And
it is supremely important that he be led to appreciate the matchless personality of the Man of Galilee,
that he be deeply stirred by the moral grandeur of
the Christ.

The sentiments of the pupil are thus built up by
his life in the group. They are moulded by the
prejudices, attitudes, ideals, hates and loves of the
persons who make up his world. This world of persons includes those who become real to him among
the characters about whom he is told, and of whom
he reads. And it exerts its most powerful influence
through the men and women, boys and girls to whom
he responds with admiration. A large number of
these sentiments are built up during childhood and
youth and they become in some cases determiners of
attitudes and conduct. Whether wholesome or unwholesome they may persist into adulthood. Not infrequently even men and women of high intellectual
attainments will be found to meet certain ideas or
situations with a response of fear, aversion, or indignation, that is altogether unjustified by the facts
in the case.

But many of the sentiments are of a more worthy
type and they add much to the enrichment and satisfaction of social life. Moreover some of them become
bound to certain kinds of acts and, through experience in a variety of situations, to the moral qualities

involved in them. Thereafter if an act, real or imagined, is seen clearly to be a case of this or that type of conduct, it tends to arouse the emotional responses that have been bound to the class of action under which the case falls. And the nature of the response will largely depend upon whether the sentiments have been developed through contact with men and women of the rank and file, or with those who are the moral heroes of the race.

The necessity of action.—For the moral sentiments to become ideals, however, another factor is necessary, namely, action. From the psychological point of view ideals are ideas to which habits and emotional responses have been connected so that they involve an impulse to act in a characteristic way. There are those who place all of the emphasis in moral training on habits. There are others who emphasize ideals almost as if they were independent of life and experience and might be imparted merely by talking about them. Both of these positions are one-sided. Ideals are quite essential to a wholesome, well-balanced, moral life, but for them to be effective they must have led frequently to activity. They will then include impulses to action as well as to feeling. For the pupil to become equipped with effective moral ideals he needs to have many experiences in which, for example, the desire to be honest is bound to honest conduct, or the love of industry is linked with habits of persistent endeavor. This does not mean that ideals are nothing more than habits. In a crisis they may lead to conduct the moral quality of which goes far beyond that of anything done by the individual in the past. And it is often in times of crisis that the true moral character of a person is revealed. For at such times the merely customary ways of acting are quite inadequate. A real moral test is faced by the athlete who, in a crucial contest, has a chance to win by breaking the rules, although his unfairness would probably not be noticed by anyone. What he does in such a situation will depend upon what he is. It will be accounted for by the quality of his moral sentiments and by the habits of fair-play which he has developed in a variety of different situations in the past. In other words his action will be in accord with the ideals which he has made a part of himself and which have become effective in his life.

It is therefore not enough that the teacher win the pupil's admiration for characters whose moral sentiments are worthy of being made his own, not enough that there be developed a love of this or that virtue; there must be many opportunities to express these ideals in conduct. And that is hardly the chronology of the matter. Ideals are perhaps seldom taught and then expressed. They are more often taught by being expressed. The deed may never fully represent the ideal. And the sentiments are, as a rule, much wider in their application than any act that is immediately possible. But unless there is action, ideals can scarcely become effective. There are men who *know* the right and desire to do it, but who fail because the habits they have formed lead to a different way of life. Almost every mature person has, at some time, prayed the prayer of the poet Drinkwater:

We know the paths wherein our feet should press,
Across our hearts are written Thy decrees;
Yet now, O Lord, be merciful to bless
    With more than these.

Grant us the will to fashion as we feel,
Grant us the strength to labor as we know,
Grant us the purpose, ribb'd and edged with steel,
    To strike the blow.

Knowledge we ask not—knowledge thou hast lent,
But Lord, the will—there lies our bitter need,
Give us to build above the deep intent
    The deed, the deed.

When the pupil has reached the highest level of conduct, his acts are peculiarly his own. He does what he desires to do; for he desires above all else to be true to his ideals. And his ideals are especially precious to him. They have become a part of himself so that he is most truly himself when he is living according to them. Thus in situations involving moral issues he is motivated not by crude instinct, nor by anticipation of the praise or blame of an immediate society, but by what he believes to be right. He may make mistakes. His knowledge may be limited and his reasoning may be faulty, but men will recognize in him a certain strength of character that is altogether worthy. Morally he is irreproachable.

One of the most striking portrayals of this type of character in recent literature is Drinkwater's Abraham Lincoln. Whatever other impressions may be left with the reader he cannot but feel something of the moral force of the Emancipator. Here was a man who, in the crucial hour of his soul's testing, held to his ideals with a grim resolution that the bitter abuse of enemies, and the sharp censure of friends, could not break down. And this, when many of his strongest impulses would have·led to a different course of action, if he had not kept the larger good constantly before him. Men of this kind do "belong to the ages." But perhaps an even more significant fact is that something of this same quality of life is found among men and women, from the humblest to the greatest, wherever they attain to genuine moral character.

How is character related to personality?—

The meaning of character is given in clear terms by McDougall in his *Outline of Psychology.* "Character," he says, "is the system of directed conative (active) tendencies. It may be relatively simple or complex; it may be harmoniously organized or lacking in harmony; it may be firmly or loosely knit; it may be directed in the main toward lower or toward higher goals. Character of the highest type is that which is complex, strongly and harmoniously organized, and directed toward the realization of higher goals or ideals. Such character may be attained by the individual whose intellect is relatively simple and ordinary. But the better organized and richer the intellect, the more efficiently will character work toward the realization of its goal" (p. 417).

The two essential elements in this conception of character are: (1) the direction of active tendencies, and (2) the systematization of these tendencies. When the actions of a person are self-directed rather than merely impulsive, they are said to be volitional. The first essential of character is, therefore, volition. The second is organization of all the tendencies into a unified and consistent whole. For character to be both strong and good, activity must be not only volitional and unified, but it must be directed toward worthy ends.

An understanding of what is involved in strong moral character requires therefore the consideration of two basic questions; What is the nature of volition? How do the sentiments and active tendencies become unified?

1. *The nature of volition.*—The clearest case of volition is that of a deliberate choice between two or more alternative lines of action, and an analysis of a situation of this kind will help to make plain the factors involved.

A college youth is sitting for an important examination upon the outcome of which much depends. He is unable to answer one of the questions but has easy access to some notes which would supply the desired information. He is confronted with the problem of choosing between a dishonest course which will bring him success and an honest course which will almost certainly mean failure. There are many impulses toward the former line of action. Since success in the examination will bring him some distinction, the tendencies to self-assertion and the desire for the approval of others impel him toward it. Moreover, he does not think the question is quite fair and he is very sure that no one except himself will know anything about his act should he choose to glance at the notes in his pocket. Yet despite the allurements of evil the youth decides upon the honest course, writes what he knows about the questions, and hands in a paper which, whether good or bad, is his own work.

In this illustration the decision of the youth was, in a thorough-going sense, an act of will. That is, it was not merely the triumph of one impulse over another, but was the act of a person. The responses made in volition are not due to desires and impulses that are unacceptable to the self. In fact, the distinctive mark of voluntary action is that the whole self is thrown upon the side of what might otherwise be the weaker motive and thereby the self becomes the determining factor. The college youth, in the situation just described, did the honest thing because he was a certain kind of person. His moral equipment made such action possible. And along with other sentiments and habits, those connected with his idea of himself played a large part. In the rather inelegant but expressive phrase of another, "He did what he did because he was what he was."[7]

Any act that is the result of choice between alternatives is in one sense an act of will even if it has no more moral significance than the selection of a blue rather than a red lead-pencil from the five-cent counter. But the special interest of this chapter is in the kind of volition which, because there is a measure of conflict, involves a more definite moral choice. In some cases it seems, to the onlooker at least, that the individual has chosen the difficult right rather than the easy wrong. He has perhaps risked his life in an effort to save an enemy when, so far as external considerations go, it would have been perfectly easy for him to have "passed by on the other side." And one who reflects upon such conduct may well ask: What kind of moral equipment is possessed by the man who is capable of so heroic a deed?

Summary of the factors in volition.—Psychology

---

[7] Chapman and Counts, *Principles of Education*, p. 137.

will probably never be able to give more than a partial explanation of this kind of moral conduct. Some of the important factors involved in it may, however, be briefly summarized. They are: (1) Ability to hold at the focus of attention the idea of the right course of action to the exclusion of other ideas—a power that is dependent, at least in part, upon the other factors to be mentioned; (2) Ideals of unselfishness, helpfulness, forgiveness, and the like, which have been built up in the manner described earlier in this chapter; (3) An idea of the self into which these ideals have been incorporated—the self the individual desires to be, but never quite becomes; (4) An attitude toward the self which involves a measure of assertiveness and what McDougall calls "the sentiment of self-regard," so that there is an effort to realize the ideal and a feeling of dissatisfaction at failure to do so; (5) The habit of a ready active response to the promptings of the better self. These five factors are the essential elements in volition where the situation is such that moral conflict is involved.

2. *The organization of character.*—But isolated acts, even though they be of high moral quality, do not constitute strong character. The sentiments and tendencies must be organized into some kind of consistent whole and the process by which this result is brought about is one of first importance in education. How, then, can the conflicting impulses and inharmonious sentiments become organized into character?

A measure of unity and the appearance of strong character is often attained by the individual whose attachment for some person, or some institution, constantly dominates his conduct. Not a few men have been enabled to "pull themselves together" and to bring into harmony the conflicting elements of their personalities by the love of a good woman. Others have achieved a certain strength by the pursuit of a professional career, or by devotion to a cause. The young and talented violinist who has glimpsed the possibility of a concert career gains a wholesome unity by bending all efforts toward the attainment of the goal. This kind of dominant sentiment or ruling passion may make a valuable contribution to moral development, but unless it is incorporated in some larger, more inclusive sentiment, it can scarcely result in genuine strength of character. For if the object of affection is removed, or if a situation in which it is not concerned has to be faced, the individual may show unbecoming weakness. An instance comes to mind of a man well-known and highly respected in the community but whose life was organized about his affection for his wife. When death took her from him the man "went to pieces" morally and dropped out of respectable society. The case is, no doubt, an extreme one, but it makes clear the essential weakness of the character that rests on sentiments of this kind only.

The essentials of strong character.—1. Strong character, on the other hand, results from the organization of the conative tendencies about an ideal of conduct with which the individual identifies himself. The nature of this ideal depends upon the sentiments and habits that have been acquired in the course of his moral growth through his responses to those whom he has loved and followed. If the constituent elements of this ideal self have been derived from the higher moral tradition rather than from an immediate society, the individual may develop a strength and independence of character that enables him to hold unerringly to his course despite the driving force of contrary winds.

2. The development of this kind of character requires, also, a wholesome attitude toward the self. There must be a strong self-regarding sentiment, a goodly measure of self-respect if there is to be a genuine effort to realize the ideal. Such an attitude is a very different thing from the self-conceit of the egotist, and it is not inconsistent with a life of sacrifice. But it is clear that the person who says: "This is the right and I will hold to it"—even if *the right* is the service of the lowly, or the love of enemies— is prompted by a kind of refined self-assertion which underlies his desire to realize the ideal.

3. Something else, too, is essential to strong character—the habit of making decisions in harmony with the ideal. By letting the ideal self sit in judgment upon conduct, and by establishing the habit of acting in accord with its promptings, the synthesis of sentiments and tendencies is brought about. "Every decision made," says Woodworth, "every conflict resolved, is a step in the further organization of the individual."[8] And if the decisions are made in harmony with a high ideal, the resultant character becomes not only strong, but good.

To this process of bringing all the tendencies into harmony, religion makes a large and unique contribution. The love of God and devotion to Christ

---

[8]Woodworth, *Psychology*, p. 529.

become for many Christians a "master sentiment" which gives to their conduct an admirable unity and consistency. And such a sentiment is not dependent upon circumstance because its object is both real and ideal. The discussion of this important matter belongs, however, in the last two chapters and it will be taken up more fully there.

Strong character is not unduly affected by change of situation or by loss of some particular object of affection. It possesses that quality of inwardness of which Jesus said so much in the Sermon on the Mount. No external conditions can destroy the ideal so long as the self holds to it. It is always there, "where neither moth nor rust doth consume, and where thieves do not break through nor steal." (Matt. 6:20.) It is always loved. It always impels toward worthy conduct.

Character and personality.—The question must now be faced as to the relation of character to personality. Here, as in so many of the divisions of psychology, no clear line of demarkation can be drawn. In a true sense both of the terms refer to what an individual really is; and neither of them is to be confused with mere reputation. Yet it is desirable that a rough distinction be made between them. (Personality is what the individual is as a whole.) (See chapter six.) It includes all of his activities in every relation of life. And the discussion of it must, therefore, include consideration of such factors as bodily constitution, temperament, native intelligence, and the like, over which the individual has little or no control. Character on the other hand, refers especially to those aspects of life that are more distinctly moral, that are self-directed and for the social good. The distinction is, of course, not absolute. It is probably true that in everything the individual thinks, and feels, and does, he in some degree helps or hinders the coming of the better day for all men. And the most thoroughly moral act may, at the same time, involve instinctive tendencies, memory, reasoning, imagination, and still others of the elements that go to make up the total life of the individual. But for practical purposes character and personality may be differentiated in the way that has been suggested. They are related as part to whole.

But that is not all that needs here to be said. Character plays a more significant role in the development of personality than that of one among a number of parts. It is the most important part. The relation is well stated by Welton. "Character," he says, "may be called the core of personality, because it contains that nucleus of purpose which determines the general trend of life, and around which all smaller purposes and ideals are more or less effectively and intelligently grouped. If character does not grow in strength and dignity the personality can but show all kinds of inconsistent qualities, and the life be marked by vascillation and ineffectiveness. Character sets up the central ideals of life."[9]

Religious education is interested in the total personality of the pupil because religion at its best has a bearing upon the whole of life. But religious education is especially concerned about character, or the achievement of moral personality. And that, says Emerson, is the greatest task God has given to man.

[9] *What Do We Mean By Education?* p. 86.

QUESTIONS—

1. Is slavery immoral? Why does the Christian attitude toward this question today differ so greatly from that of Christians in past generations?

2. What criticism would you make of the view that morality is "the intelligent choosing of ideals and ways of action that are in harmony with the good of society"?

3. What are the four levels of conduct according to McDougall? Distinguish clearly between them and give examples.

4. Can you recall instances in your own experience as a child or as a youth when the approval of an immediate group was rejected for the sake of a higher approval? Did you think of that higher approval in terms of parents, teachers, friends, Jesus, or God? Or did you think of it as the approval of your best self?

5. What are the moral sentiments? How are they built up? Why are they important factors in the development of moral personality?

6. What is the function of habit in moral training? How does your church school provide for the cultivation of habits of right conduct?

7. Why is mere instruction in moral precepts so often ineffective in securing right conduct?

8. Are you able to analyze some moral decision of your own into the five factors in volition given in the text?

9. Is there an irreconcilable conflict between the following statements? Strong character requires a wholesome attitude toward the self. Strong character results from losing oneself in the service of humanity. Why? Why not?

10. What principles of moral training can you draw from the matters considered in this chapter?

REPORTS AND INVESTIGATIONS—

1. Make a study of the characters that are admired most by children and young people. Perhaps you could have the members of some class write down the ten characters, living or dead, real or imaginary, which they admire most. Analyze the results. How far are the characters drawn from the movies? General literature? Present day life? History? The Bible?

2. Secure from a number of the teachers in your church school statements of the ways in which they seek to develop the moral character of their pupils. How far do they confront their pupils with concrete moral problems? How far do they provide opportunities for actual practice in doing the right thing?

3. Report on the programs of the Boy Scouts, Camp Fire Girls, or other similar groups, from the standpoint of their value for moral training. What are their points of strength and of weakness?

4. Give instances of conduct that seemed to be clearly self-chosen, and of conduct that seemed to be merely impulsive or imitative. How far do you consider ''what others will think'' in deciding moral questions? At what age do you think it possible for conduct to be moral in the highest sense?

5. Write out some principles of moral training that you think might be helpful to teachers in the church school. The following key words may be suggestive: *association, admirations, motivation, volition, habituation, reflection, unification.*

REFERENCES—

Chapman and Counts, Principles of Education, chap. ix. Houghton Mifflin.

Hadfield, J. A., Psychology and Morals, chaps. x-xii.

McDougall, William, An Introduction to Social Psychology, chaps. viii-ix.   J. W. Luce and Co.

—, Outline of Psychology, chap. xvii.   Scribners.

Norsworthy and Whitley, Psychology of Childhood, chap. xiii.   Macmillan.

Sharp, Frank C., Education for Character, chaps. xi-xiii. Bobbs-Merrill.

Welton, J., What Do We Mean by Education?   chap. ii. Macmillan.

Woodworth, Robert S., Psychology, chap. xx.   Henry Holt.

CHAPTER IX

RELIGIOUS EXPERIENCE

How is Personality Conditioned by Religious Experience?

The main reason for the existence of the church school, and one reason for the existence of the Christian home, is that religion may be taught. Yet this part of the total educational task can never be carried on by itself. The teacher of religion must teach a great many other things besides. His subject matter includes ethics, history, geography, Biblical literature, hygiene, philosophy, and no doubt numerous other things. On the other hand, any or all of these subjects may be taught in such a way as to have little or no positive religious significance. They do not in themselves, no matter how effectively presented, constitute the teaching of religion. What the teaching of religion must mean, if the words are chosen with care, is that the materials and methods of education are used in such a way that the religious experience of the pupil is guided and enriched. To suggest something of what is involved in this guidance of the religious life, and to show how it contributes to the total personality, is the work of the present chapter. The specific questions to be considered are: (1) What is the nature of religious experience? (2) Where does religious experience begin? (3) What are the factors in religious growth? (4) How does religion affect conduct and personality?

WHAT IS THE NATURE OF RELIGIOUS EXPERIENCES?—

Definitions of religion are numerous, conflicting, and for the most part, of little value. Yet some conception of what religion is every teacher must have. And there is no view that meets with a wider acceptance today than that religion is a way of life. This phrase, however, is not meant to be a definition. It indicates rather a way of thinking about religion.

It suggests an approach to the subject that will, in the quickest and most direct manner, bring the essentials into relief. The view, as it is usually stated, includes the idea of a certain high quality of life— "life at its broadest and best"—and quite frequently it is given added force by linking with it the words of Jesus: "I come that they may have life, and may have it abundantly" (John 10:10).

Religion as life is a wholesome and an exceedingly valuable conception. It tends to keep thought about religion from centering wholly upon some mere segment of experience or upon any particular psychological process. It would not permit the identification of religion with intellectual belief, with emotional experience, or with any single institution such as the church or the priesthood. Moreover those who urge this view would remind the reader that in this book the present chapter is not the only one that deals with religion. From the beginning the discussion has been of tendencies and processes that make up the life of the pupil. And it is the pupil who is religious, not just some part of him. Native tendencies habits, ideas, reasoning, emotional responses, attitudes, ideals—all are involved in the experience of a person who, at his best, lives a religious life. Thus Tracy says, "Religion is neither apart from life, nor a part of life, but life at its highest and best."[1]

One of the most salutary features of this view is that it brings religion and morality into such close relation. Religion, at its best, has always been highly moral, but sometimes the two aspects of life have

---

[1] *The Psychology of Adolescence*, p. 185.

fallen apart. Even zealous churchmen have, at one and the same time, been piously devoted to religious practices while they were cruelly oppressing their fellows. At least certain kinds of moral defects have been looked upon as something apart from the religious life. It is a wholesome and thoroughly Christian emphasis that brands all wrong attitudes toward members of the human family not merely as defective morality, but as defective religion. "If a man say, I love God, and hate his brother he is a liar: for he that loveth not his brother whom he hath seen, cannot love God whom he hath not seen" (1 John 4:20).

Misconceptions to be avoided.—But certain possible misconceptions must be guarded against if religion is to be conceived as a way of life. The statement may easily lead to confusion of thought and to unsound practice.

1. There is the danger that religion shall be thought of in such broad terms as to lose any specific and definite meaning. If religion is everything it is nothing. There is a sense, of course, in which religion is rightly considered the total response of the whole life. But this point-of-view may easily be overemphasized until one seems to be saying that all aspects of life are equally religious—that blacking my shoes is as much a religious act as overcoming a temptation or offering a prayer. There is good reason for considering the matters discussed in the preceding chapters as dealing throughout with religion. There is also good reason for setting forth in the present chapter *those aspects of experience which, if properly guided, give to all the rest of life its religious quality.*

2. Religion as a way of life is open to another pos-

sible misconception. There are those who would interpret it to mean the identification of religion with morality; and this view is gaining a certain currency today because it is supported by some of the best writers upon the Psychology of Religion. It is clear, however, that to identify religion and morality is not merely to depart from the commonly accepted usage of the words, but is to make of Christianity simply a glorified ethical system. To be religious—in any thoroughly Christian sense—is to be good; but to be good is not thereby to be religious. The emphasis in present day thought that brings religion and morality together is wholly commendable. It will, nevertheless, render small service to men if it causes them to lose sight of all distinctions between the moral and the religious life.

Religion and morality.—Because religion at its best includes morality, the growth of ideals and their systematization (as discussed in chapter VIII) are fundamental aspects of the religious life. But religion is not merely the striving after ideals. It is even more than devotion to some single ideal, though that ideal be pursued with a love strong enough to result in harmony of life and strength of character. The distinctive mark of religion is the conviction that the One who gathers to himself all of man's ideals is a real Being, and that by dependence upon him the higher way of life is made possible. The man whose morality stops short of religion may follow the path of duty blindly, and in spite of fate; but the religious person finds in the universe "a power not ourselves that makes for righteousness."[2] He has a life-

---

[2] Matthew Arnold, *Literature and Dogma*, viii, 1.

directing conviction that in his moral struggles he is not alone, and that his ideals are not merely human constructions, but are, in some sense, grounded in Reality. Religion is not merely striving for an ideal. It is doing so with the help of God.

If then religion is to be conceived as a way of life, it must be made clear that what is meant is life in God. The unique element in religion is its cosmic significance—its assurance that ''in doing our duty and in abiding by our standards *we somehow have the very heart and soul of things with us and are aligning ourselves* with the eternal.''[3] Religion requires God. And it requires a God who is within the life of man, yet more than it; who is accessible to human thought, but greater than it.

Professor Weigle draws an analogy between the physical forces which sustain life and those spiritual forces upon which the religious person feels himself to be dependent. Physical life, he says, is made possible by the meeting within our bodies of unnumbered physical forces that are not our own. The forces that hold our bodies together fill the Universe. We do not sustain them; they sustain us. Moreover, on the human level, we receive life as a gift from certain spiritual forces—the love which ante-dated our being, for example, or the moral ideals of the home into which we are born. Religion maintains that the Universe itself has such spiritual forces. Man did not create them; they sustain him. And they will further strengthen and enrich his life if they enter fully into his consciousness and he adjusts him-

---

[3]Baillie: *The Roots of Religion in the Human Soul,* p. 110.

self properly to them. It is this adjustment that con
stitutes religion.[4]

If the religious life is thoroughly Christian there
can be no lessening of emphasis on moral and social
values; no neglect of the service of man for the sake
of the service of God. God is not indifferent to the
things men prize—their highest desires and purposes,
their intellectual, aesthetic, social and ethical ideals—
He "loves and values them too."[5] There are rational
grounds for being moral; moral grounds for being
rational; and both rational and moral grounds for
being religious. The Founder of Christianity excluded forever from the Christian ideal any kind of
religious life that neglects its moral and social obligations when he said: "Inasmuch as ye did it not unto
one of these least, ye did it not unto me" (Matt. 25:
45).

Religious experience at its best.—Religious experience, at its best, is thus seen to involve two basic
factors. It is the experience of the person whose life
is lived in devotion to the highest ideal known to
him, and in dependence upon and fellowship with
God for the attainment of the ideal.[6] The ideal,
so far as the Christian is concerned, includes the
application of the spirit of Christ in all the situations of life, both individual and social; and
God, as found by the Christian, is the one who was
revealed in Jesus and who is made accessible through
following him. The ideal is a way of life which God
desires that man shall realize; the dependence is

---

[4]From unpublished lectures of Professor Weigle. Used by
permission.
[5]Baillie: *The Roots of Religion in the Human Soul*, p. 131.
[6]See D. C. Macintosh, *The Reasonableness of Christianity*, p.
40-43, and *Theology as an Empirical Science*, p. 237 f.

upon a God who is a real being and whose character and will represent the supreme ideal.

Like all the rest of life, religious experience is a development. As the child grows toward maturity he becomes able to approximate more and more of the ideal. Furthermore, the consistency and extent of the devotion to the ideal, and the degree and quality of his fellowship with God are matters of growth. This view does not deny the reality of God's dealings with men. It simply recognizes the orderliness of His ways.

For the most truly religious person, then, the whole of life is a religious experience. The common task becomes, for him, a work of God, and moral effort gives a new sense of the worth of ideals and of their ground in Reality. In his failure, in his repentance and trustful resolution, he finds "a Power which can help, deliver, illuminate, and gladden."[7] In the service of his fellows he comes to know a Fellow-Worker who labors at his side. And in prayer and the worship of God he gains strength for his moral needs and a vision that satisfies the soul.

The whole life of the pupil may thus come to have a religious quality. But it will gain this quality only by reason of his conscious dependence upon God in fellowship and worship. It is therefore with this particular phase of religious experience—with this specific religious adjustment—that the present chapter is especially concerned. "Prayer," says Sabatier, "is religion in act; that is, prayer is real religion."[8]

---

[7] L. P. Jacks, *Religious Perplexities*, p. 60.

[8] *An Outline of the Philosophy of Religion*, quoted by Wm. James, *The Varieties of Religious Experience*, p. 464.

WHERE DOES RELIGIOUS EXPERIENCE BEGIN?—

The life of conscious dependence upon God, like any other worthy manner of life, is an achievement. It has its natural roots, and its supernatural ground, but for its full development there must be the commitment of the self to the cultivation of it, and to the direction of its growth. Although man may be "incurably religious," his experience does not reach the Christian level until moral personality has been attained and he chooses to live the religious life.

But the roots of religion run deep into human nature and social experience. And if there is to be any effective guidance of religious growth, the sources of the religion of childhood must be understood and, as far as possible, controlled. The teacher will, therefore, be interested in knowing in what sense religion may be considered instinctive and how far it is to be traced to social and environmental influences. The question involves the problem of the relative importance of heredity and environment, a problem over which there has been much fruitless controversy. What man possesses by nature is potentiality. What he becomes in reality will depend upon the combined working of nature and nurture. And this is as true of religion as it is of any other aspect of life.

Religion is instinctive in the sense that it has a basis in the original nature of man. Psychologists today are unable to find any single religious instinct. but it is clear that man's native equipment (reviewed in chapters two and three) is such that he tends to become religious. Fear and submission, curiosity and wonder, love, parental impulses, the desire for fellowship and the impulse to trust—these and other original tendencies are the psychological basis of the religious attitude toward the universe. In the few cases of which there are records, where individuals have grown to manhood with very meagre social contacts, they seem to have developed a crude religion of their own.

Any adequate religious experience, however, is dependent upon social and environmental factors. An extreme case may perhaps be of value in illustrating this truth. A child born in the heart of pagan Africa will have a very different kind of religious life from that of the person born in a Christian home in America. The difference is chiefly due to environment. It grows out of the vast disparity in social structure and education.

The roots of religion.—The natural roots of religion may, therefore, best be traced to the interaction of the individual with his environment. Four phases of this process are of special significance in the development of religion. They are: conversation and instruction, or what is said to the child; the behavior of adults, or what is done before the child; nature and the child's reactions to it; and social experience, or the child's responses to life in the group.[9]

1. *Instruction* is by no means the earliest nor the most important factor in the religion of childhood. Long before the child can understand the things that are said to him he has received many religious impressions of a negative or of a positive sort. And his own activities and experiences are always more real

[9] From unpublished lectures of Professor Weigle on *The Psychology of Religion*. The discussion throughout this chapter draws considerably upon these lectures. The material is used by permission.

than anything that comes to him simply through the medium of words. The proper function of instruction, as will be shown presently, is more to explain experience than to be a precondition of it. Nevertheless the wholesome development of the religious life is impossible without instruction. The child needs information about religion as well as religious habits and attitudes. He needs to know how God has dealt with men in times past, and what they have learned of His purposes and requirements.

It is not easy, however, to make this religious instruction vital and meaningful. And there are those for whom the difficulties in the way seem almost insurmountable. The suggestion has been made that religious instruction should not be given the child because he accepts uncritically whatever is told him, because he is such a literalist, and because his imagination often leads him to fill in the gaps of his knowledge with the most grotesque details. But these traits are merely the limitations of the child's immaturity. They are not peculiar to religion. And to deny him religious instruction because of them is no more reasonable than would be the refusal to instruct him about all other aspects of life for the same reasons. This kind of error in the child's reasoning is no more serious in the field of religion than it is, for example, in the realm of science.

Yet the teacher must be on his guard lest he accentuate the difficulties of the child by telling him things that are untrue. Sound instruction must always be in a form that will make it intelligible; that is, it must as far as possible be in terms of the child's own experience. But this principle does not require the teaching of falsehoods. The child needs the truth—the best truth the teacher knows —if he is to be saved from later mental conflicts of the kind that are so damaging to faith. For one who is so taught, growth will mean not destruction but fulfillment and will proceed naturally with the expansion of his powers.

2. It has long been observed that actions speak louder than words. And this observation is especially true in religious training because religion is a way of life. *The behavior of adults* before the child may be much more important and influential than the things they say. The two factors should, of course, be in harmony; but, where they are not, the principles lived will be more powerful than those merely spoken about. Religion cannot be effectively taught in a home where the practice of it is ignored. If children were to become more conscious of the nature of their own responses to adult behavior, they would often cry out with Emerson, "How can I hear what you say when what you are is thundering in my ears?"

But the deepest roots of the child's religion lie in his own experiences, and the wise teacher will keep as close to them as possible. Conversation and instruction are important in the interpretation of experience and in the further guidance of it; but they do not create it. Nothing contributes more to the child's religion than his reactions to nature, and his own social contacts.

3. *The physical environment* calls forth from the child a variety of responses. Included among them are many of those that go to make up the religious attitude—fear, curiosity, wonder, gratitude, reverence,

and the like. Thunder and lightning, sun and moon, trees, birds flowers—all are reacted to in ways that have significance for religion. A six-year-old child in conversation with her younger sister was heard to remark: "God makes the prettiest things I ever saw." It was a beautiful Spring day. The first roses had just been gathered and a bunch of them in a vase was a source of delight to the children. Standing by an open door, and looking upon a "world made new," the older girl improvised a song the words of which were written down by a listener in the next room:

> "God makes the pretty rain;
> God makes the pretty sun;
> God makes the beautiful world;
> God makes the pink roses . . .
> God makes the flowers and people,
> And I like this world."

The words used in this song of appreciation show that the child had received religious instruction. Perhaps the more significant thing, however, is the character of the child's response to nature. The instruction gave meaning to the experience; but the experience gave reality to what had been taught.

4. Probably the most important factor in the child's religion is his *social experience*. By his responses to life in the group he builds up many attitudes that are essential to the religious adjustment. It is as the child loves and is loved; as he approves and is approved; as he deals fairly with his associates, co-operates with them, and cares for those who need his help—that the life of trust and fellowship is made

possible for him. Through such experiences the sentiments of a wholesome social life are built up and,
if they are acquired in a religious group, many of
them will center in the object of religious devotion.
God is in these groups and the child will find him
there. The happy fellowship, the love, service, and
worship, will mould his attitudes and bring him genuine satisfaction. In responding to them he will
make a response, also, to the One upon whom the
members of the group acknowledge their dependence
through submission, thankfulness and reverence. And
he will make the response long before it is a conscious,
self-directed act.

The relation of instruction to experience.—As the
child becomes able to understand language, and as
his imagination develops, there is a need for religious
instruction to supplement, explain and clarify his
experience. But there is little value in his learning
to say much about being thankful if he has never
really felt grateful for anything; and his soul may
be seriously harmed by his talk of being God's helper,
if he has never done anything to help forward the
divine purpose in the world. What the child needs
most is fellowship in groups that are dominated by
the Christian spirit; for "instruction which is rooted
and grounded in fellowship is vital and meaningful,
while instruction without fellowship lacks motive and
content."[10] It is the child's social experience that
gives substance and reality to his religious ideas. It is
to his life in Christian groups—especially the home
and the church—that the most important source of
his religion is to be traced.

[10]*The Teaching Work of the Church*, p. 48.

Religious experience may thus begin in the nursery. At first it will be a kind of borrowed experience, but the child may early begin to make it more truly his own. Given the proper guidance, his life in relation to God will gradually become a more conscious adjustment. Perhaps in adolescence it will reach full consciousness and there will be a step of self-commitment to the life of devotion and service. But religious growth, if it is to be wholesome, must not be forced. The religion of childhood is a relatively simple thing. It does not require an elaborate theology. Some theology there will have to be; for the pupil's questions must be answered. But all subtle and abstract formulations of religious truth belong to a later period of life. The closer the teacher stays to the child's own experience the more vital his teaching will be. And there will be many ways in which this experience can be given a religious interpretation. The responses of the child to nature may help to make real a God of beauty and power; his social experience may serve to unveil a God of love; through the approval and disapproval of his conduct by those whom he loves, he may learn something of a God of righteousness; in his efforts to do kindly, helpful deeds—"to create more love in the world"—he may come to understand a God who labors with men for the good of man; and in his struggles to do the right he may find a God who touches the balance on the side of good conduct.[11]

[11]The last of these experiences is no doubt more typical of adolescence than of childhood, but that some children gain help in self-control through prayer seems undeniable. Mrs. Mumford tells of a five-year-old boy who was finding prayer a help in overcoming a bad habit. One day he volunteered the information, "When you ask God to help you do anything, you have to try your very hardest yourself, then he does the last little bit you can't manage. If he did it all, it would be spoilings."— *The Dawn of Character*, p. 165.

Thus even within the limitations of childhood, God may be a reality.

In tracing the roots of religion to human nature and social experience there is no suggestion that religion can be confined within the cramping walls of a narrow naturalism. It is the Christian belief that through the pupil's experience and instruction in the Christian Society, through his devotion to ideals and his attitude of dependence, he is brought into touch with the living God. The personality and character that result from the life of devotion and service are not merely human products; and the conviction of being in harmony with the Eternal has deeper roots than the imagination of man. Their full meaning can be fittingly indicated only in terms of the grace of God and the work of the Holy Spirit. In the words of another: "What we have referred to, on the human side, as the growth and development of character, is to be described, on the divine side, as the work of the regenerating, enlightening, and sanctifying Spirit of God. The correlate of man's discovery is God's revelation; the correlate of learning, God's teaching; the correlate of human growth, God's nurturing care."[12]

WHAT ARE THE FACTORS IN RELIGIOUS GROWTH?—

Religious experience, like all other experience, is ever-changing. The passing years and the expanding horizons of life modify the pupil's ideals and the intensity of his devotion. There are changes also in the nature and quality of his fellowship with God. And while it is impossible here to describe these

---

[12]Weigle, *The Teaching Work of the Church*, p. 51.

changes in detail, some attention must be given to the causes underlying the more important of them. For convenience the factors in religious growth may be designated: developmental, environmental, and moral.

1. Developmental factors.—As the child becomes a youth, as youth passes into manhood, and as manhood approaches old age, many changes which profoundly affect the religious life are wrought in the individual. Some of these are due merely to physical and mental growth, or decay. They are the inevitable accomplishments of the maturing body and mind, or —in later life—of the gradual decline of the faculties. The religion of childhood is "religion within the limits of the child's mental powers, and circumscribed by the boundaries of his mental horizon."[13] It is necessarily concrete, is somewhat formal and external, and although feeling is an important element in it, there is none of the higher, more refined emotion which is considered almost essential to adult religious experience. The period of adolescence brings to the individual the capacity for this higher emotion and the religious life is thereby given a deeper feeling tone. It tends also to become more subjective and personal and, as the intellectual powers grow stronger, to become more rational. The religion of adulthood —an extremely varied phenomenon—is modified by reason of the attainment of maturity. There are tendencies toward conservatism in thought and action, and often a greater interest in the doctrinal and the practical aspects of religion. What religion means in old age will depend in part upon the physi-

---

[13]Tracy: *The Psychology of Adolescence,* p. 188.

cal and mental health of the individual, and religious experience will be colored by the whole outlook on life.

These changes in the religious life are gradual, continuous, and, for the most part inevitable. In so far as they can be separated from the other factors—and that is, of course, only in a rough, approximate way—they are not the achievements of moral personality but are natural processes which in some cases open up opportunities for moral growth and in others set limitations to it. Yet it is upon these developmental changes that the emphasis has been placed in many studies of religion which have become guides for educational practice. This has been especially true in studies of adolescence. The pronounced physical and psychical changes during these years have been spoken of almost as if they, in themselves, were religious phenomena. Thus conversion was declared to be "the altruistic irradiation of sex maturing" and the "new birth" was considered inevitable because it was identified with the birth of the procreative powers. One result of this tendency was that an exaggerated importance was attached to such experiences as the "sense of sin" (as distinct from a consciousness of actual transgression), "religious awakening" and "adolescent doubt." Its influence is still seen in those discussions of adolescent religion that make religious interest almost wholly a matter of the developing powers. There is, of course, ample evidence that most people who join the church do so during adolescence.[14] But environmental influences and the char-

[14]See Athearn: *The Indiana Survey of Religious Education,* I, pp. 371-378.

acter of the whole social structure are important contributing factors in bringing about this result.

2. Environmental factors.—Many of the factors that modify religious experience must, therefore, be traced to the environment. The changes that come during adolescence are due not only to the youth's expanding powers but to his expanding world, and to religious training. Psychological study makes it plain that the teaching and expectations of the different religious groups greatly affect the character of adolescent religious experience. The suggestion is made by Pratt that even the so-called natural skepticism of youth—at least in its more extreme and negative forms—would not be nearly as common as it is if it had not been so widely advertised.[15] However that may be, it is certain that the religious difficulties of youth are often due quite as much to inadequate religious training, and to efforts at adjustment in a new and complex world, as they are to the expansion of the mind and the heightening of the rational powers. It is also clear that proper educational guidance during these years will do much to assure a wholesome religious development.

Religious experience is modified by the social environment, in varying degrees, throughout the whole of life. And not only the local environment—the church and the community—but also the forces at work in the larger world, are factors in the growth of the individual. Social groups, education, economic pressure, institutional loyalties, ''the spirit of the age'' —these and other influences play upon him and deeply affect his religious life. They may weaken or destroy it;

---

[15]*The Religious Consciousness*, p. 177.

they may force it into a cramped and rigid formalism; or they may heighten its moral quality and widen its usefulness and vision. What the outcome will be, will depend partly upon the nature of these environmental influences, but it will be largely determined by the character of the individual and the quality of his religion. An important factor will be the degree of moral and spiritual independence he has achieved.

3. Moral factors.—Many important changes in religious experience are, therefore, due to moral factors. They result from the heightening of ideals, from the moral choices of the individual, and from his self-commitment to the life of devotion to the *highest,* and of dependence upon the greatest. They are, of course, not independent of the processes of development, nor of environmental influences. In actual life they will often be quite inseparable from them. Yet a proper understanding of religious growth is impossible unless the distinction here made is kept clear. Just as strong character was seen to require freedom from the domination of environment, so genuine religious growth cannot be thrust upon the individual. It will rather come about through his commitment of himself to the higher life, through his choices of the better way, through his increasing acquaintance with God and dependence upon him in fellowship and worship. It will be made possible by a religious education that provides for this kind of growth—that guides the experience of the pupil and yet encourages him to go beyond his teachers; to choose, to seek, to make new ventures along "the

mystic way" and in the practical application of his religious ideals.

Morality and religion are thus seen once more to be, not identical, but inextricably bound together. Religion becomes moral and the whole of religious experience, while it overflows morality, has nevertheless moral significance. From this point of view sin is "a willed acceptance of a wrong thing, knowing it to be wrong." A life of sin is lived by a person who repeatedly and consciously chooses the lower values. Conversion is not merely an emotional experience, nor the act of joining the church, but is a turning about from a life of sin to the higher and better way.[16] Decision is the conscious commitment of the self to the higher life—a life which the individual has already begun to live although chiefly by reason of his being carried along in the fellowship of the Christian group. Perseverance is a continuance in the way; and growth is finding in it new and deeper meaning, more and better kinds of loving service, and an ever deepening conviction of its ground in Reality. And this whole experience involving conversion or decision, perseverance and growth, insight, helpfulness and assurance, is at once moral and religious for it is achieved through dependence upon the divine being. The higher life is a life properly adjusted to both man and God.

The religion of maturity will, then, be devotional,

---

[16]This is only one of the many different meanings given to the word conversion in ordinary usage. It is not its common theological meaning. The position taken here is that it would be better to give the word its true etymological significance of "turning round" and to use some other word—perhaps *decision* —to designate the act of self-dedication of an individual who has been brought up "in the nurture and admonition of the Lord." (Eph. 6:4). For a discussion of the term conversion, see A. J. W. Myers: *Educational Evangelism*, p. 103-111.

intelligent, and practical. From the standpoint of educational method it will be maintained and enriched by prayer and worship, by study, and by active participation in those enterprises that seek to bring men, and the conditions of life, into harmony with the will of God. The religious person will not be unaffected by the baffling problems of the social environment. But in the midst of them he will not lose God. Neither will he, by shutting his eyes to the condition of his fellows, cherish God in selfish isolation. In devotion to the higher life he will find the divine Being to be great enough and good enough for his moral needs, and in dependence upon him he will acquire insight and power for the task of building a more brotherly world; he will gain "strength for the journey and courage to face the road."

How does religion bring about these results in conduct and personality?—

In the foregoing discussion the influence of religion upon moral conduct has been taken for granted. Such a position would seem to be justified by the experience of the race—especially Christian experience. But the question as to how religion affects conduct is one in which psychology is interested, and it requires brief consideration at this point. Psychology, of course, views the matter from the human side and therefore it deals with only a part of the total process. It is, however, a most significant part and it will be helpful for the teacher to consider it.

The question itself—although in a form that is quite common—is not well stated; for religion does not so much affect conduct, as constitute it. Religion is conduct, at least in part—the conduct of the person who lives in conscious dependence upon God. And in the case of the Christian religion, it includes the highest ideal of conduct known to man. Yet there is point to the inquiry. What it seeks to discover is how the consciousness of God—that which gives to religion its specific character—contributes to moral conduct and personality.

Before facing this question it should be noted that there are other aspects of life besides those that are specifically moral, and that the life of personal communion has worth in itself. "Religion no less than beauty or companionship, is required by men in the simple fulfillment of life."[17] It is part of the glory of man that he can "glorify God and enjoy him." This truth, however, needs to be placed alongside two others. On the one hand, the life of worship cannot be called Christian if it weakens the sense of social obligation; and, on the other, the life of moral endeavor cannot reach its full power apart from dependence upon God.

Religion and conduct control.—The religious consciousness contributes to conduct control both directly and indirectly. Its indirect effect is the result of a certain refined emotional quality which it gives to all experience. This heightening of the tone of life is a kind of marginal response. The most devout Christian cannot continue to keep God in the center of consciousness. He is obliged to turn from the One to the many; to give his attention to the exacting details of the work-a-day world and of Christian service. In fact these activities must occupy by far the largest portion of his life. Yet throughout all of

---

[17] Chapman and Counts: *Principles of Education*, p. 344.

his varied experiences, though he be beset with difficulties and trials, he may have in the margin of his mind a sense of hopefulness and trust, a feeling of being "at home in the universe," that tends to color everything he does. The total effect of this attitude upon conduct must be very great, although to analyze it in detail is perhaps impossible. It can be confidently said, however, that where this response is the result of Christian fellowship and teaching, it predisposes the individual toward moral courage and strength; it gives him a measure of self-possession in face of the unexpected, and it strengthens his desire to do the right.

The more direct contribution of religion in the control of conduct is also a matter of first importance. It results from the fact that the religious consciousness is, to so large an extent, a consciousness of God in relation to man. The nature of this contribution may be suggested by a threefold statement:

1. The consciousness of God is a powerful motive for right conduct. It was seen in chapter eight that the moving power of ideals lies in their personal derivation and in their becoming the pupil's own so that reaching or approximating them is an act of self-realization. Religion adds a unique element to this motivation. The ideal, say that of love for an enemy, is no less man's own, but it is seen as the desire also of God. It is a part of His will and purpose. And it gains a personal warmth and a heightened attractiveness because there are gathered to it the sentiments of love and devotion that have been built up about the religious object. The "readiness" of the individual to do what needs to be done

is increased, and he is given power—at once internal and external—for the attainment of the ideal.

2. Moreover, when a good purpose is being carried through to completion and when a good act has been done, the consciousness of God tends to fix the habit firmly in the life. It intensifies the satisfaction that accompanies the act and thus, according to the law of effect, increases the probability of habituation. The act has the approval of the ideal self and of God. And this approval, for the Christian at least, is not that of a being who is a mere device of the imagination. The intensity of the satisfaction is largely dependent upon his conviction that, in following the right course, he is "aligning himself with the Eternal."

3. In the pursuit of that purpose which is at once the desire of the soul and the will of God, and by the evaluation of conduct before the ideal self in the presence of God, the conflicting currents of impulse and low aim are turned into the channel of the Good Life. Faced with a situation involving, say, the conditions of the workers in his factory, the employer who is a religious man will not be prompted by impulses to economic gain alone, but will feel the drawing power of that comprehensive ideal which embraces all the higher values of life—the purpose of God.[18] And the consciousness of God will add to his power of acting in harmony with this purpose, and to his satisfaction in so doing. In this way character becomes unified and stabilized. Sometimes a single act, a moment of "turning about" and

---

[18]See Bower: *The Curriculum of Religious Education,* pp. 111-114.

of intensified consciousness of God, is of vast significance in the attainment of unity. But the maintenance of the higher life and progress in it, is possible only through continuous and consistent devotion to the ideal, in constant, and often conscious, dependence upon God. And this life of devotion and dependence makes the largest possible contribution to the growth of effective personality.

QUESTIONS—

1. How would you justify the view that religion is best conceived as a way of life? Answer possible objections to this view.

2. What is the relation between religion and morality from the Christian point of view?

3. Do you agree with the statement that if the whole life of the pupil comes to have a religious quality it will do so largely because of "his dependence upon God in fellowship and worship"?

4. Why is the child's social experience all important in determining the quality of his religious life?

5. What criticism would you make of the use of the following lesson material in teaching first grade children? "The Father, the Son, and the Holy Ghost are one God. The three persons together are called the Trinity."

6. Does the natural and social explanation of religious growth exclude the operation of the spirit of God? Why? Why not?

7. What changes in your own religious life would you say have been due chiefly to (a) developmental factors? (b) environmental factors? (c) moral factors?

8. What is the meaning of the term conversion? Do you think the author's distinction between conversion and decision is sound? Why? Why not?

9. How does the consciousness of God contribute to moral character and personality? Supplement from your own point of view what is said in the text.

10. Do you think that adequate moral training is possible without religion? Give the reasons for your position.

REPORTS AND INVESTIGATIONS—

1. Gather a number of illustrations of religious responses of children, especially those showing gratitude, appreciation, reverence, and similar attitudes. Have you observed cases where the thought of God helped the child to control his conduct? Describe any such incidents.

2. Secure brief written answers from a number of children to such questions as: What is God like? Why do we pray? Why do we go to church? What do you like best about Jesus? What does it mean to be a Christian? Note the differences in the answers according to the age and background of the children. Point out cases where you consider the inadequacy of the child's religious ideas is due to faulty training, and others where you think it is the result of his own limitations.

3. If suitable books are available (such as the study of the pupil in the Specialization units of the Teacher Training Course) report on: (a) The religion of childhood, (b) The religion of adolescence, and (c) The religion of adulthood. Illustrate the likenesses and the differences between the periods by your own observations where possible.

4. Report on the practice of your church as to receiving children and young people into its membership. Do the children feel themselves to be outsiders until they take formal membership in the church? What differences are made in receiving into membership a child who has had a sound Christian training and a mature person whose life has been lived in open violation of Christian principles?

5. In the department of your church school with which you are most familiar, what specific provision is made to stimulate and to develop in a wholesome way, the pupil's consciousness of God? Suggest where improvements might be made.

REFERENCES—

Baillie, John, The Roots of Religion in the Human Soul, chap. iii. Doran.

Brightman, Edgar S., Religious Values, chap. v. Abingdon.

Coe, George A., A Social Theory of Religious Education, chaps. xi-xiv. Scribners.

—, The Psychology of Religion, chaps. i, iv, viii, x. The University of Chicago Press.

Mumford, Edith R., The Dawn of Religion in the Mind of the Child. Longmans, Green and Co.

Myers, A. J. W., Educational Evangelism, chaps. ii and vi. National S. S. Union, London.

Pratt, James B., The Religious Consciousness, chaps. i and v-vii. Macmillan.

Tracy, Frederick, The Psychology of Adolescence, chap. xiii. Macmillan.

CHAPTER X

CHRISTIAN PERSONALITY

How is Christian Personality Attained?

As you enter upon the last chapter of this study of the pupil it will be well to glance back over the ground that has been covered. In chapter one there was a brief introductory discussion of the nature of education, special attention being given to the place of the pupil in the teaching process. The body of the book has been devoted to the consideration of three basic problems. (1) In chapters two, three, and four, the native equipment of the pupil was described. (2) Then followed, in chapters five and six, an account of *the way in which specific* changes are made in the life of the pupil. (3) The last three chapters, seven, eight and nine, have shown how, in and through these changes, *personality develops*. Because of the special interests of the teacher of religion particular attention has been paid to the moral and religious aspects of personality.

The discussion throughout the book has been from the viewpoint of the Christian teacher. Chapter ten, however, will make more explicit this Christian point of view, and will survey the whole process by which Christian personality is built up. It constitutes, therefore, something of a review and summary of the book. The two main divisions of the chapter deal with the questions: (1) What is meant by Christian personality? and (2) How can this kind of personality be attained?

WHAT IS MEANT BY CHRISTIAN PERSONALITY?—

The Christian is a follower of Christ. Anyone who sincerely responds to the call of the Son of God attains a measure of Christian personality. But the teacher's ideal for the pupil is that his whole life may be thoroughly Christian. And while this goal may never be quite attainable, it is, nevertheless, an alluring ideal for the person who has once glimpsed it. The degree to which it can be approximated by the pupil will depend, to a large extent, upon the kind of religious education he receives.

The statement was made in chapter nine that no view of religion meets with wider acceptance today than that which describes it as a way of life. When the Christian religion is viewed from this standpoint, the essence of Christianity is seen to be "Jesus' Way of Living," and this phrase, like the others, is gaining recognition. The conception is, in the main, a wholesome one. It rings true to the emphasis placed upon life and character in the teaching of Jesus himself. But it, too, is open to possible misunderstanding. There should scarcely be any need of saying that Jesus' way of living involved a basic religious adjustment. It was a manner of life that was motivated, sustained, and given meaning by devotion to the purpose of the Father, and by conscious dependence upon Him. Moreover it should be clear that the kind of religious adjustment within reach of the Christian today is made possible through the life and work of Jesus himself. If morality is devotion to ideals, and religion (in its specific and definitive sense) is dependence upon God, then *Christianity involves both morality and religion raised to their highest terms and bound together in a life.* It was such a life that Jesus himself lived. It is to such a life that he calls his followers.

The way of life that is offered to men by Christianity thus includes an ideal and a means of progressively realizing that ideal. The Christian identifies himself with Christ and the endeavor to realize the ideal-self leads to growth in Christlikeness. It is by following Christ, also, and not by disputatious arguments about him, that men find reality in the life of dependence; for their conviction of "the infinite Friendliness"[1] is deepened, and they bring themselves into touch with the spirit of the living God.

A test of Christian personality.—The Christian way of life requires a Christian person to live it. Perhaps the most practical test of Christian personality is, therefore: Does it exercise and express itself in life-situations by meeting them "in the spirit and way of Christ"?[2] If it were truly said of an individual that in every phase of life he acted in this spirit and manner, his personality could, in the fullest sense, be called Christian. And perhaps the best indication of the degree to which the pupil has attained the goal is the number and kind of life situations in which his conduct harmonizes with this principle. The teacher will not forget, of course, that the manner of meeting one situation is always dependent in part upon how other situations have been met; that what Christ did in the city, or on the plain, was not unrelated to his conduct on the mountain side; that the "spirit and way of Christ" includes conscious dependence upon God and the kind of courage and strength that flow from it.

What this following of Christ means, objectively and in detail, is not easy to state. It could be determined only by a careful analysis of modern life and by the judgment of Christ's best interpreters as to what is the Christian thing to do in this situation and in that. New situations are constantly aris-

---

[1]L. P. Jacks: *Religious Perplexities*, p. 90.

[2]Shaver: *The Project Principle in Religious Education*, p. 40.

ing in the changing civilization of today and the follower of Christ is ever confronted with new problems. Yet there are basic human impulses and relationships that are, in one sense at least, changeless; and there are certain Christian ideals of life that retain their meaning despite the passage of time. Some of the larger features of the Christian ideal for the individual and for society are clear enough. Its dominant note, according to both Jesus and Paul, is unselfish love. It would include among the traits of Christian personality, in one form or another, such qualities as trustfulness, reverence, love of Christ, repentance for wrong-doing, hopefulness, friendliness, courage and self-giving.[3] It would involve also the manifestation of such traits in all the varied relationships of life, and the constant endeavor to secure these values not for the self alone but for all men.[4] The Christian ideal includes a society that will make possible for every one the fullest development of Christian personality of which he is capable.

It is sometimes urged that there is little value in

[3]Twenty-two basic traits of Christian personality have been selected by the International Council of Religious Education as guides in the construction of the new International Curriculum. These traits with both negative and positive elaboration are listed in *Research Service Bulletin No. 5.* The key words are: Co-operation, courage, creativeness, dependability, faith, forgiveness, Goodwill, health-mindedness, honesty, humility, joyousness, love, loyalty, obedience, openmindedness, penitence, purity, purposefulness, reverence, self-control, self-respect, spirituality. *Research Service Bulletin No. 5,* p. 49-58.

[4]The areas and relations of life in which Christian personality will function are classified by the Curriculum Committee of the International Council as follows: (1) Health Activities, (2) Educational Activities, (3) Economic Activities, (4) Vocational Activities, (5) Citizenship Activities, (6) Recreation (7) Sex, Parenthood, and Family Life, (8) General Life in the Group, (9) Friendship Activities, (10) Aesthetic Activities, (11) Specialized religious Activities. Each of these areas of human experience is subdivided into the six basic relationships of life: (a) Personal (b) Home, (c) School, (d) Church, (e) Other community relations, and (f) Relations beyond the Local Community.—See *Research Service Bulletin No. 5,* p. 42-48.

the listing of traits because they are abstractions and are, to so large a degree, subjective. But the words have meaning and, from the standpoint of one who observes the conduct of others, they represent certain ways of acting that are recognizable. It is true that they require definition and concrete illustration if they are to be made thoroughly practical standards of judgment for the teacher to use; but the task of so defining and illustrating them does not fall within the scope of this book. In a general way, however, men know what hopefulness, and courage, and friendliness, and gratitude toward God, mean; and the wise teacher is constantly on the lookout for the appearance of these and other Christian traits in the lives of his pupils.

But these qualities of life may also be viewed from the standpoint of the pupil himself. For him they are, or may become ideals. And the strength of their impelling power will depend upon the kind of religious education he receives; upon the way in which these ideals are built up in his experience. If they are learned through contact with great Christian personalities—especially that of Jesus himself, and through their being tested in the crucible of life, the love of them will predispose the individual, in meeting all kinds of situations, to Christian conduct.

The inward spirit and the outward act.—The mere externals of conduct can, of course, never be a completely adequate test of Christian personality. A truly Christian deed must be in the spirit as well as in the way of Christ. The pupil may act in a Christian way, so far as his outward behavior is concerned, merely because he has been told to do so by teacher,

or parent, or by some other authoritative voice. Or
his act may be simply the result of habits that have
been developed under social compulsion. Cases have
been observed of a child forced to say his prayers
under the threat of a switch which lay within easy
reach of the parent, and of a college student who
continued to pray the prayer of her childhood, ''Now
I lay me down to sleep.'' It would seem, too, that
the behavior of many adult Christians remains on
the level of the authoritative and the habitual. Religious education must, of course, make use of these
types of behavior and they have an important part
to play in its task of building character. But it
seeks ever to bring the pupil to the place where his
acts, while in harmony with, the highest Christian
standards, possess also the inward moral quality of
self-chosen, purposeful conduct. Freedom is, therefore, an essential factor in fully developed Christian
personality. ''For freedom did Christ set us free''
(Gal. 5:1). In following Christ the mature Christian is, to use Luther's phrase, ''the most free lord
of all.'' He is lured on by an ideal that is loved
and is freely pursued and he has little need of external restraints or promptings.

Ultimately the goal of the Christian teacher is the
christianizing of the whole personality of the pupil.
It is that the pupil may come to possess the knowledge, ability, attitudes and ideals that will enable
him to meet all life situations in the spirit and way
of Christ. But just as external factors may force
conduct into the Christian mould even where the true
Christian spirit is lacking, so may the individual
who desires to act in a Christian way be kept from

doing so by forces over which he has little or no control. As was pointed out in chapter seven his conduct may be very deeply affected by such factors as bodily constitution, hereditary tendencies, or unwholesome environment or training. If a measure of cheerfulness, for example, is an element in Christian personality, some persons may be kept from completeness in this regard by defective bodily structure or functioning. Even the degree and quality of the individual's consciousness of God is dependent, in part, upon intellectual and emotional capacity and development. And the ability to do the Christlike thing in a complex situation of business or politics is by no means independent of a knowledge of economics or of political science.

Now, religious education is interested in all of the factors that help or hinder the attainment of its objectives. It cannot achieve its full purpose without christianizing, in home and society, the conditions of life which contribute so largely to character and personality. It cannot be blind even to physical factors; for the correction of a physical defect may, in the case of some child, be the indispensable condition of a wholesome attitude or of a loving deed. It must give consideration to the whole life of the pupil in all his relationships if it would help him toward his fullest possible development. Nevertheless the main concern of the teacher of religion is to make Christian the central ideals of the pupil's life—his spirit, desires, and purposes. It is to secure from the pupil a continuous and voluntary commitment to the Christian way, in conscious dependence upon God.

The practical objective of religious education is, therefore, that the pupil should become as Christian as he can be; that, within the limits of his abilities and conditioning environment, he should approach as nearly as possible to the ideal of meeting every situation in a Christian way. He may fail to do the Christian thing because he lacks necessary information, or because he does not possess the ability to see clearly all the implications of his acts; but his desires are purged of their unworthy elements. He seeks first the Kingdom of God and his righteousness. He finds satisfaction in conduct that is, to the best of his knowledge and understanding, in harmony with the spirit of Christ.

This does not mean, let it be said emphatically, that the Christian may rest content in ignorance, or that he may lightly excuse his faulty conduct by pleading his inability to understand moral issues. One of the essential traits of Christian personality is a desire for growth, a spirit of enterprise and discovery, a constant searching for more light upon the question as to what it means to be a Christian. Religious education must give knowledge as well as inspiration, it must stimulate thought as well as feeling, it must encourage its best pupils to do their best thinking upon the problem: Where does the way of Christ lead in the complex life of today?

A forward-moving goal.—Christian personality is, therefore, a forward moving goal. In one sense it is ever attainable, yet never attained. It is by no means a state to be once for all achieved; for changing conditions and new knowledge bring new obligations and wider opportunities for the expression of the Christian spirit. What Christian personality meant a hundred years ago is not what it means today, nor is its meaning today what it will be a hundred years hence. Jesus Christ still walks far in advance of the race. It is ever true that:

> New occasions teach new duties;
>   Time makes ancient good uncouth;
> They must upward still, and onward,
>   Who would keep abreast of truth.
>   —Lowell: *The Present Crisis.*

And in the life of the individual Christian, also, there must be continuous growth. It was after many years of Christian service that Paul wrote: "Not that I have already obtained, or am already made perfect: but I press on" (Phil. 3:12).

Yet, in a true sense, Christian personality can be attained. The term may well be applied to the person whose life is predominantly Christian, judged by the best Christian standards of his day. Henry Drummond, for example, could be said to have had a Christian personality, at least according to the judgment of D. L. Moody, for Moody said of him, "That man is more like Jesus Christ than any other man I know." Moreover there have been in every generation at least a considerable number of Christians— some of them known to fame and others long since forgotten by the world—whose spirit and manner of life, whose attitude toward God and man, was sufficiently Christlike for it to be said of them that they achieved Christian personality. And wherever religious education really reaches its objective a similar statement can be made concerning those whom it has nourished and whose moral and religious growth it has guided.

A person who, through the expression of his own ideals and purposes, manifests the essential Christian traits in his relations to man and God, and who seeks ever to revise his standards and manner of life on the basis of his Christian experience and his deepening insight into the meaning of the Christian spirit —that is what is meant by the attainment of Christian personality.

How can this kind of personality be attained?—

Christian personality, if it is attained, is largely the achievement of the pupil. Yet it may be that adverse circumstances make impossible for a given individual, or group, any such attainment. It is the business of the church, and especially of the teacher of religion, so to guide the development of the pupil as to make most probable his reaching the Christian goal. To say in detail how this can be done would be to repeat all that has been written in the preceeding chapters and to review the whole program of the church. But, by way of summary, certain large aspects of the process may well be outlined here. If the pupil attains Christian personality he will do so by reason of his fellowship in the Christian group; his self-commitment to the Christian way; and his dependence upon God.

1. *Christian fellowship.*—Christian fellowship there must be, if Christian personality is to be attained. And the earlier the pupil is introduced into this fellowship the more thorough and permanent its influence upon him is likely to be. It has been made

clear in earlier chapters that the processes which modify original nature are at work long before they are consciously chosen acts of the pupil; and that the most important source of the child's religious life is his social experience. Before there is self-direction in any true sense a bent has been given to the personality. And even the kind of self-control that the pupil attains—perhaps the determination of whether he shall gain genuine self-control at all—depends largely upon the character of the social group which is the matrix of his early life.

But fellowship implies much more than a passive absorption of the virtues of the group. As the term is used here it means a normal, wholesome sharing in the life of the family, the church and the community. It may come about through a variety of activities—listening to stories, and telling them; singing hymns, and playing games; worshiping with others, and praying for them; doing the work of a class-president or electing some one to that office, and carrying on the business of class or society. In the life of the group the pupil enjoys what Professor Coe aptly calls, "the specific happiness of being a member of society."[5] And Christian fellowship should heighten the tone of that happiness, whether it is found through the activities of the family hour at home, or through intelligent participation in the worship and missionary giving of the church.

The social contacts of the pupil, both real and imaginary, will expand in an ever-widening circle. If the spirit of the group which cradles his early years is truly Christlike, he will come to feel his

Coe, *A Social Theory of Religious Education*, p. 80.

sympathetic relation to the people of other nations and of other races. He will have intercourse, too, with those who in ages past have lived valiantly the good life. He will identify himself with the great company who have heard the call of Christ and will know something of the meaning of "the communion of the saints."

The impressionable years.—But it is more especially the fellowship of the impressionable years to which attention is here being called. The experience of the pupil in the Christian group will, in the manner described in earlier chapters, predispose him toward the higher life. It will equip him with habits and attitudes, give him knowledge, cultivate in him religious and moral sentiments, and help him acquire ideals and purposes that are essential to Christian personality. And many of these elements may be so thoroughly built into his life that they become a permanent possession that no later experience can eradicate. The child who has been reared in a Christian family—whether the home or the larger Christian group—may change many of his ways as he ventures forth into the larger world, but, in the words of Bushnell, "The odor of the house will always be in his garments, and the internal difficulties with which he has to struggle will spring of the family seeds planted in his nature."[6]

There is a very illuminating passage in Will Durant's *Transition* in which he describes the influence upon his life of those stories and pictures of Christ that saturated the atmosphere of his childhood home. "I was filled with a great love for this man," he

---

[6]Bushnell, *Christian Nurture,* 1916 edition, p. 78.

writes, "so much that to this day, when I should be ready to admit the historical uncertainty that enshrouds him, his figure gathers round it, in my mind, a thousand tender memories, and endless emotional reverberations. I thrill yet at the mention of his name, and hunger yet for the ideal life he wished mankind to live; if to love him and hear him gladly is to be a Christian, then, skeptic and pagan though I be, I am a Christian too, and Christ is still my God.'"[7] Whatever may be thought of Doctor Durant's total attitude, and however much it may be regretted that other aspects of his early religious training were not as wholesome as this one, there are but few Christians who would fail to appreciate the value of these strong sentiments toward Jesus Christ. They have, no doubt, contributed very greatly to the personality of the writer who, despite the "Great Change," has about him so much that is Christian still. There are many other important factors in the equipment of the pupil for the higher life, but without the development of powerful moral and religious sentiments, Christian personality cannot be attained. And childhood and youth is preeminently the time for building up the sentiments.

2. *Christian thinking and doing.*—The Christian life involves self-commitment to the way of Christ. In and through the pupil's fellowship in the group there will come to him innumerable opportunities to choose between the higher and the lower values. In fact, the constituents of Christian experience are largely such choices made under a great variety of circumstances. The situations, which may be either

---

[7] *Transition: A Mental Autobiography,* pp. 21-22.

real or imaginary, vary greatly in complexity. They range all the way from the simple decision of the child to tell the truth and accept punishment for a misdeed, to the martyr's choice of death rather than the surrender of his cause. Whenever the pupil identifies himself with the character in the story who does the Christian thing, he is choosing the higher value. Whenever he listens to the teaching of prophet or apostle and responds to a truly Christian message with whole-hearted acceptance he is committing himself to the Christian way. But even more important in character formation are his choices whenever he faces an actual situation in his own life, and with a clear understanding of the issues involved, decides upon the Christian course of action, and carries it through to completion. Christian thinking and doing are effective builders of wholesome personality.

One of the most significant choices in the life of the individual is that full commitment of the self to the way of Christ which takes place in the act of decision or of conversion. (See the discussion of these terms in chapter nine.) But the pupil who has been nurtured in the Christian group will have had many experiences of choosing the Christian way before the time when he positively identifies himself with the followers of Christ. And in making this decision he will be acting in harmony with the system of ideals and purposes he has been building up through the years. Moreover his acts of self-commitment to the way of Christ will not end on the day of decision. There will be times that call for rededication; and occasions, too, when, after a period of perplexity, there will be illumination. At such times he will choose either the light or the darkness, and in so doing he will discover new richness and depth in his religious experience, or he will settle into the smug complacency of a merely nominal Christian life.

Practice in choosing the Christian way.—The kind of religious education that would develop Christian personality must, therefore, give the pupil practice in choosing the Christian way and in following it. The whole life of the family and of the church, if it is permeated by the Christian spirit, will provide many opportunities for this kind of purposeful activity. But there is a need that more attention be given to the matter in building curricula and in carrying on the teaching process. For this reason the project principle is a most valuable guide to the teacher of religion. A project is virtually a bit of pupil-activity—usually a group enterprise of some kind—that is *self-chosen* and therefore entered into heartily; that is carried to completion; and that leads to some result which is felt by the pupils to have worth. Other things being equal, the more nearly the activity resembles real life, and the more it involves the pupil's own thinking of the problematic type, the greater its educational value. There are many good reasons for the use of the project principle in religious education but none that are more important than this: that project teaching provides the pupil with numerous opportunities to choose and to carry out high and worthy purposes under the guidance of a teacher of mature Christian experience.[8]

[8]See, in this connection, Shaver's discussion of the criteria for selecting Christian education projects. Shaver: *The Project Principle in Religious Education*, pp. 47-50.

It is clear that wherever the activities of church school groups are of this character, the pupils will receive valuable training for meeting future life-situations in the spirit and way of Christ.

The result of Christian thinking and doing, as was pointed out in chapter eight, is the unification of character and personality. Every decision made on the Christian level tends to Christianize the central ideals and purposes of the pupil's life—his ideal self —and thus to bring harmony to all of his experience. He has a determining motive in meeting all of life's situations. He is devoted to the Christian ideal. He desires wholeheartedly to walk in the way of Christ.

3. *Christian worship.*—But the attainment of full Christian personality requires power and vision, and these are the fruits of a life of dependence upon God. Religious education differs from general education not so much in what it omits as in what it includes. It seeks to bring about the adjustment of the pupil not merely to his physical and to his human environment, but to God. This adjustment is, of course, not possible apart from human fellowship, nor is it independent of the pupil's thinking and doing as he faces the concrete situations of life; yet it cannot be wholly identified with these phases of his experience. It is rather a complex response that includes all of these particular adaptations—and more. And that something more is all-important. It is the most distinctive aspect of the religious adjustment. It is the essence of what takes place in the act of worship, or prayer.

Worship must not be identified with the emotional side of religion, nor with reflection upon failures in human conduct. It involves rather the whole personality. And it may, in the end, turn away from the problems of life to the One in whom all problems are resolved. It is "a personal approach to God"[9] in which the consciousness of dependence is quickened and the worshiper seeks harmony and finds power. Whether it be the prayer of the individual in his closet, or the "Te Deum" of the worshiping group, the act is one of approach to God which leads to a deeper sense of fellowship with the divine Being.

The proper attitude toward God—like the proper adjustment of man to society or to nature—has to be learned. And the Christian message declares that the life and work of Jesus Christ portrays this attitude and provides a means whereby it can be achieved in the lives of his followers. It maintains that as men respond wholeheartedly to the call of Christ, and act upon his truth, they will discover the way to the Father. They will find an answering response in the universe to their yearnings after a fuller life. They will lay hold on God.

There is, then, a worshipful life. It is lived by the person who is related, in a truly Christian way, to his fellows and to God. But the teaching of the New Testament, as well as the testimony of Christian experience, is that this kind of life is made possible by times of worship—occasions when the approach to God is fully conscious, and "spirit with spirit can meet" in direct, personal intercourse. It is here that religion has something unique to offer men. Social fellowship and the inspiration of the crowd they may have without religion. Some sort

---

[9]Weigle and Tweedy, *Training the Devotional Life*, p. 6.

of moral training may be provided on the level of a thorough-going humanism. But worship makes possible a kind of fellowship with God that is available nowhere else. If teachers of religion fail to guide the pupil into a full, rich experience of Christian worship, their failure is at the most crucial point in the whole enterprise of religious education.

The fruits of worship.—What worship does in the life of the individual cannot be indicated by a simple tabulation of results. The relation of God to the world and to man is, in the Christian view, so intimate, and the needs of men are so varied, that the fruits of worship defy classification. Yet the divine response is dependable. Its effects in human experience can be recognized. And, in the broadest of terms, it may be said that true worship gives power and insight for the moral life. In conscious dependence upon God, the person who is devoted to the Christian ideal finds courage and strength. Christianity, as Principal Jacks has said, does not so much remove the enigmas of life, as it does give men courage in the midst of their perplexities. A few years ago an eminent sociologist, addressing a group of students, advised his hearers not to enter the field of social service unless they could take with them an adequate religious faith. Without religion, he, said, their work was likely to be vitiated by a growing pessimism, or to be rendered futile by a radicalism of the impatient and superficial type. The life of dependence gives strength for moral endeavor. It makes available to the Christian, as he strives to walk in the way of Christ, the sustaining energy of the spirit of God.

The experience of worship, at its best, is also a source of moral and spiritual enlightenment. Religious insight does not come by reasoning alone, but by contact with God. There is an emphasis today upon problem-solving as the technique for religious teaching, and the value of this method has been pointed out a number of times in this study of the pupil. But the principle must not be applied in too narrow and exclusive a way. There are other types of experience which contribute to the richness and worth of life, and which are by no means without moral significance. One of them is the heart of worship—communion with God. The new insight of the Great Apostle which had so much to do with keeping Christianity a universal religion, was not the result of "group thinking," but of devotion to Christ and of communion with God. And if it be urged that Paul's was a unique case, the same thing may be said of the insight of Luther and of other great spiritual adventurers. The limitations of the ordinary Christian no doubt preclude the possibility of the profound originality of such leaders, but may not the process be somewhat similar in the lesser concerns of life? There is always a need for clear thinking upon religious problems, but the possibility of a Christian outcome as a result of group thinking, depends not only upon correct reasoning, but upon the character and spirit of those who make up the group. It would seem that there is the greatest likelihood of a Christian result where the members of the group, individually and as a company, are following after the Christian ideal in conscious dependence upon God.

In worship and prayer the vision of the Christian is clarified. His attitude for the time being is not that of problem-solving, but of contemplation and fellowship. Yet he returns to his tasks with a new sense of their worth and meaning and with a deeper conviction of the reality of the unseen. It is through this life of dependence, as well as by their Christian thinking, that men will gain a clearer vision of what it means to follow Christ in the complex life of to-day or, let it be said, of tomorrow. It is here, too, in work and worship, that faith and trust are made strong. There comes to the individual an added assurance that the values men hold dear will not perish; and he gains a measure of preparation for the unexpected and the unpredictable. His belief in Him who "brought life and immortality to light" (2 Tim. 1:10) is given the religious quality that makes it faith, and he is enabled to face even the remote future with confidence and hope.

QUESTIONS—

1. In what sense can it be said that the essence of Christianity is "Jesus' Way of Living"? What are the elements of strength and of weakness in this view?

2. Can you suggest a better test of Christian personality than the one proposed in the text, viz., that the Christian person is one who meets life-situations in the spirit and way of Christ?

3. Why can the externals of conduct never be a completely adequate test of Christian personality?

4. What cases have you known of Christians whose failure to do the Christian thing was due to lack of information or to inability to see clearly all of the implications of their conduct? To what extent do you consider them responsible for their failure?

5. Do you agree with this statement from the text? "What Christian personality meant a hundred years ago is not what it means today, nor is its meaning today what it will be a hundred years hence."

6. Of what importance in the growth of Christian personality is the building up of strong religious sentiments? Where, in the program of religious education, are these sentiments most effectively developed?

7. Why is the project principle an especially valuable guide in the work of the Christian teacher?

8. What are some of the activities of your church which are not commonly thought of as belonging to the educational program but which, nevertheless, give valuable training in Christian thinking and doing? Should they be considered as a part of the educational work of the church?

9. How much attention is given by your church school to the problem of guiding the pupils in the experience of Christian worship? Criticize the statement, ''If teachers of religion fail to guide the pupil into a full, rich experience of worship, their failure is at the most crucial point in the whole enterprise of religious education.''

10. What would you say is the chief contribution this course has made to your life, or to your equipment for the work of the teacher?

REPORTS AND INVESTIGATIONS—

1. Think of the most Christian person you have ever known. List ten traits possessed by this person and compare them with similar lists prepared by other members of the class. Discuss the points of agreement and of disagreement. What do you consider to be the most essential traits of Christian personality?

2. Recall instances of persons known to you who have manifested certain wholesome traits in one situation (perhaps in the home or at church) and almost the opposite traits in other situations (say, in business or politics). How do you account for these differences? What is their significance for religious education?

3. Study the life and work of your church (or of your home, or your community) from the standpoint of their approximation to the Christian ideal. How far do they provide a society in which the growing child may experience a truly Christian fellowship? What are the most conspicuous negative elements? What can be done to improve the situation?

4. Report on the program of some department of your church school as to its guidance of the pupils in (a) Christian thinking and doing, and in (b) Christian wor-

ship. List in detail what is being done in the way of service and recreational activities, projects, carefully prepared worship services, and pupil participation in planning the work of the department.

5. Prepare for the final examination. The leader will announce the kind of examination that will be used but, whatever plan is followed, the preparation should include a review of the main topics treated in the text and the class discussions. The student will find it helpful to prepare a list of fifty questions covering these items. He should also be ready to submit his observation notebook to be examined by the class leader.

REFERENCES—

Baillie, John, The Roots of Religion in the Human Soul, chap. iv. Doran.

Bushnell, Horace, Christian Nurture, chaps. i-iv. 1916 Revised edition. Charles Scribner's Sons.

Coe, George A., A Social Theory of Religious Education. Consult index: Conversion, Christian experience, Fellowship, Thought and Action, etc. Scribners.

Macintosh, D. C., The Reasonableness of Christianity, chaps. ii and iii. Scribners.

Shaver, Erwin L., The Project Principle in Religious Education, chaps. iv, x, and xi. University of Chicago Press.

Weigle, Luther A. The Training of Children in the Christian Family, chaps. i, iii, xii, and xiii. Pilgrim Press.

Weigle and Tweedy, Training the Devotional Life, chaps. i-iii, vii-ix. Pilgrim Press.

BIBLIOGRAPHY

Allport, F. N., Social Psychology. Houghton Mifflin.

Averill, L. A., Psychology for Normal Schools. Houghton Mifflin.

Baillie, John, The Roots of Religion in the Human Soul. Doran.

Berman, L., The Glands Regulating Personality. Macmillan.

Betts, G. H., How to Teach Religion. Abingdon.

—, The Mind and Its Education. Appleton.

Betts, G. H., Hawthorne, M. O., Method in Teaching Religion. Abingdon.

Bernard, L. L., Introduction to Social Psychology. Holt.

Brightman, E. S., Religious Values. Abingdon.

Bushnell, Horace, Christian Nurture. Scribners.

Chapman, J. C., and Counts, G. S., Principles of Education. Houghton Mifflin.

Coe, Geo. A., A Social Theory of Religious Education. Scribners.

—, Education in Religion and Morals. Revell.

—, Psychology of Religion. University of Chicago.

Colvin, S. S., and Bagley, W. C., Human Behavior. Macmillan.

Freeman, F. C., How Children Learn. Houghton Mifflin.

Gates, A. I., Psychology for Students of Education. Macmillan.

Groves, E. R., Personality and Social Adjustment. Longmans Green.

Hadfield, J. A., Psychology and Morals. McBride.

Hartshorne, H., Childhood and Character. Pilgrim Press.

Healey, W., Mental Conflicts and Misconduct. Little Brown.

Kilpatrick, W. H., Foundations of Method. Macmillan.

Kitson, H. D., How to Use Your Mind. Lippincott.

Leighton, J. H., The Field of Philosophy. Adams.

Macintosh, D. C., The Reasonableness of Christianity. Scribners.

Martin, H., Formative Factors in Character. Longmans Green.

McDougall, Wm., Outline of Psychology. Scribners.

—, An Introduction to Social Psychology. Luce.

Mumford, E. R., The Dawn of Religion in the Mind of the Child. Longmans Green.

Neumann, H., Education for Moral Growth, Appleton.

Norsworthy and Whitley, Psychology of Childhood. Macmillan.

O'Shea, M. V. (Ed.), The Child: His Nature and His Needs. Children's Foundation.

Overstreet, H. A., Influencing Human Behavior. Norton.

Pratt, James B., The Religious Consciousness. Macmillan.

Pyle, W. H., The Psychology of Character. Warwick and York.

Roback, A. A., The Psychology of Character. Harcourt Brace.

Sharp, Frank C., Education for Character. Bobbs Merrill.

Shaver, Erwin L., The Project Principle in Religious Education, University of Chicago.

Soares, T. G., Religious Education, University of Chicago.

Starch, D., Educational Psychology. Macmillan.

Terman, Lewis M., The Measurement of Intelligence. Houghton Mifflin.

Thorndike, E. L., Educational Psychology. Vols. I, II, III. Teachers College.

Tracy, Frederick, The Psychology of Adolescence. Macmillan.

Watson, John B., Psychology from the Standpoint of a Behaviorist. Lippincott.

Weigle, L. A., The Pupil and the Teacher. Doran.

—, The Training of Children in the Christian Family. Pilgrim Press.

Weigle, L. A., et al, The Teaching Work of the Church. Association Press.

Weigle, L. A., and Tweedy, H. H., Training the Devotional Life. Pilgrim Press.

Welton, J., What Do We Mean by Education? Macmillan.

White, W., The Mechanisms of Character Formation. Macmillan.

Woodworth, R. S., Psychology: A Study of Mental Life. Henry Holt.

INDEX

251

ALEXANDER II

and the

Modernization of Russia

is one of the volumes
in the

TEACH YOURSELF HISTORY
LIBRARY

Edited by A. L. ROWSE

Teach Yourself History

VOLUMES READY OR IN PREPARATION

ALEXANDER II

and the

Modernization of Russia

by
W. E. MOSSE

NEW YORK
THE MACMILLAN COMPANY

PRINTED IN GREAT BRITAIN

General Introduction to the Series

THIS series has been undertaken in the conviction that there can be no subject of study more important than history. Great as have been the conquests of natural science in our time—such that many think of ours as a scientific age *par excellence*—it is even more urgent and necessary that advances should be made in the social sciences, if we are to gain control of the forces of nature loosed upon us. The bed out of which all the social sciences spring is history; there they find, in greater or lesser degree, subject-matter and material, verification or contradiction.

There is no end to what we can learn from history, if only we would, for it is coterminous with life. Its special field is the life of man in society, and at every point we can learn vicariously from the experience of others before us in history.

To take one point only—the understanding of politics : how can we hope to understand the world of affairs around us if we do not know how it came to be what it is? How to understand Germany or Soviet Russia, or the United States—or ourselves, without knowing something of their history?

There is no subject that is more useful, or indeed indispensable.

Some evidence of the growing awareness of this may be seen in the immense increase in the interest of the reading public in history, and the much larger place the subject has come to take in education in our time.

This series has been planned to meet the needs and demands of a very wide public and of education—they are indeed the same. I am convinced that the most congenial, as well as the most concrete and practical,

5

approach to history is the biographical, through the lives of the great men whose actions have been so much part of history, and whose careers in turn have been so moulded and formed by events.

The key idea of this series, and what distinguishes it from any other that has appeared, is the intention by way of a biography of a great man to open up a significant historical theme; for example, Cromwell and the Puritan Revolution, or Lenin and the Russian Revolution.

My hope is, in the end, as the series fills out and completes itself, by a sufficient number of biographies to cover whole periods and subjects in that way. To give you the history of the United States, for example, or the British Empire or France, *via* a number of biographies of their leading historical figures.

That should be something new, as well as convenient and practical, in education.

I need hardly say that I am a strong believer in people with good academic standards writing once more for the general reading public, and of the public being given the best that the universities can provide. From this point of view this series is intended to bring the university into the homes of the people.

A. L. ROWSE

ALL SOULS COLLEGE,
    OXFORD.

Contents

Dates are given according to our present Gregorian Calendar. In Alexander's day, Russians used the Julian Calendar which was then twelve days behind the Gregorian. Where it was desirable to give a date in both styles, they have been placed side by side.

'Experience shows that the most dangerous moment for a bad government is usually when it begins to reform itself.'
—ALEXIS DE TOCQUEVILLE

'No despot can make happy a country which his predecessors have made unhappy. The traces left by centuries of oppression cannot be wiped out by imperial decree. That is the tragedy of Alexander II.'—KURD VON SCHLÖZER

Preface

WHILE the names of Peter the Great and Lenin have become household words, that of Alexander II, Emperor of all the Russias from 1855 until his assassination in 1881, is familiar only to the specialist. Yet the 'Tsar Liberator' is associated with a social transformation hardly inferior in importance to the reforms of Peter or Lenin's October Revolution. B. H. Sumner says: "The emancipation of the serfs (1861) and the other reforms of the sixties marked the watershed between the old and the nineteenth-century Russia, much as the reign of Peter the Great marked that between the old Muscovy and the New Russia."[1] In spite of his less dynamic personality, Alexander II deserves to rank with the two great innovators among the makers of modern Russia.

If the effect of Alexander's reign is to be summed up in a single phrase, it may be said to mark the transition in Russia from a semi-feudal to an early capitalist economy. Two measures in particular helped to accelerate the process. The liberation of the serfs increased the available force of mobile free labour. The construction of railways stimulated the growth of Russian industry. Together with a great expansion of banking and credit facilities, these developments laid the foundations of an 'Industrial Revolution' which has continued without intermission until the present day.

The economic transformation of Alexander's reign

[1] B. H. Sumner, *Survey of Russian History* (second revised edn., London, 1947), p. 352.

9

found its reflection in the social sphere. The liberation of the serfs accelerated the decline of the landowning nobility. It assisted the more prosperous peasants but hastened the pauperization of the poorer. At the same time the expansion of Russian industry swelled the numbers of the industrial proletariat. The progress of banking and commerce increased the importance of capitalist entrepreneurs. In their cumulative effect these changes undermined the position of the gentry in Russian social life.

This development in its turn had political repercussions which received a measure of recognition in Alexander's administrative reforms. The abolition of seigneurial jurisdiction reduced the authority of landowners over their peasants. The creation of all-class zemstvos destroyed the administrative monopoly of officialdom and gentry. By the introduction of conscription, the theoretical equality of all the Tsar's subjects in the matter of military service was recognized. A radical reform of the law-courts and the adoption of the jury system reduced the power of the bureaucracy. Finally, a relaxation of the censorship regulations allowed the growing intelligentsia to engage in the public discussion of political questions. Russian political journalism, and with it the growing influence of 'public opinion', date essentially from the time of Alexander II.

For these reasons, it seems hardly too much to say that Alexander II carried out a revolution from above as important in its effects as the movements which in 1848 had elsewhere called students and workers to the barricades. By his autocratic power he gave Russia what the United States of America won only after four years of bloody civil war. Moreover, if Russia, after her defeat in the Crimea, was able to maintain her position as a European power, she owed this in no small measure to the reforms carried out under his direction. The Great Reforms make Alexander II an important figure in the history of nineteenth-century Europe.

Chapter One

Unreformed Russia

WHEN Alexander II ascended the throne in 1855 Russia, by European standards, was a poor and backward country. Of the sixty million inhabitants of European Russia (excluding the non-Russian fringes), some fifty million were peasants. As against this, the number of workers employed in industry was insignificant. In 1825, there had been some 210,000 industrial workers. By 1855 their numbers had risen to about 483,000. Of these many still returned to their native villages for the harvesting season. Well over nine-tenths of the people lived permanently in the villages. Commercially, Russia was undeveloped. In 1847, when the value of her exports reached 134 million rubles, the share of purely Russian firms was less than 2 per cent. The rest was in the hands of foreign or predominantly foreign firms. Communications were rudimentary. The condition of the roads was deplorable. Railways were in their infancy. A proposal in 1835 to build a comprehensive network of railways had been opposed by the Minister of Finance on the grounds that it was unnecessary, costly, and a danger to 'public morals'. Railways encouraged 'frequent purposeless travel, thus fostering the restless spirit of our age'. None the less, the first line, totalling only 16½ miles,[1] was opened at this time. The first major line, that linking St. Petersburg and Moscow, was constructed between 1842 and 1851 by American engineers with

[1] The Russians measured their distances in *versts*. One verst equals 0.66 mile.

American capital. In consequence, Russia, by 1855, could boast of a grand total of some six hundred and fifty miles of railway.

The major symptom of Russian backwardness was the persistence of personal bondage or serfdom. In 1835, some 10·9 million *male* serfs lived on estates belonging to the hereditary nobility, whilst another 10·6 million were settled on state lands. In 1859, their numbers were about 10·7 and 12·8 million respectively. In that year serfs of both groups, together with their families, numbered above 40 million. Agricultural serfdom imposed on the serf a heavy economic burden. Of the land belonging to an estate, he was allowed to cultivate a part for his own use. The remainder was farmed directly by the landowner or the local administrator of state property. For the share of the land which he was allowed to farm for himself, the serf was obliged to make to the landowner (whether a squire or the state) a payment in cash or in labour. The first was known as *obrok*, the second as *barshchina*. The geographical distribution of the two forms of payment varied. Where a proprietor had an abundance of fertile land which he wished to farm on his own account, he would demand from his serfs as much labour as possible. Where, on the contrary, he had at his disposal more servile labour than was needed to cultivate his own fields, he would put the superfluous serfs on *obrok*—that is to say, he would allow them to go and work wherever they wished in return for a fixed yearly payment. The first case was common in the fertile grain-producing provinces south of Moscow, the second in the barren regions of north-eastern Russia. A special group of landowners' serfs were the house-serfs, described with much justification as 'domestic slaves rather than serfs in the proper sense of the term'. Their number, which during the first half of the nineteenth century was steadily increasing, may by 1855 have reached a million and a half.

The legal power of the owner over his serfs was subject to no effective limitation or control. "The owner", said the law, "may impose on his serfs every kind of labour, may take from them money dues and demand from them personal service, with this restriction, that they should not thereby be ruined, and that the number of days fixed by law should be left to them for their own work." The last proviso referred to a law of 1797 limiting the maximum of *barshchina* to three days a week and confining it to week-days. These provisions were difficult to enforce. Whilst three days of *barshchina* a week were normal, four and even five days were not unknown. Moreover, the distribution of the labour days owed to the lord was nowhere clearly defined. Some owners during the short ploughing and harvesting seasons would force their serfs to work continuously on the home farm to the neglect of their own plots.

The economic exploitation of the serfs was backed by the power of the state. For any offence committed against himself or anyone under his jurisdiction, the owner was permitted by law to inflict on his serf a punishment not exceeding forty lashes with the birch or fifteen blows with a stick. In actual fact, none of the serfs and very few of the proprietors knew that the law placed any sort of restriction upon the right of chastisement. No limits were observed in practice. So long as the proprietor refrained from the habitual practice of inhuman cruelty, the authorities never thought of interfering. Flogging in the stables was accepted as a common feature of Russian village life; in the towns it formed part of the regular duties of the police and the fire-brigade. Infinitely more dreadful to the serf than either birch or stick was the owner's right to present him to the authorities either as a recruit or for transportation to Siberia. It was assumed, in theory, that such punishments would be resorted to only in extreme cases; in fact, the authorities accepted without question any serf presented to them. The owner's threat to enrol a serf as a soldier was an instrument of blackmail and extortion which rarely failed of its purpose. Finally, where an owner had driven his serfs to insubordination or mutiny, he had the legal right to call in the police and the military to restore order. Such punitive expeditions, as a rule, ended in an orgy of floggings.

Such were the economic and legal aspects of serfdom. What the institution meant in terms of human suffering and degradation is hard to describe in words. For the ordinary peasant, serfdom meant a life of backbreaking work, grinding poverty, dirt, ignorance, and superstition. It meant utter subjection to the whims of owners and their stewards, brutal floggings and cringing servility, relieved by occasional drunken orgies as the only means of escape. The domestic serf often led a lazy, idle existence, but on the other hand he was in closer relation with an often brutal and always tyrannical master. Serf girls and women, particularly, suffered the consequences of their subjection. The case of the landowner in south-western Russia who claimed the literal fulfilment of the *ius primæ noctis* was, no doubt, an exception. However, all accounts of the period agree that in their dealings with serf girls and women the majority of Russian landowners knew little or no restraint. "Half the landowners killed by their serfs", wrote Alexander Herzen, a shrewd observer of the Russian scene, "die for their deeds of valour on the field of love." Peter Kropotkin, 'repentant nobleman', sensitive offspring of an old princely family, after recording in his memoirs some of the things which he saw in his father's house, continues:

"These were things which I myself saw in my childhood. If, however, I were to relate what I heard of in those years it would be a much more gruesome narrative : stories of men and women torn from their families and their villages and sold, or lost in gambling, or exchanged for a couple of hunting dogs, and then transported to some remote part of Russia for the sake of creating a new estate; of children taken from their parents and sold to cruel or dissolute masters; of flogging 'in the stables', which occurred every day with unheard of cruelty; of a girl who found her only salvation in drowning herself; of an old man who had grown grey-haired in his master's service and at last hanged himself under his master's window; and of revolts of serfs, which were suppressed by Nicholas I's generals by flogging to death each tenth or fifth man taken out of the ranks, and by laying waste the village, whose inhabitants, after military execution, went begging for bread in the neighbouring provinces, as if they had been the victims of a conflagration. As to the poverty which I saw during our journeys in certain villages, especially in those which belonged to the imperial family, no words would be adequate to describe the misery to readers who have not seen it."

No serf could marry without the owner's consent. What is more, he must, if ordered, marry the person selected for him. Kropotkin describes an instance—one landowner once asked another: "Why is it, General, that the number of souls [male peasants] on your estate increases so slowly? Probably you don't look after their marriages." A few days later, the general called for a list of the inhabitants of his village. He picked out the names of all young men who had just attained the age of eighteen and of the girls just past sixteen—the legal ages for marriage in Russia. Then he wrote on a slip of paper: "John to marry Anna, Paul to marry Parashka", and so on with five couples. The weddings must take place in ten days' time, the following Sunday but one. A cry of despair rose from the village. Women young and old wept in every house. Anna had hoped to marry Gregory; Paul's parents had already talked to the Fedotovs about their girl. In any case, this was the season for ploughing not weddings, and what wedding could be prepared in ten days? Dozens of peasants came to see the landowner; their womenfolk took pieces of fine linen to his wife to secure her intercession. It was of no avail. The master had fixed the date of the weddings, and so it must be. On the appointed day, the processions made their way to church, the women wailing as they did at funerals. Parashka refused to be married to Paul. The squire, informed of the fact, sent a messenger to the priest: "Tell that long-maned drunkard [the Russian priests wore their hair long and, on occasion, were not averse to drink] that if Parashka is not married at once, I will report him to the archbishop as a drunkard. . . . Tell him he will be sent to rot in a monastery and that I will exile Parashka's family to the steppes." When the message was delivered, Parashka's mother fell on her knees, imploring her daughter not to ruin the whole family. Parashka continued saying "I won't", but in a weakening voice, until at last she stood silent. The nuptial crown was placed on her head and she made no further resistance.

Not every Russian landowner—they numbered a quarter of a million—was either a monster or a libertine. Cases of sadism and inhuman cruelty, although far from infrequent, were exceptional. But even in 'normal' conditions, serfdom was sad enough. Old Prince Alexis Kropotkin was neither vicious nor particularly brutal; his serfs and his servants classed him among the better masters. His son recorded some incidents in his household. The maid Polya (Pauline) had been taught to make fine embroidery and become an artist at her work. She had been given some education, and become a companion rather than a housemaid. When it became apparent that Pauline was going to have a child, her furious mistress had her hair cut short and exiled her to the dairy. The father of the child, serf of another landowner, implored permission to marry her. As he had no money to offer, his request was refused. In the meantime, another husband had been selected for Polya. 'Bandy-legged Filka' had as a child been kicked by a horse and had not properly grown. His legs were crooked, his feet turned inwards, his nose was broken, and his jaw deformed. To Filka, the unhappy Polya was married by force, after which the couple were sent away to work as peasants on one of the prince's estates.

Gerasim Kruglov had been educated at the prince's expense at the Moscow Agricultural Institute. A brilliant pupil, he passed his examinations with distinction and was given a gold medal. The director of the Institute urged Kropotkin to give Kruglov his freedom to let him study at the university (where serfs were not admitted).

"He is sure to become a remarkable man, perhaps one of the glories of Russia; it will be an honour for you to have recognized his talents and to have given such a man to Russian science."

"I need him on my own estate", the prince replied to numerous applications made on the young man's behalf. On the estate there was nothing for Kruglov to do. After he had made a survey, he was ordered to sit in the servants' hall and wait at dinner. Kruglov's looks showed his disappointment. The princess (Kropotkin's second wife) thereafter took special pleasure in humiliating him. One day in the autumn she asked him to go and shut the entrance gate which a gust of wind had opened. "You have a porter for that", answered Kruglov, tried beyond endurance. For this action, he was placed under arrest and chained, to be sent away as a soldier.

A conversation between Peter Kropotkin and his father some time after the liberation of the serfs epitomizes the spirit of serfdom. "You must agree, father," said the younger man, "that you often punished your servants cruelly and without sufficient cause." The old prince did not deny the charge. "With these people", he replied, "it was impossible to do otherwise." Then, after a thoughtful pause, he continued :

"But what I did was hardly worth speaking of. Now, take Sablev for example : he looks so soft and talks so gently, but he was really terrible with his serfs. How many times did they plot to kill him! I, at least, never took advantage of my maids. But that old devil Tonkov carried on in such a way that the peasant women were going to inflict a terrible punishment on him ... Good-bye; *bonne nuit* !"

One of the terrors of every male serf was the possibility that he might be made a soldier. The armies of Nicholas numbered just over a million in 1826; some twenty years later their numbers had increased by about four hundred thousand. There was then no conscription. When a levy of recruits was ordered, the landowners and administrators of state domains had each to supply a certain number of men (calculated at so many for every 1000 male souls). As a rule, the village communities kept a roll of potential recruits, and sometimes decided by lot who was to go. Even here, interference from the owner or his steward was not uncommon. The domestic serfs, on the other hand, were entirely at the mercy of their lord. If he was dissatisfied with one of them, he could send him to the recruiting-board (even when there was no levy) and get a recruiting receipt. Such a receipt had considerable money value, as it could be sold to anyone whose turn it was to become or to provide a soldier. It could also be kept by the owner against the next recruiting levy.

The giving away of domestic serfs as recruits was a very common occurrence. Kropotkin describes the situation. When it became known that one of the servants was to be sent to the recruiting-board, gloom spread over the household. The victim was placed under guard in the office to prevent him getting away. When the allotted man was taken out under escort, all his fellow servants surrounded him. He made a deep bow, asking forgiveness from everyone for his offences. If his father and mother lived in the same village, they came to see him off. He would bow to the ground before them. His mother and other female relatives would intone their lamentations as at a burial and in the same words. Then the victim would enter on his twenty-five years' service.

The recruit was torn from his family and his native village. If he had children, they were taken away to a military orphanage to be brought up as soldiers. His wife—it would be truer to say his widow—was left to her own devices. After three years, she was legally allowed to remarry. His village knew him no more.

In the days of Nicholas conditions in the army were hard and discipline was cruel :

"Blows from the officers, flogging with birch rods and with sticks for the slightest fault, were normal affairs. The cruelty that was displayed surpasses all imagination. Even in the Cadet School, where only sons of the aristocracy were educated, a thousand blows with birch rods were sometimes administered, in the presence of the whole School, for a cigarette— the doctor standing by the tortured boy, ordering the punishment to end only when he ascertained that the pulse was about to stop beating. Whereupon the bleeding victim was carried away unconscious to the hospital."

Even this was gentle compared to the punishment meted out to common soldiers :

"When one of them appeared before a Court Martial, the sentence was that a thousand men should be placed in two ranks facing each other, every soldier armed with a stick of the thickness of a little finger . . . and that the condemned man should be dragged three, four, five and even seven times between these two rows, each soldier administering a blow. Sergeants followed to see that full force was used. After one or two thousand blows the victim, spitting blood, was taken to hospital and attended to, in order that the punishment might be completed when he had more or less recovered from the first part of it. If he died under the torture, the execution of the sentence was completed upon the corpse."

Tsar Nicholas and his brother Michael knew no pity. No sentence was ever lightened. General Timofeev, a heartless martinet but a great favourite of the Emperor, would order a soldier to be flogged almost to death for a mistake made during a parade.

Any soldier who survived his service found a hard lot awaiting him at the end. He had lost his place in the village. His wife had remarried years before. His children had disappeared into the 'cantonist schools'. He had learnt no trade and had little inclination to work. He became a tramp or a beggar. Moltke, hardly a sentimentalist, was moved during a visit to Russia at the sight of a Crimean veteran begging outside the Kremlin :

"There stood the man who but a few short months ago had shed his blood for his country. Now he was begging outside the Kremlin, in the very heart of the empire which has grown great, exists and will continue to exist thanks to its faithful, pious, brave and neglected soldiers."

After serfdom and the army, officialdom formed the third great pillar of unreformed Russian society. The number of officials (*chinovniks*) exceeded half a million. Their name, for the Russian public, was synonymous with extortion and corruption. A Russian nobleman, in a memorandum submitted to Alexander II shortly after his accession, declared :

"All power is centred in the hands of the *chinov-niks*. Casting a glance at the middle and lower spheres of the official world, we see a savage and greedy horde which has taken possession of Russia and enjoys without inhibition the rights of conquerors. It plunders all classes of people, robs the Imperial Treasury. . . . Having bound the hands of Ministers by centralization, paper formalism and countless signatures, having freed itself in this manner from every inspection and verification on the part of the central government, being everywhere the persecutor of freedom of expression which is . . . so much feared by thieves and plunderers, this Tartar horde, yclept Bureaucracy, robs and bullies Russia, producing a general discontent."

Corruption was especially prevalent in certain branches of the administration. The Ministry of Communications enjoyed a particularly unsavoury reputation. It had become, under the Minister Kleinmichel, "a veritable abyss of corruption and abuses, which swallowed up immense sums without the slightest advantage to the Empire". A typical piece of ingenious fraud is described by the Swedish Minister at St. Petersburg. Some years after the accession of Alexander II the astronomer Struve, when carrying out trigonometrical surveys outside St. Petersburg, adopted as his base one of the main roads leading to the capital. Struck by the curious nature of his results, he decided to measure his base, duly equipped with milestones registering the distances. Much to his surprise he discovered that each of the alleged miles was short by several yards. On measuring further roads, Struve made the same discovery. The roads had been constructed under Count Kleinmichel's régime. In fact, every department of the administration connected with construction or supplies was riddled with corruption. During the Crimean War, the military supply departments—at the soldiers' expense—were 'dishonoured by plundering such as history will shudder at'. The officials of the special Exchequer Courts in each province were profitably employed. Annual gifts from the district cashiers, the brandy farmers, and local contractors helped to keep them in funds. Their most lucrative operation, however, was recruiting, which, in official slang, they referred to as their *harvest*. Their methods were simple and effective.

In more exalted spheres transactions, if more refined in form, were hardly different in spirit. Count Vladimir Adlerberg I, Minister of the Imperial Household and all-powerful favourite of Nicholas I, kept a mistress, a lady married to a minor official. *Madame de* Bourkov, once a simple Latvian servant-girl, had made a career for herself, and was now, under a different name, a partner in a St. Petersburg fashion shop. People who desired a favour from the Court were well advised to pay a visit to the shop. There they might acquire a pair of gloves, at a grossly excessive price, after which their petitions were more likely to be successful.

Corruption shaded imperceptibly into the crudest forms of extortion. This was the chosen field of the rural police. Its victims were to be found more particularly among the religious minorities subject to special restrictions. They included Jews, Mohammedan Tartars and Bashkirs, sectarians, and, above all, the primitive Finnish tribes of north-eastern Russia and the miserable natives of Siberia. The Finnish tribes, 'poor, timid, stupid people', formed a regular gold-mine for the Russian officials. Inspectors of police and others would pay the Governor (the highest official in each Province) double the usual sum to be appointed to a district inhabited by Finns. The reason is easy to see :

"If the land-surveyor is travelling on business and passes a native village, he never fails to stop there. He takes the theodolite off his cart, drives in a post and pulls out his chain. In an hour, the whole village is in a ferment. . . . The elder come to pay their respects: the surveyor goes on measuring and making notes. They ask him not to cheat them out of their land, and he demands twenty or thirty roubles. They are glad to give it and collect the money; and he drives on to the next village of natives."

If the police found a dead body, they dragged it around for a fortnight—the frost made this possible— through the Finnish villages. In each village they declared that they had just found the corpse and meant to start an inquest. The people, to escape the inquest, paid the blackmail demanded of them. With Russian peasants, on the other hand, there were limits to what could be achieved.

The law courts of unreformed Russia took their general character from the rest of the administration. They were staffed by *chinovniks* and shared all the faults of the executive branch of government. In addition, they had distinctive shortcomings of their own. Proceedings were secret and in writing. Since a single civil suit could—in certain circumstances—pass through eleven courts, and since delays were profitable to the officials, law-suits dragged on for years. The judges enjoyed neither independence nor respect.

In practice, for the mass of the Russian people, the law did not exist. It was the upper classes and foreigners who were its principal victims. The latter, in particular, might have to choose between the hazards of the 'courts' and submission to frauds of the grossest kind. The state of the 'courts' and the near impossibility of enforcing the payment of debts was an important factor in retarding Russia's economic development.

The general condition of the Russian administration requires some accounting for. Officials in the lower ranges received a remuneration so miserable that they could not live on their pay alone. The poverty of *chinovniks* who had the folly to be honest, or were inexpert at gathering in their 'harvest', is illustrated by the two clerks in a provincial office who, during the wet season, reported for duty only on alternate days—they possessed only one pair of boots between them. Such poverty, combined with deplorable moral and educational standards, inevitably turned men into bribetakers. In fact, corruption was considered scarcely reprehensible; it was taken for granted in all official circles.

Every form of administrative iniquity and abuse, moreover, was carefully protected by the absence of legal responsibility and by administrative secrecy. No official could be prosecuted without his superior's permission. Since the plunder was shared among all ranks of the administrative hierarchy, such permission was rarely granted. An official who was able to 'stimulate' the goodwill of his superiors was immune from prosecution. There was no control by the Russian public over the conduct of officials since the assemblies of nobles, established by Catherine the Great, dealt almost exclusively with the affairs of the nobility. The most effective protection of officialdom, however, lay in the secrecy of administrative action. No budget was published, and the entire financial administration was thus shielded from the public gaze. Judicial proceedings took place in secrecy. Discussion of administrative abuses was permitted only in the purely literary form of a work like Gogol's 'Government Inspector'. The censorship prevented any discussion of the conduct of individual officials. Not till the refugee Alexander Herzen published his *The Bell* (*Kolokol*) in London were specific abuses exposed. In these circumstances, officialdom enjoyed almost complete immunity. Infrequent inspections organized by the Senate (the highest judicial body of the empire) may have had some effect in the localities under review, but could not alter the general spirit of the administration.

The evident defects of this vaguely oriental system of administration had been aggravated by Nicholas I's heavy-handed paternalism.[1] Brought up and trained as a soldier, the Emperor became a fanatical devotee of uniformity, obedience, and discipline. Civilian officials and even students were put into uniform. Everything in the empire was arranged according to the principle of hierarchical subordination. Steeped in the military tradition, Nicholas liked to refer to his vast empire as his 'command'. A military spirit pervaded the administration. Members of the Tsar's military establishment, aides-de-camp who had distinguished themselves on the parade ground and whom he knew personally, were promoted to the highest offices of state. The inevitable outcome of this development had been further to undermine the spirit of legality in Russian public life.

The most typical institution of Nicholas's régime was the 'Third Division of His Majesty's Own Chancery', the all-powerful security police commonly known as the 'Third Division'. The activities of this body— created after the Decembrist Rising of 1825—were ubiquitous. According to its historian, "there was no aspect of Russian life that would escape its control". The government, it was felt, "had to know what was going on among the people, what were their thoughts, what they talked about, what occupied them; it became necessary to penetrate into men's hearts and most secret thoughts". Moreover, not content with spying and prying, the Third Division frequently "assumed judicial functions and determined the guilt of persons in matters which had nothing to do with public safety". The state police was, in fact, a state within the state. Its Director was a member of the Committee of Ministers; indeed, his position at times resembled that of a Prime Minister.

[1] In the description of Nicholas I's system of government use has been made of the excellent account in the second volume of Michael Florinsky's *Russia: A History and an Interpretation* (New York, 1953).

Two successive heads of the Division had been amongst the closest intimates of the Tsar.

After the Polish insurrection of 1830–1, the heavy hand of Russian repression had fallen both on the Congress Kingdom (the autonomous state set up by the Treaty of Vienna, of which the Tsar was the ruler) and on Russia's western provinces (the territories acquired in the partitions of the eighteenth century, where the landowning gentry was mainly of Polish nationality). In both areas together, some 5,000 estates were confiscated. It is estimated that roughly one-tenth of all noble estates in the Congress Kingdom were involved. Some 30,000 families of Polish noblemen from the western provinces were deported to the Caucasus, Siberia, and the lands beyond the Volga (officially, this policy was termed 'resettlement'). In Warsaw, Field-Marshal Paskievich, who ruled the Congress Kingdom from 1832 until his death in 1856, carried out a policy of ruthless Russification and suppression of Polish autonomy. In the Kingdom and the western provinces alike, no effort was spared to suppress Polish cultural life. There were heavy reprisals against the Catholic Church. Severe (and successful) pressure was brought to bear on the Uniats (who preserved the Greek-Orthodox ritual whilst recognizing the authority of the Pope) to rejoin the Orthodox Church. The Polish universities of Warsaw and Vilna were closed. Instruction in Polish secondary schools in the Kingdom had to be conducted in Russian. Any mention of even the most celebrated Polish writers was prevented by the censorship.

It was not Polish intellectual life alone that had suffered from the repression following the revolutions of 1830. In Russia also, Count Uvarov, as Minister of Education (1833–49), had introduced a system based on "the truly Russian, conservative principles of orthodoxy, autocracy and nationality, our last anchor of salvation and the best guarantees of Russia's strength and greatness". Uvarov had constructed his 'intellectual dams' in the schools and universities of the empire; the censorship and the Third Division saw to it that writers and journalists conformed to the principles of the official 'party line'.

The revolutions of 1848 removed the last vestiges of intellectual freedom. In September 1849, even Uvarov resigned because he was thought too liberal. His successor, the obscurantist Prince Shirinsky-Shikhmatov immediately destroyed what little remained of university autonomy and academic freedom. Deans of Faculties were ordered to supervise the contents of academic teaching. Study of philosophy and of European constitutional law was discontinued, the teaching of logic and psychology entrusted to professors of theology.

At the same time the censorship became still more severe. Censors began to delete terms like 'forces of nature' from text-books on physics and 'free currents of air' from cookery books. (It was held that they might have a political significance, and, indeed—faced with the censorship terror—journalists and writers did resort to a variety of subterfuges.) The name of the great writer Gogol could no longer be mentioned in print. Almost every government department, down to the Post Office and the Imperial Stud, could exercise ill-defined functions of censorship over matters concerning its own province. It could happen that an article written by a high official of the Ministry of the Interior was banned by the censor at the request of the Ministry of Education. A censor declared that "if one were to count all officials in charge of censorship, their numbers would greatly exceed that of books published every year".

Intensification of the censorship was accompanied by a determined attempt to keep Russians from 'contagious' contact with the West. Passports for foreign travel became practically unobtainable. Study at foreign universities, so common in an earlier age, was no longer to be thought of. Nicholas's 'Iron Curtain' was almost as effective as that erected by his latter-day successors.

It was under these conditions that in 1853 the Russian government blundered almost unwittingly and ill-prepared into war with England and France. Nicholas's elaborate diplomatic system produced in the hour of need no friends but many enemies. Still worse, owing in part to Russian backwardness, lack of railways and administrative inefficiency and corruption, still more to a faulty strategy,[1] the Russian armies on which all the care of the régime had been lavished, did not justify the high hopes of the Russian public. It was this that gave the death-blow to Nicholas's system of government. Many members of the upper classes had acquiesced in that system—however reluctantly—because it had raised Russian prestige in Europe. Now it was revealed that the military colossus stood on feet of clay. Of a peace-time army of around one million and a quarter only 350,000 could, after heroic exertions, be brought to the field of battle. The heavy sacrifices made for the army had been in vain : the system of Nicholas stood condemned.

The Tsar himself understood the extent of his failure. The last months of his life were darkened by a realization that his life's work lay in ruins. On March 2, 1855, the 'Iron Autocrat' died broken-hearted; rumour even spoke of suicide, and it is certain that he had of set purpose neglected an attack of influenza from which he was suffering. With the death of Nicholas, a pillar of the old régime came crashing to the ground.

[1] Strategically the defence of the Crimea was a costly blunder. Could the ill-organized allies have invaded the interior? What, in such an event, would have been the outcome of the conflict?

Chapter Two

The New Emperor

ALEXANDER, son of Nicholas, the new Emperor of All the Russias, was born in Moscow on April 29 (April 17 o.s.), 1818. His mother, Alexandra Feodorovna (before her baptism into the Orthodox religion she had been Princess Charlotte of Prussia) was the daughter of Frederick William III of Prussia and Queen Louise. The later Frederick William IV and William I were her brothers. Until her death in 1860, she maintained the closest ties with her family in Berlin. Young Alexander, almost 'with his mother's milk' imbibed a strong affection for Prussia and things Prussian which remained with him throughout his later life. In 1829, at the age of eleven, he paid his first visit to Berlin. His grandfather had appointed him colonel-in-chief of the Third Prussian Uhlan Regiment. The child, until the end of the visit, refused to appear in anything but his new Prussian uniform. It was the beginning of a life-long association with the Prusso-German army.

Alexander's early education bore a dual aspect. From the tender age of six, as befitted a son of Nicholas, he received a military training composed of drills and parades. From 1829 onwards he attended the annual cadet camps organized under his father's personal supervision. Even his Christmas presents were of a martial nature. Thus in 1831, his loving parents gave him a bust of Peter the Great, a rifle, a sword, a box of pistols, a parade uniform, and a set of china cups and saucers depicting Russian soldiers of different arms. However, whilst the young prince found pleasure in

29

parades and reviews, he showed little interest in the
more serious aspects of military science. In the autumn
of 1832, the Tsar complained of this to Captain
Merder, his military tutor, and himself drew up a
syllabus for the study of fortifications and gunnery;
Alexander, reluctantly, had to apply himself to these
subjects. In fact, he never acquired the slightest interest
in scientific soldiering; throughout his life he remained
a passionate addict of the parade-ground and the
military review.

Nor did the civilian side of his education produce the
desired results. The civilian tutor of the Tsarevich—
and it is impossible not to recognize in the choice the
hand of the Empress—was the romantic, 'liberal', and
humanitarian poet Zhukovsky. When, in 1826, the
tutor-elect submitted a detailed programme for the
future development of his charge, he declared that its
overall purpose was to be 'education for virtue'. Early
in 1828, this education was begun in earnest. Soon the
tutor had to remonstrate against excessive parades. In
July, after Alexander had passed his first examination,
Zhukovsky declared himself satisfied with the result;
yet through his report runs an undertone of anxiety
about his pupil's lack of diligence. Merder, in his diary,
recorded the opinion he had formed of Alexander's
character. The prince had a natural inclination to what
was good. He had, however, a disposition to vagueness
and hesitation when faced with obstacles or difficulties.
The rest of Alexander's life would confirm the accuracy
of the observation. The following year, Zhukovsky in
his turn complained once again of the Tsarevich's lack
of application. Alexander did not like lessons but preferred to play and roam about in the open air. In fact,
he would never feel attracted to reading or study, whilst
the desire for the open air foreshadowed a life-long
passion for the chase. In 1831, there were further
laments about apathy in the face of difficulties. Other
defects made their appearance. Merder told Nicholas

of his son's arrogance, disobedience, and quarrelsome disposition. Later in life Alexander on occasions showed himself to be extremely vindictive.

At the same time the child displayed a certain emotional sensibility and good nature which also would not be lacking in the later Tsar. During a walk with Merder along a St. Petersburg canal, Alexander (just thirteen years of age) noticed on one of the barges moored to the quay an old workman covered with a dirty mat, shaking and groaning. The child rushed across a plank, bent over the old man and asked him questions. When Merder, disapproving, followed Alexander on to the barge, he saw the boy wiping away the old man's tears with his handkerchief. Merder took a gold piece from his purse and gave it to Alexander—who left the coin on the old man's chest.

When, during the autumn of 1832, Merder developed heart attacks—not entirely unconnected with his pupil's wilfulness—Alexander at once changed his behaviour. He visited his invalid tutor regularly. When Merder had to go abroad for his health, Alexander used to write to him every Saturday. When he died in Rome in the spring of 1834, the Tsarevich wept bitterly. Throughout his life, Alexander was apt to burst into tears on formal or moving occasions.

Emotional outbursts were coupled with a certain good sense—already noted by Merder—which rarely left Alexander in later life.

In the spring of 1837, Alexander's formal education was declared to be complete. In spite of his lack of application, the future Emperor had acquired a good knowledge of Russian, French, German, Polish, and English. He had listened to lectures from Speransky, Russia's most distinguished statesman and jurist, on the laws of the Russian Empire. However, in spite of every effort, the Tsarevich had remained obstinately 'non-intellectual'. The future glories of his reign in the realms of literature and music left him cold and unappreciative. Neither the Romanov nor the Hohenzollern strain was literary or artistic.

The completion of Alexander's formal education was followed by a tour of the Russian Empire extending over seven months. The Tsarevich was accompanied, among others, by Zhukovsky, who spared no pains to influence his pupil in the direction of pity and humanity. Although almost drowned in official reviews and receptions, the Tsarevich found time to visit the huts of the peasants. He heard their complaints, he saw their wretchedness. Again, during his visit to western Siberia (the first ever paid by a Romanov), Alexander met some of the exiled Decembrists (the military conspirators against Nicholas I in 1825) and addressed them with kindliness. Encouraged by Zhukovsky, he sent a special messenger to his stern father asking for an alleviation of their lot. Great was his joy—and even more that of the good Zhukovsky—when Nicholas sanctioned a real improvement in the conditions of their exile. In remote Viatka, amidst the forests of north-eastern Russia, Alexander met a more recent exile—young Alexander Herzen. At the instigation of Zhukovsky, the prince asked his father to permit Herzen's return to St. Petersburg. Nicholas replied that this would be unfair to the other exiles, but permitted an improvement in Herzen's condition (exile in a town nearer Moscow). Herzen has left a portrait of his youthful benefactor. The young prince, he noted, had not his father's stern expression. His features suggested rather good nature and indolence. Although barely twenty, he was already growing stout. The few words he addressed to Herzen were friendly, and he had not "the hoarse, abrupt, utterance of his uncle Constantine".

The educational value of Alexander's tour was limited. In the course of seven short months, he had to visit no fewer than thirty provinces. Official engagements occupied most of his time. Yet the Tsarevich gained impressions of lasting value. He wrote to one of his tutors: "With my own eyes . . . I have seen our mother Russia, and I have learnt to love and respect her even more. Yes, we may be proud that we belong to Russia and call her our motherland." His genuine patriotism was a marked characteristic of the later emperor. Alexander's travels in Russia were followed by a grand tour of Europe to crown his official education. Again, as in his tour of Russia, the educational effects, to Zhukovsky's grief, were reduced by an excess of official engagements. During the tour (at Ems in 1839) the Marquis de Custine had an opportunity of twice getting a close view of the heir to the Russian throne. Custine noted that Alexander was stout for his age. Also that he had a melodious voice, which was unusual for his family. The expression of his face was gentle and well-meaning. However, the contrast between the youthful, smiling eyes and the constant contraction of the mouth appeared to suggest a lack of frankness and perhaps some hidden grief. His movements were graceful and noble; his manner was modest but without timidity. Truly the model of a prince, the French observer exclaimed with admiration. A second scrutiny, however, produced a less favourable impression. The prince's grace and noble bearing were indeed undeniable, but his face, in spite of its youth, now appeared inferior to his figure. The complexion was no longer fresh. The eyes betrayed a melancholy beyond his years. The face was round, Germanic rather than Slav, but the Greek profile recalled classical cameos. Custine noted a power of dissimulation frightening in one so young. (Was he remembering, consciously or unconsciously, the personality of the prince's uncle, Tsar Alexander I?) Above all, Custine again noted that the Tsarevich appeared to be suffering.

This last observation—although he hardly knew it—did credit to the Frenchman's perspicacity. Alexander, at this moment, was under a violent emotional strain : he was desperately in love with little expectation of a happy outcome. To find for him a suitable wife had been one of the principal objects of the Grand Tour. When the subject had first been mooted, the Tsarevich, then under the influence of the charms of a ballerina, had shown complete indifference. However, on passing through Darmstadt, he had fallen violently in love with the Princess Mary, the Duke's young daughter, then barely fifteen years of age. At once he had told his aides : "She is the woman of my dreams. I will never marry anyone but her." He had written forthwith to his parents (who had expected to find their future daughter-in-law at the court of Karlsruhe), asking permission to marry Mary. In reply, he had been told to hasten his return to St. Petersburg, where the matter would be discussed. Alexander, impatient and disappointed, confided to a member of his suite that, rather than renounce Mary, he would give up the throne. He had no wish to reign. He only wanted to find a worthy wife to grace his hearth and give him the highest happiness on earth—that of a husband and father.

Back in St. Petersburg, Alexander told his parents of his resolve. Nicholas demurred and, in the face of his son's impetuosity, gave the reason for his objection. Mary's father, Grand Duke Louis II of Hesse-Darmstadt, after two years of married life and the birth of two sons, had decided to end conjugal relations with his wife. Duke and Duchess had begun to live apart. The Duchess had led her own life and was credited with numerous frailties. In the spring of 1823, some fourteen years after these events, the court of Darmstadt learnt with amazement that she was pregnant. In July, a son was born.[1] Louis II, to avoid a scandal, assumed the paternity of the child. Everyone knew the true father, a man of such inferior station that nobody dared to name him. The following year the Duchess was delivered of another child by the same father : the Prin-

[1] Prince Alexander of Hesse, ancestor of the Battenberg (Mountbatten) family.

cess Mary. Alexander declared that this revelation
made no difference to his determination that he would
abandon the succession rather than live without Mary.
Reluctantly Nicholas yielded. In the spring of 1840, the
couple were formally betrothed. In December, Mary
was received into the Orthodox Church as Maria
Alexandrovna. In the following spring, Alexander and
Mary were married with the traditional pomp and
ceremonial appropriate to the occasion. The Tsarevich
had shown that he could be stubborn when he meant
to get his way.

There followed years of idyllic family happiness.
A first child, a girl, died soon after birth, to the grief of
the parents. But during the years which followed four
sons and a daughter were born. Mary made a favourable impression on her new relations and on her future
subjects. All agreed that she combined great beauty
with perfect distinction. In spite of her youth, her tastes
were of a serious kind. She devoted herself to charitable
works, whilst her piety was the delight of the Holy
Synod. The only fault the Court could find in her was
some stiffness and formality of manner. Alexander—
lavishing upon his wife consideration and affection—
was enjoying the idyll which he had declared the object
of his life's ambition.

Tsar Nicholas, however, would not allow his son to
forget that he must one day be Emperor. Alexander
was ordered to attend the meetings of the Council of
Ministers. He was appointed Chancellor of Helsingfors
University. Membership of other governmental bodies
followed. In 1846, and again two years later, he presided
over secret committees set up to study the problem of
serfdom. In 1849, he succeeded an uncle as Colonel-in-
Chief of all military schools and colleges. The Guards
and Grenadier regiments were placed under his command. Moreover, Alexander now began to act as Re-
gent during his father's (sometimes prolonged) absences
from the capital. He became familiar with the

personnel of the higher administration, civil as well as military. In fact, thanks to the care and forethought of his father, he was perhaps the best-prepared heir-apparent ever to ascend the Russian throne.

Introduced in this manner to the practical affairs of state, Alexander had become an increasingly convinced believer in his father's system of government. Scrupulously and with boundless veneration for his stern parent, he had carried out the different tasks assigned to him. Nicholas had rewarded this devotion with unlimited confidence. Alexander, under his influence, accepted the methods as well as the principles of the régime. In the committees on serfdom, he defended the interests of the landowning nobility. The revolutions of 1848 strengthened his conservative outlook. Yet his approach to the problems of government differed in some respects from that of Nicholas. The Swedish Minister at St. Petersburg noted that, if he had inherited his father's profound sense of duty, he understood that duty in a sense more consonant with the development of 'progressive' Russian thought and with the needs created by the advance of civilization.

Indeed, for all his repressive policies, even Nicholas I had been a consistent advocate of practical reforms and the removal of abuses. He described serfdom as a 'flagrant evil', and during his reign no fewer than nine secret committees wrestled with the problem of preparing its gradual abolition. Under the enlightened administration of P. D. Kisselev, the lot of the state peasants at least was considerably improved. Nicholas applauded Gogol's 'Government Inspector'. Throughout his reign he tried to bring some order into the jungle of the Russian legal system. During the early thirties, Speransky brought to a successful conclusion his great codification of the laws of the empire. Later, a committee under Bludov for years struggled with the problem of reforming the Russian courts. In fact, in bringing about far-reaching administrative and social reforms

Alexander was not departing from his father's system of government, but rather carrying forward his programme of reform to greater purpose.

In spite of his careful training, Alexander was reluctant to accept the overwhelming responsibility of imperial rule. Indeed, he once went so far as to express the wish not to survive his father, but fate willed it otherwise: on March 2, 1855, Nicholas I died, and Alexander Nicolaevich was Emperor of All the Russias. Shortly before the end, the dying emperor had addressed his son : "I hand over to you my command, but unfortunately not in such order as I should wish. I am leaving you many labours and anxieties." Alexander replied : "I hope that there [in Heaven] you will pray faithfully for your Russia and that I may receive assistance." "I shall faithfully do so", Nicholas answered. On the day after his accession, Alexander repeated this conversation to the members of the Imperial Council. "Reposing my trust in the prayer of my unforgettable father and in God's help, on which I have always relied and shall continue to do, I ascend the throne of my ancestors."

The accession of Alexander II was greeted by the Russian public with feelings composed in equal measure of uncertainty and hope. Some had heard rumours that he favoured the liberation of the serfs without land, others that he would faithfully protect the interests of the nobility. Many entertained hopes that a new reforming age was dawning. "A new era", wrote one of these, "has begun in our public affairs; may it also be a new era in the moral and social existence of every Russian." The Swedish Minister at St. Petersburg reported that, although for the present the government's attention was absorbed by the war, it was expected that, once peace was concluded, the new emperor would turn his attention to the urgent problems of domestic administration. Much was expected of him in this sphere. His excellent intentions were known.

Without possessing his father's eminent qualities, he yet had intelligence and a profound sense of duty. He understood this duty, moreover, in a more 'modern' sense than Nicholas had done.

Whatever the future might hold, however, the war had to be ended first. Since the beginning of February, allied attacks on Sevastopol had redoubled, and it was becoming doubtful whether the heroic defence could be continued much longer. Nicholas, before his death, had agreed to a meeting with allied representatives in neutral Vienna to discuss the terms of peace. Alexander now declared that he was ready to agree to the terms already accepted by his father. However, if the coming discussion did not offer the prospect of an honourable peace, he would "go bravely into battle at the head of his faithful Russia and the entire Russian people". In fact, the talks in Vienna ended without result: the allied representatives, who had agreed to terms not unacceptable to Russia, were disavowed by their governments.

Alexander was forced to stake everything on the defence of Sevastopol. When the French captured important sections of the city's fortifications, the Russian commander, Prince Michael Gorchakov, requested permission to evacuate the fortress. The Tsar would not hear of it. Should Sevastopol itself be overrun, the Crimea must be held at all costs. It was Nicholas's faulty strategy carried to the extreme. During June the position of the defenders surprisingly improved. Alexander called for offensive operations: Gorchakov, against his better judgment, carried out the unsuccessful attack on the Chernaya which cost the Russians 8,000 casualties. Three weeks later the allies opened a fierce bombardment in preparation for a general assault. Gorchakov, convinced that defence was hopeless, evacuated the city on the night of September 8–9. Its defence had cost the Russians more than 100,000 killed and wounded.

Undaunted, Alexander continued the struggle. His manifesto announcing the loss to the Russian people struck a defiant note. He admonished Gorchakov not to lose heart but to remember 1812 and trust in Providence. Sevastopol was not Moscow, the Crimea was not Russia. Two years after the fire of Moscow, the victorious Russian armies entered Paris. "We are the same Russians still, and God is with us." The banner of St. Sergius, which had been with Peter the Great at Poltava and with the Russian home guard in 1812, was dispatched to Gorchakov's headquarters in the Crimea. At a council of war in Moscow it was decided to hold the Crimea. Nicolaev at the mouth of the Bug (Russia's second naval arsenal) also must be placed in a state of defence. Alexander himself went to that town to supervise the work. He remained for six weeks, and before returning to St. Petersburg visited his troops outside Sevastopol. He returned to the capital encouraged by the spirit he had seen in his armies.

However, his principal advisers, led by Nesselrode, the aged Foreign Minister, felt the need for peace. It was known that neutral Austria and the allies had agreed on terms of peace to be submitted to Russia in the form of an ultimatum. Sweden had signed a treaty associating herself with the Western powers. The King of Prussia, Russia's only friend, sent word that he might be forced to join the allies. Complete isolation threatened Russia. Still Alexander was unwilling to yield. "We have", he wrote to Gorchakov, "reached the limit of concession compatible with Russian honour. I will never accept humiliating terms, certain that every true Russian feels as I do. All that is left for us, crossing ourselves, is to march straight ahead and defend by united effort our native land and national honour."

At the end of December, an Austrian envoy presented the terms concerted with England and France. Not only was Russia asked to consent to the neutralization of the Black Sea, but also to cede some territory in

Bessarabia to remove her from the navigable portion of the Danubian estuary. The terms were hard and, in the Tsar's opinion, dishonourable. Would he agree, even at this price, to end hostilities which no longer offered any hope of success?

When Alexander consulted his advisers, all agreed that Russia needed peace, but all were reluctant to accept the Austrian terms. It was decided to make counter-proposals, but the Austrian government remained firm. Unless its terms were accepted unconditionally, it would break off diplomatic relations. When the Tsar put the issue again to his Council, all present declared that peace was an absolute necessity. Nesselrode in particular feared that, by the following year, Russia might be faced with a general European coalition. She might be effectively blockaded and her economic future impaired. Sooner or later, she would be forced to make peace, and later on the terms might be still more onerous. Other speakers feared that the Crimea and the Caucasus, even Finland and Poland, might in the end be lost. A continuation of the war would lead to bankruptcy. If Russia continued hostilities, she might be reduced to the state of Sweden after the death of Charles XII. If she now accepted terms which did not impede her development, she would, within a few years, be as powerful as she had been before the war. A peace concluded at present, therefore, need only be a truce. Postponed by a year or two, it would leave the empire in a state of exhaustion from which it would take decades to recover. Unconditional acceptance of the Austrian terms, however unpalatable, was a necessity.

The final decision, however, rested with Alexander alone. Whilst deeply impressed with the prudence of the counsels he had received, he felt passionately, as a soldier, that acceptance of the ultimatum would be a shameful act. Russia was undefeated. She still had a numerous army; she had her historic memories, her patriotism, her powers of endurance. Her immense territory and severe climate opposed difficulties to any invader. She might follow the example of 1812 and await the enemy at home. Such were the views of Alexander's military entourage, of many patriotic ladies in the two capitals, and, in general, of people who had no official responsibility. Alexander was in sympathy with this view; its principal spokesman was his younger brother, Constantine. Indeed, after the meeting of the Council, a 'passionate discussion' between the two brothers took place in the apartments of the Empress-dowager. Alexander drew his brother's attention to the difficulties of the situation : Prussia threatened to join Russia's enemies; the losses in manpower were vast (Russia's total loss of life in the war has been estimated at around 600,000); the raising of new recruits was becoming more difficult; last, but not least, the country's financial resources were exhausted. With a heavy heart he had, therefore, decided to accept the Austrian terms. With a deep sense of his responsibility, Alexander took the first important decision of his reign.

On March 30 peace between Russia and her enemies was signed in Paris. Alexander announced the event to the Russian people in a manifesto which contained the first official promise of internal change. "With the help of divine Providence, which has always protected Russia's welfare . . . may her internal well-being be strengthened and perfected; may truth and mercy reign in her courts; and may there develop in all spheres the urge towards enlightenment and every form of useful activity. May everybody, under the protection of laws equally just for all and giving all equal protection, enjoy the fruits of his honest labour." It was a promise to the Russian public that the character of the administration would change.

Even before the signing of the peace, the government had already taken measures which showed that a new spirit was abroad. Within a month of his accession,

Alexander withdrew the vexatious restrictions against religious sects. The Minister of the Interior responsible for the persecution of the sectaries was dismissed. Warned about malversation in the Army's supply services, the Tsar ordered a strict inquiry. A foreign diplomat sympathetic to reform rejoiced at the dismissal of the Ministers of the Interior and Communications "as if we had gained two major victories over the enemy". Before the end of the year a more tolerant régime had been introduced for the Catholic Church in Poland. Restrictions on intellectual life were relaxed. Students were once more admitted to the universities without limitation; young scholars were again sent abroad at public expense; works prohibited by the censor could again appear in print. It was known, moreover, that the Tsar had ordered the complete overhaul of the censorship regulations. No one in Russia was left in doubt that a period of 'thaw' had begun.

The 'thaw' assumed impressive proportions with Alexander's coronation at Moscow in September 1856. Favours announced in the Coronation Manifesto went beyond what was usual on such occasions. Substantial concessions were made to the Tsar's poorest subjects : tax arrears amounting to forty million roubles were cancelled; regions severely hit by the war received tax exemptions; a juster distribution of the poll-tax was promised. All recruiting was suspended for three years. The institution of the cantonists[1] was abolished, and 80,000 children of soldiers were thus, at one stroke, returned to their families. Jews were relieved from special taxes. Restrictions imposed on Polish nobles in the western provinces were removed. There was a wide amnesty for political prisoners; the surviving Decembrists were allowed to return, as well as hundreds exiled in 1849. A concession greeted with delight by the upper

[1] These were the sons of men called up for military service who were compulsorily brought up as soldiers in military orphanages.

classes was the removal of the heavy passport fee imposed under Nicholas. The 'iron curtain' painstakingly erected by the last Tsar was being removed by his heir.

Another important development was being started. In October 1855, a committee had been set up to study foreign railway legislation. On the day the conclusion of peace became known in St. Petersburg, Alexander met Baron Stieglitz, Russia's foremost and wealthiest financier. "The peace is signed; we must profit by it", the Tsar remarked. Encouraged by the Tsar, Stieglitz journeyed to Paris to discuss railway finance with French banking interests. An agreement was reached between a consortium organized by Stieglitz (which included the Crédit Mobilier, Péreire and Fould of Paris, Hope of Amsterdam, and Baring of London) and the official Russian representatives led by Kleinmichel's successor, Chevkin. The new company was to construct five major lines, which would at the same time promote the export of Russian grain through the Baltic and Black Sea ports, and facilitate the movement of troops towards the south and west. The Russian government guaranteed a fixed rate of interest on the sums spent by the consortium, provided the cost of construction did not exceed a specified maximum per mile.

From the early measures of the new ruler, it might well appear that Russia was set on the road towards 'democratization' and internal development. However, it soon became apparent that the new Tsar was not only benevolent but also weak. Granville, Queen Victoria's special envoy at the coronation, considered him "well-intentioned but weak as water". He looked "intelligent and amiable", but did not give the impression of having much strength "either of intellect or of character". This weakness, which would have done little damage in a constitutional ruler, was a great liability in an autocratic one. A faction-fight at the very centre of power had begun almost at the moment of Alexander's accession. It weakened the authority of the government, reduced the popularity of the Tsar, and came close to plunging the empire into chaos.

Nicholas I in his day had been surrounded by a small closed clique of favourites—the Adlerbergs, Baranovs, Shuvalovs, and Orlovs. The less-favoured members of the Court nobility hoped, after the change of ruler, to deprive this camarilla of its exclusive enjoyment of imperial favours. However, Nicholas's circle had already succeeded in establishing its ascendancy over the heir-apparent. His accession was followed by new favours. Adlerberg Junior, Alexander's personal friend and companion (a good-natured gambler), was given a palace and an annual grant of 20,000 roubles for its maintenance. Baranov received a present of 300,000 roubles. Orlov sold back to the state for twice that sum a palace Nicholas had given him the previous year. Shuvalov obtained for his son Peter—a simple colonel aged thirty—the responsible position of Chief of Police in the capital, at a salary of 80,000 roubles. Petersburg was unfavourably impressed by the appointment of one so young and inexperienced.

The favours shown to members of the camarilla infuriated the Court nobility. In revenge, they now professed a desire for honesty in public affairs little in accord with Russian tradition. There was severe criticism of the depredations made on the public funds. The camarilla replied with an attempt to remove hostile influences from the Tsar's entourage. The most important of these was the Empress Mary. Even before Alexander's accession, the Empress had waged a bitter struggle to save her easy-going husband from the damaging influence of his companions. To do this, she had taken upon herself a share in the responsibilities of government. Every night, after retiring with the Emperor, she read to him important papers and discussed impending measures of the government. Indolent by nature and trusting her judgment, Alexander often listened to her advice. This did not suit the camarilla. It was insinuated that the Empress wished to germanize Russia; she was given the malicious nickname of 'bourgeoise allemande' (one is reminded of Marie Antoinette, 'l'Autrichienne'). Unfortunately for the Empress, these attacks coincided not only with a pregnancy (in the spring of 1857) but also with an attachment formed by Alexander for Princess Alexandrine Dolgoruky, one of her maids of honour. The camarilla created for the princess the position of an official mistress; kind 'friends' then exaggerated the affair to the Empress. On the advice of a confessor in league with the camarilla, she had the imprudence to reproach her husband with his infidelity. The result was an estrangement, even a temporary separation. The object of the camarilla was achieved.

To forget his domestic troubles, Alexander, now eager to avoid his wife's company, gave himself up to a life of dissipation in the company of his old friends. It was now that he first gave full rein to his lifelong passion for the chase, particularly bear-hunting. The Empress changed her tactics. She resolved—to regain some influence and restore some semblance of normal relations—to turn a blind eye to her husband's infidelity. She struck up an alliance with the other female members of the imperial family, especially the dowager-empress. Thanks to this, she was able to regain at least part of her former influence. She did much to confirm the Tsar in his resolution to liberate the serfs, and later played a fatal role as the protectress of the Pan-Slav movement.

Whilst at the centre of power intrigue succeeded intrigue, discontent was rapidly spreading among all classes of the population. There was unrest among the peasantry in the interior of the empire; the gentry felt alarm at the prospect of changes in the institution of serfdom; numerous officials had lost their posts in the interests of economy or as part of the campaign against corruption. Officers, especially in the favoured Guards regiments, were irritated by frequent changes in uniforms and by alterations in military regulations. Many were threatened with premature retirement as a result of large cuts in the military forces. The small *rentiers* were hit by a reduction in the rate of interest paid by government savings-banks. (This had been intended, apart from economy, to divert capital into railway construction.)

People blamed the Emperor for their many and varied discontents. The British Minister at St. Petersburg reported that although Alexander was by universal consent "an amiable and well-intentioned man", everybody considered him a weak ruler. The complaints of his want of capacity and decision grew "daily louder and louder". Criticism of highly placed individuals and government measures was becoming widespread, especially in St. Petersburg. Officers in a fashionable restaurant put forth a drawing of a bear with the head of the Emperor and the words "he who goes a-hunting loses his job" ("*qui va à la chasse, perd sa place*"). In part, this orgy of criticism was the natural reaction to the iron rule of Nicholas, the inevitable consequence of a relaxation of the reins of government. However, the result of the ferment was to weaken the prestige and authority of the Emperor and his government. This would be felt severely the moment the government attempted to make changes more far-reaching than minor 'liberal' concessions. It would then appear that a well-meaning 'thaw' did not of necessity promote the more serious task of reform.

Chapter Three

The Tsar Liberator

BEHIND the ferment caused by the great 'thaw' lurked Russia's basic social problem, the question of the future of serfdom. "The question of questions, the evil of evils", a high official confided to an acquaintance, "the first of all our misfortunes, is serfdom". All other evils of Russian life—and they were numerous—were connected with this cancer, and would lose much of their gravity by its removal. The question was not a new one : both Alexander I and Nicholas I had made half-hearted and unavailing attempts to pave the way for the abolition of serfdom. The opposition of the gentry and of most of the higher officials had frustrated their designs. Alexander II, from his experience as president of two secret committees, knew the difficulties of the task. Yet the policy of gradual liberation was a tradition which he had inherited from his father. Both shared the conviction that, sooner or later, serfdom would have to go. The experience of the Crimean War, moreover, had made clear to everyone that fundamental reforms at an early date could no longer be avoided if Russia was to retain her position among the powers.

Alexander's conversion to the necessity for abolition had been a gradual process. In the secret committees over which he presided he had, on the whole, defended the interests of the landowners. However, as he himself told Turgeniev, the latter's 'abolitionist' *Sportsman's Sketches* had left their mark on his impressionable mind. A general conviction of the need for reform combined with unrest among the peasant soldiers returned

47

from the Crimea completed his conversion. Soon after his accession, rumours began to circulate that he favoured the abolition of serfdom. On April 11, 1856, he had made his first public pronouncement on the most important problem of his reign. He told representatives of the Moscow nobility : "For the contradiction of certain unfounded reports, I think it necessary to tell you that I do not at present intend to abolish serfdom; but certainly, as you well know yourselves, the existing manner of owning serfs cannot remain unchanged. It is better to abolish serfdom from above than to await the time when it will begin to abolish itself from below. I request you, gentlemen, to consider how this may be achieved, and to submit my words to the nobility for their consideration."

Shortly after his return to St. Petersburg, the Tsar consulted the Minister of the Interior about the best method of introducing a policy of 'gradual endeavours towards the liberation of the privately owned serfs'. The Minister, Lanskoy, recommended as a first step the preparation of a plan for liberation by stages. In consequence, he was asked to collect the relevant information from different ministries and to prepare a historical résumé on the evolution of serfdom and proposals made for its limitation since the time of Peter the Great. He was also told to use the coming coronation in Moscow for a private sounding of visiting marshals of nobility (the elected leaders of the local nobility in districts and provinces).

These preparatory measures reveal two aspects of Alexander's intentions at this stage. In the first place, he envisaged the abolition of serfdom by gradual stages rather than its immediate suppression. In addition, rather than bring about this emancipation by the action of the government alone, he hoped to obtain the co-operation of the Russian nobility. (Both these notions Alexander had inherited from his two immediate predecessors and their advisers.)

The first attempt to enlist the support of the nobility was a failure. The speech to the Moscow nobles, similar remarks to some marshals of nobility visiting St. Petersburg, repeated hints from Lanskoy to the marshals, produced not the slightest effect. The representatives of the nobility simply replied that they did not know on what principles the government intended to base its policy; they could not elicit those principles by themselves.

Alexander, therefore, decided that the first step must be taken by the government. In accordance with Russian administrative practice, he set up a secret committee under his own presidency. In his absence, it would be presided over by Orlov, the President of the Imperial Council. Orlov, then seventy-one years of age, was known as a convinced defender of serfdom. The majority of the committee was composed of officials hostile to abolition. Lanskoy alone, a Freemason who under Alexander I had sympathized with the Decembrists, was well-disposed. His only support was likely to come from Jacob Rostovtsev, one of the Tsar's adjutants-general.

Alexander himself opened the first meeting of the committee. He explained that several of his ancestors had tried, at various times, to improve the lot of the serfs. Their efforts had met with little success. Serfdom had now outlived its day and the time had come to consider "with due care and deliberation" arrangements which would lead to its eventual abolition. With regard to these, the résumé drawn up by the Ministry of the Interior raised a number of important questions. Was all the land, including that at present farmed by the serfs for their own use, to be considered the property of the landowners? If so, should there be legal recognition of the peasants' customary right of use? Again, should the owners be compensated for the loss of their serfs' services and such land as they might be asked to surrender? If so, to what extent should the burden of the operation be borne by the exchequer? It was for the committee to consider these questions and submit their recommendations.

Russian official procedure was slow and cumbersome, and the work of the committee was not advanced by the fact that there was profound disagreement amongst its members. The majority, led by Orlov, Adlerberg Senior, Gagarin, Panin (the influential Minister of Justice), and Muraviev (Minister of Imperial Domains), considered all reform to be both premature and dangerous. Their aim was to 'apply a brake', to prevent liberation, and, if unavoidable, to reduce its scope to an inescapable minimum. Lanskoy, the protagonist of emancipation, was supported only by some senior officials of his own Ministry. Without the backing of the Emperor, he had no hope of success.

While the committee was blocking all action, the Ministry of the Interior had worked out its own plan of emancipation. Lanskoy proposed that, for the time being, all land should remain the legal property of the landowner. The peasants should simply be protected in their customary right to form part of the estate. They should not pay for their *personal* freedom (the complete severance of *all* ties which bound them to their former owners). Their huts and farmyards (homesteads) would become their personal property, for which they would make payments to the owner spread over a period of ten to fifteen years. At the end of this 'period of transition', they would obtain full independence. In the intervening period, all necessary legal arrangements for the termination of serfdom would be made. Since all land remained in law the property of the squire, he would receive no compensation. The peasants would pay for the part of the estate allocated for their use either in money or in labour. No financial intervention by the government would be needed. The new system might be introduced gradually in the various provinces of the empire.

While this plan was in preparation, the Emperor had been abroad (summer of 1857). At Kissingen in Germany, he met Kisselev, who had been a warm protagonist of emancipation under Nicholas I. "I am more than ever determined", Alexander confided to his father's trusted adviser, "but have no one to help me in this important and pressing matter." Kisselev noted in his diary that the Tsar was clearly determined to carry through the emancipation but was meeting with difficulties on all sides.

On returning to Russia, Alexander discovered to his annoyance that the secret committee had made no progress whatever. He therefore appointed his brother Constantine, a radical reformer, a member of that body. Under his influence some headway was made. At this point matters were accelerated by an unexpected development. About the middle of November, Nazimov, the Governor-General of Lithuania (which embraced the provinces of Kovno, Grodno, and Vilna) arrived at St. Petersburg with a petition from the local nobility. The nobles of the three provinces requested permission to give *personal* freedom to their serfs while retaining possession of all the land. (Similar arrangements had already been introduced in the Baltic provinces under Alexander I.) The majority in the secret committee, to whom the matter was referred, supported the proposal. They hoped that it might pave the way for a general liberation without land throughout the empire.

The petition brought by Nazimov and its support by the secret committee impelled Alexander to his first decisive intervention in the liberation struggle. He declared categorically that the Lithuanian request for landless liberation must be rejected. Instead, the committee should take steps at once to draft legislation based on Lanskoy's proposals. After liberation, the peasants should receive their homesteads as their own property. They must retain the right to cultivate the land they were farming at present in return for a fixed rent in money or labour dues. Three meetings of the committee sufficed to formulate these principles. On December 2 (November 20 o.s.), Alexander signed the celebrated Rescript (an imperial order addressed to an individual, usually a high official) to Nazimov, containing his reply to the petition of the Lithuanian nobility. The Governor-General was instructed to form committees in each of the three provinces. These were to consist of the provincial marshal of nobility as president, one elected representative of the nobility for each district (the administrative sub-unit of the province), and two experienced landowners appointed by the Governor. Each committee should prepare a draft project of liberation based on the following principles: the landowners retained ownership of all the land; the peasants would, however, acquire their homesteads after payments spread over a fixed number of years; they would have the *use* of such land as was necessary for their subsistence and for the payment of taxes, for which right they would pay the owner in money or labour. Manorial jurisdiction would be preserved. When the work was completed, each committee would elect two delegates to a Commission for the whole of Lithuania, which would also include one experienced landowner from each province appointed by the Governor, and a representative of the Ministry of the Interior. The Commission would then bring together the three separate projects and submit to the Governor a plan for the whole of Lithuania. The latter would forward the plan to the Ministry of the Interior for submission to the Tsar.

The Imperial Rescript was accompanied by an instruction from Lanskoy to Nazimov. This stated clearly (as the Rescript had omitted to do) that after a twelve-year period of transition, it was intended to abolish serfdom. At the end of this period it would be illegal to sell serfs, to give them away, or to transplant them against their wishes. It would also become illegal to turn them into domestics. In fact, steps would be taken first to limit and finally to abolish the class of domestic serfs. If the landowners of Lithuania felt unable to accept these proposals, their objections must be stated in their final project.

Neither the Rescript nor Lanskoy's instruction was originally intended for publication. Yet only two days after signing the Rescript, Alexander communicated the content of these documents to the marshal of nobility of a central Russian province with the words: "I have decided to carry this matter to its conclusion and hope you will persuade your nobility to help me." Two days later, Lanskoy addressed a circular to the governors and marshals of nobility of all the provinces of European Russia. With it, he enclosed a copy of the Rescript and of his instructions to Nazimov—"for information and action should the nobility of your province express a similar desire". Thereafter, the matter no longer concerned the nobles of Lithuania alone but the whole of the Russian nobility. Would the rest of the nobles now take the initiative which Alexander desired?

The Tsar expected the nobles of his capital to take the lead. On December 21, he received a delegation come to thank him for his presence at a ball. Having thanked the marshal for his hospitality, he observed that their Governor-General (whilst ordinary provinces had simple Governors, those of special importance, or sometimes groups of provinces, were administered by Governors-General) had explained to them his wishes in the peasant question. It was his firm resolve that the matter should be settled. The principles laid down by him were oppressive to neither side. "I hope", the Tsar concluded, "that you will show a sincere interest in this matter, and will turn your attention to a class of people who deserve that their situation should be justly assured. Further delay is impossible; the matter must be dealt with now and not postponed to a distant future. That is my unshakable resolution." Turning to the

Governor-General, he added : "I ask you to co-operate with and lead the nobility; help them if there are difficulties." Thus were the Emperor's intentions revealed for the first time to the Russian public. Official publication of the Rescript to Nazimov followed. A decisive step had been taken; to stop now would be virtually impossible.

In any case, nothing was further from the Emperor's mind. On January 20, 1858, the hitherto secret committee on peasant matters became officially the "Main Committee on the Peasant Question for the Review of Projects and Suggestions concerning the Peasantry", known more briefly as the Main Committee. By the end of the year, forty-four provincial committees and two covering a group of provinces were wrestling with their draft projects for liberation. The policy embodied in the Rescript to Nazimov which was now being carried out marked Alexander's third approach to the problem. His speech at Moscow in the spring of 1856 had been part of an unavailing attempt to prod the nobility into taking the initiative. The setting up of the secret committee had ushered in an unsuccessful effort to draft a peasant statute with the help of officials in St. Petersburg. Now the Tsar was trying to achieve better results by combining direction from the centre with local initiative. The new approach contained two novel features. For the first time in Russian history, a Tsar had appealed to the entire nobility of the empire to co-operate in a major legislative enactment. Moreover, by the publication of the Rescript, he had for the first time submitted a burning question to the general Russian public. Both the nobility, therefore, and the intelligentsia (students, journalists, doctors, and members of professional groups in general) now entered the lists as champions or opponents of emancipation. The future of serfdom had become the issue of the day.

The announcement that the Tsar intended to liberate the serfs split the whole of Russian society into two

groups, the abolitionists and the 'planters'—by which
name the opponents of liberation soon came to be
known, thanks in no small part to the journalistic genius
of Alexander Herzen, the revolutionary socialist in
exile. The 'abolitionists', writers, journalists, and university professors with a sprinkling of merchants and
liberal officials, at once began a public campaign to
demonstrate their support for the Tsar. In January
1858, a great banquet at the Moscow Merchants' Club
was addressed by a succession of distinguished professors and publicists representing every shade of Russian
opinion. When the well-known editor Michael Katkov
proposed the health of the Tsar, he was greeted with
prolonged cheers. The loudest applause of all, however,
was reserved for Kokorev, the self-made millionaire
spokesman of the Moscow merchants.[1] Kokorev appealed to his fellow merchants to subscribe to a great
redemption fund to help the peasants pay the landowners for their homesteads and such land as they
might receive after liberation. All the merchants, he
declared with truth, were descended from the peasantry. They all—and particularly the farmers of spirits,[2]
of whom he himself was one—owed their wealth to
money paid by peasants. What an opportunity to show
their gratitude today! The banquet was followed by
others organized by Kokorev at which enthusiastic
speeches by scholars and literary men were followed by
ovations before the portrait of the Tsar.

The Russian press, which had received permission
at last to discuss the peasant problem, shared in the

[1] This is how Kokorev was described by a Swedish diplomat:
". . . a spirit farmer, who by this trade as well as by other more
or less legal methods, has acquired an immense fortune. . . .
There is not a single industrial enterprise of any importance
which does not number him among its founders; not a single
well-written article in an economic journal of which he is not
the author. He is the hero of Russia's rising industry."
[2] The sale of *vodka* was a state monopoly farmed out to
merchant-entrepreneurs, who frequently made large fortunes.

abolitionist enthusiasm. In its issue of February 15, Herzen's *Kolokol* (published in London but with a considerable circulation inside Russia) carried the famous article 'After Three Years', which began and ended with the words 'Thou hast conquered, O Galilean!' Chernyshevsky, another radical journalist, compared the task undertaken by Alexander to that of Peter the Great. Young Peter Kropotkin, then a student in the Cadet School, later recalled how "all intellectual St. Petersburg was with Herzen, and particularly with Chernyshevsky. . . . I remember how the officers of the Horse Guards, whom I saw every Sunday after church-parade at the home of my cousin, used to side with Chernyshevsky, the leader of the advanced party in the emancipation struggle. The whole disposition of St. Petersburg, whether in the drawing-rooms or in the streets, was such that it was impossible to go back."

More directly useful to the Tsar than the enthusiastic but rather ineffectual support of the intelligentsia and the merchants was the assistance and encouragement of two other groups. Of these, the first consisted of a handful of reformers in the government itself. Lanskoy, the Minister of the Interior, had from the start been the driving force behind the policy of liberation. He, in his turn, leant heavily on his two younger and more energetic assistants, Soloviev and Nicholas Miliutin. The latter in particular—owing to his enthusiasm and technical knowledge—had soon become a leading figure in the abolitionist ranks. Another prominent supporter of emancipation was Alexander Gorchakov, the diplomat who, shortly after the Crimean War, had become Minister of Foreign Affairs. A school-fellow of the poet Pushkin, brought up in the 'liberal' atmosphere of Alexander I's early years, he was a reformer by personal inclination. In addition, his desire for a political *rapprochement* with France militated in the same direction. Early in 1858 a foreign observer recorded that Gorchakov "still wished to move forward like a student" and spoke of nothing but 'progress'. Another foreign diplomat at the end of 1859 went so far as to speak of "the omnipotent influence which Prince Gorchakov has enjoyed these last three years". His was a powerful influence on the side of the abolitionists.

More important even than these official influences—which were, after all, more than counter-balanced in the official sphere by the Orlovs, Panins, and Muravievs—was the existence of prominent abolitionists in the Tsar's immediate entourage. The Empress Mary, who, by resigning herself to her husband's infidelities had regained much of her influence, was a warm supporter of the abolitionist cause. So, curiously enough, was Alexandrine Dolgoruky, the mistress who had supplanted her in Alexander's affection. (She is the heroine of *Smoke*, one of Ivan Turgeniev's novels.) The third in this triumvirate of feminine influences (and this was characteristic of Alexander) was the Tsar's aunt by marriage, the Grand-Duchess Helen (a former Württemberg princess). A woman of wide cultural interests, her musical and literary *soirées* had become the meeting place of all that was cultured and enlightened in St. Petersburg society. Her interests, however, were not confined to culture. She aspired to a political role, and, at two important junctures her influence over her nephew was considerable. The first of these was during the liberation struggle. It was in her salon that Alexander met the leading abolitionists, Miliutin, Samarin, Cherkassky. It was she who provided him with much of the information he needed to carry out his task. Moreover, her assistance proved invaluable to another abolitionist member of the imperial family, the Grand-Duke Constantine. Alexander's younger brother was a reformer heart and soul; with an enthusiasm which usually outran discretion, he had thrown himself into the struggle against the powerful 'planters'.

The opponents of liberation formed a powerful phalanx composed of two distinct elements. They were led by a group of influential Ministers, headed by Orlov and Panin. The former, late in 1857, was described by a shrewd observer as 'still the first man of the empire' and 'the soul of the government'. Panin, the other 'planters'' leader, was described as a "*grand seigneur* in the fullest sense of the term; *un homme d'autrefois* immutable in his principles". When he came to realize that he could no longer please his sovereign, he retired rather than, as he himself said, "bow his grey head before the idol of progress".

Orlov, Panin, and their supporters in governmental spheres knew that liberation would mean the end of the existing social order and were determined to fight it to the end. They attempted—not without some success—to frighten the Tsar with the spectre of a peasant rising which, they claimed, would inevitably follow the abolition of serfdom. If these were the generals, their army consisted of the great majority of the provincial gentry resolved to fight for its land and its privileges. On every one of the provincial committees set up to prepare the projects of emancipation, the 'planters' formed the majority. Only an enlightened minority, varying in size, was prepared to apply conscientiously the principles laid down by Lanskoy on the Tsar's behalf. The majorities had no thought but opposition or obstruction. In effect, therefore, the 'planters' controlled both the Main Committee and all the provincial committees. It looked doubtful whether, in the face of their opposition, it would prove possible to apply the policy of the Rescript.

In fact, by the spring of 1858 matters were once again grinding to a standstill. The immediate problem was to establish a measure of uniformity in the proceedings of the many provincial committees. This was the first time in Russian history that locally elected bodies had been called upon to discuss matters of such vital importance. Moreover, it was clear that they were discussing the problem in a spirit at variance with the intentions of the government. The indefatigable Ministry of the Interior proposed to issue new directives. A draft instruction laid down that the object of the emancipation was the complete independence of the peasants from their former masters and their endowment with land. This draft, submitted by Lanskoy to the Main Committee, was duly rejected by that body. The Tsar, through his confidant Rostovtsev, ordered the issue of a new directive which paid more attention to the hereditary rights of the nobility. Under Rostovtsev's influence, the principles of the draft were modified. It was now declared the object of imperial policy that the serfs should become personally free and enjoy the hereditary use of their huts and farmyards. The redemption of these would be voluntary within a period to be laid down. The question of land allotments for the liberated serfs was passed over in silence. The new programme readily won the support of the Main Committee. It was confirmed by the Tsar and transmitted by Lanskoy to the provincial committees for their guidance. The Ministry of the Interior had suffered a major defeat at the hands of the 'planter' majority.

Moreover, the new circular coincided with the decision of the government to restrict the unfettered discussion of emancipation. The publication of the Rescript to Nazimov had been followed by a lively press discussion. Censorship had been lenient, and extreme as well as moderate views had found expression. Amongst those who advocated radical solutions was Professor Kavelin, the Tsarevich's tutor in Russian law, who had published two articles on the subject. His analysis of relations between the government, the landowners, and the serfs had led to three drastic conclusions. The existing legal relationship between owners and peasants must be terminated, since for a long time to come no Russian court would decide impartially between members of the two groups. The peasants, moreover, must retain all the land which at present they farmed for their own account. Lastly, compensation to the owners should be paid by the exchequer, although it might later be recovered from the peasants. These proposals—particularly the suggestion that the peasants should retain all land which they held at present—were judged harmful and dangerous. The Tsar accepted the verdict of the Committee. Kavelin lost his position as tutor to the Tsarevich; the censor who had passed the offending articles received a reprimand. The Committee itself drew up a circular which laid down that in future all discussion of the peasant question must be limited to the official programme. With the circular of May 4, 1858, all serious discussion of liberation in the Russian press came to an end.

The Tsar, having made important concessions to the 'planters', was now anxious that some progress should be made. He took one of the heroic decisions of his career and resolved to tour the provinces of northern Russia to appeal in person to the local nobility for support for his policy of liberation. He was away from St. Petersburg for a month. His first stop was at Tver, where he was, perhaps, least likely to meet with a hostile reception. "I now entrust to you", he told the nobles, "a matter important to you as it is to me, that of the peasants. I rely on you to justify my confidence. The duty of dealing with this important matter has been laid on men elected from your midst. Use your best judgment, reflect carefully, seek the most advantageous manner of placing the peasantry in a new situation, make your arrangements to suit local conditions, in a manner offensive neither to the peasants nor to yourselves, on the basis of the fundamental principles which I have laid down in my Rescripts. You know how close to my heart is your welfare; I hope that the well-being of your peasants is no less dear to you." Five days later, in addressing the nobility of the province of Kostroma, Alexander repeated the key phrases of his campaign. On August 31, he spoke to the nobles of Nizhni, on

September 4 to those of Vladimir. On the 12th he addressed severe reproaches to the recalcitrant nobility of the Moscow province. On the 15th there followed a speech in a persuasive tone at Smolensk; three days later yet another at Vilna. Wherever Alexander went, he announced that deputies would be called to St. Petersburg for the final deliberations.

The Tsar's tour marks a turning-point in the development of the peasant question. It gave him an opportunity to declare in public his determination to carry the matter to a successful conclusion. His own impressions, moreover, were on the whole encouraging; he gained the conviction that there would be no systematic obstruction. Wherever he had gone he had found at least a minority of the nobility sympathetic to liberation on the terms laid down by the government.[1] The 'people' everywhere had shown its delight at the prospect of emancipation. Returning to St. Petersburg in an optimistic mood, the Tsar said to Lanskoy: "You and I have jointly started this peasant matter; we will see it through together."

Almost at the same time as Alexander, Rostovtsev had returned to St. Petersburg after a prolonged sojourn in Germany. For some time he had been conscious of his lack of intimate knowledge of the problem and had therefore determined to spend some time thinking it over. The conclusions he reached largely coincided with those already reached by the Tsar. In consequence, from this moment until his death in 1860, Rostovtsev became the Tsar's *alter ego* in the struggle for liberation. Now, in consultation with Rostovtsev and Lanskoy, Alexander decided to have their joint policy put forward in the Main Committee under his own presidency.

Meanwhile, a change had occurred in the Commit-

[1] It is, however, worth noting that the Tsar during his tour did not visit the 'planters'' strongholds in the Black Earth Belt. He confined himself to provinces where economic conditions made liberation with land less offensive to the nobility.

tee's composition. Earlier in the year, infuriated by the obstructionist tactics of the majority, the Grand-Duke Constantine had lost his temper. He told Orlov that he "greatly doubted the sincerity of these gentlemen who . . . instead of removing difficulties, did what they could to increase them". When Orlov rejoined that this was an aspersion on the honour of the Russian nobility, the Grand-Duke declared that the Russian nobility were not even good enough for him to spit on. (According to another version, he merely observed that there was no such thing as a true nobility in Russia.) The members protested to the Tsar, and early in October Constantine left for a naval cruise in the Mediterranean.

In his place, the Tsar himself assumed an active role in the Main Committee. For four important meetings in October and November, he never left the chair. He declared that as the first projects of the provincial committees were beginning to reach St. Petersburg, he would lay down certain principles. From the first moment the new law was published, the peasants must gain the feeling that there had been a definite improvement in their lot. At the same time, the landowners must see that their interests had been safeguarded. The firmness and vigilance of the local authorities must not be relaxed for one moment; no disturbances of any kind must be tolerated. The Minister of the Interior should ask all provincial committees to submit, together with their projects, detailed memoranda on the way in which the peasants' lot would be bettered by their proposals. Moreover, as projects reached the Ministry of the Interior, they should be studied individually to make sure that they did not depart from the principles laid down by the government, and examined to see how far and in what manner they improved the condition of the private serfs.

Having laid down the procedure to be followed, the government had to wait for the local committees to complete their work. In these, bitter battles were raging among the members, representing at least three distinct points of view. Diehard 'planters' everywhere were fighting a rearguard action to save all land for the gentry. On the other hand, influential and well-educated nobles, including, as a rule, the members appointed by the Governors, were ready to co-operate wholeheartedly with the government in the implementation of its programme. Between the two groups stood those—and they formed the majority in most committees—whose sole desire was to save for their order the maximum of material advantage.

The divisions in the committees led to inconveniences not anticipated by the government. In the first place, they were productive of delay: hardly a single committee was able to submit its project by the date appointed. More serious was the fact that most provincial committees produced two, sometimes three, different projects. This meant a great deal of extra work for the sub-committee set up to examine them. And since two of its four members (Panin and Muraviev) were bitter opponents of liberation, the sub-committee threatened to become an impassable bottleneck.

Foreseeing this difficulty, Lanskoy had already recommended replacing the sub-committee by two Commissions under the auspices of his own Ministry. One of these would deal with principles common to all the projects, the other with local peculiarities. On February 16, 1859, the Tsar accepted the suggestion, and Rostovtsev, himself favourable to the new scheme, became president of the two Commissions. Prominent among the members were Lanskoy's assistants, Miliutin and Soloviev. Miliutin from the start was one of the key members. In March, when a vacancy occurred for the post of Deputy Minister of the Interior, Lanskoy at once recommended his indefatigable assistant. The Tsar, who did not know Miliutin personally, was only too familiar with his reputation among the 'planters' as a red revolutionary. The Grand-Duchess Helen, who passionately supported Miliutin, arranged that he should be privately presented to the Empress Mary. "This is Mirabeau beginning his secret meetings with Marie-Antoinette", the 'planters' at Court murmured after their first meeting. The Empress was able to dispel the Tsar's distrust; he appointed the 'red' official Acting Deputy Minister. Rostovtsev, who respected Miliutin's knowledge and sincerity, followed his advice in the selection of 'experts' from the provincial committees. In consequence, the members invited to join the Commissions belonged almost invariably to the liberal minorities of the provincial committees. Among the most prominent were the Slavophils, Samarin and Cherkassky. Some opponents of liberation also found a place; in spite of their inclusion, however, the Commissions were the first official bodies in Russia which had an 'abolitionist' majority. This fact, more than anything else, assured that the emancipation was finally carried out on terms not too widely divergent from those laid down by the government.

The bulk of the work fell on the shoulders of Miliutin. The Acting Deputy Minister of the Interior possessed outstanding ability, unrivalled knowledge of the problems, and a capacity for hard work. Rostovtsev jokingly described him as 'our Egeria'. The two men—the prime architects of liberation—soon agreed to combine the two Commissions into one (known as the Editing Commission), which was then subdivided into separate sections to study the administrative, economic, judicial, and financial aspects of liberation. This was the body on which would finally fall the task of drafting the emancipation laws.

On March 18, such members of the Commission as had already reached St. Petersburg, were presented to the Emperor. Alexander expressed the hope that they would successfully complete their task. He added: "All I desire is the good of Russia. You are called upon, gentlemen, to accomplish a great task. I shall know how to value your efforts. The matter, I know, is delicate. My choice has fallen on you: I have heard about each of you from your president; he has recommended every one of you. I am convinced that you love Russia as I love her and will honourably do your duty. You will justify the confidence I place in you." Rostovtsev would report to him regularly on their progress. "I hope that, together, we shall bring this work to a successful conclusion. May God help you in this difficult task; I will not forget you. Farewell." Then, after kissing Rostovtsev, Alexander left the hall.

The first meetings of the Commission showed that Rostovtsev's ideas had evolved in a liberal direction. He now recommended liberation with land, a redemption operation assisted by the government, and the reduction to a minimum of the period intervening between serfdom and complete liberation. Soon a difference of opinion arose between the majority and the 'planters' led by P. P. Shuvalov (Marshal of Nobility of St. Petersburg) and Prince Paskievich (son of the former Field-Marshal). Rostovtsev, on the Tsar's behalf, had explained that the period of transition was to end as soon as the redemption of homestead and allotment was completed. The principle had been accepted by the Commission, but the 'planters' objected that the land should remain the legal property of the present owners, whilst the peasants should enjoy the right of hereditary use. They insisted on recording a minority opinion. When the Tsar ruled that this opinion was not to be included in the printed minutes of the Commission but simply to be appended to its final report, they asked leave to resign. The minority view became the subject of a bitter discussion in a plenary meeting of the Commission. Miliutin, Soloviev, and Cherkassky, in opposing the 'planters', argued that the arrangement proposed by the minority would simply continue serfdom in a modified form. Unless the peasants were made owners of their allotments, their economic dependence would continue, and their 'freedom' would have little meaning. On receiving the minutes of the discussion, Alexander ordered that the views of the majority should prevail. However, Shuvalov and Paskievich "sacrificing their personal views" should remain in the Commission and "participate in its labours with their former energy". The decision, typical of Alexander's methods, fore-shadows the appointment of Panin as Rostovtsev's successor as President of the Editing Commission.

Shortly after this incident, the Tsar received a letter from Paskievich, once more re-stating his views. Alexander's comments reveal what his own opinions were. Where Paskievich observed that it appeared to be the government's intention to convert the serfs into landed proprietors, the Tsar wrote that this was a fundamental condition from which nothing would induce him to recede. Against some comment on the right of the peasants to refuse to acquire land Alexander observed: "After which the owners would chase them off the land and leave them to roam the country." Where Paskievich noted that the proposals of the majority could be introduced only by force, Alexander commented : "Yes, if the nobility persist in their obstinacy." A recommendation that full personal freedom should be granted only three years after the publication of the statute provoked the rejoinder : "From the very first day of publication." However, Alexander did agree that redemption must be voluntary. Where Paskievich protested his sincerity, the Emperor regretted "the false point of view". Paskievich's protests remained without result. His had been a rearguard action on behalf of liberation without land. It had been defeated by the majority in the Editing Commission supported by the Tsar. From this time onwards, the 'planters' would fight no longer about the principle of liberation with land but about the size of the allotments.

In the meantime, attention had shifted once again to

the provincial committees. By the end of July the great majority of these had completed their drafts. In almost every case, two separate projects were submitted, representing respectively the views of the 'planter' majority and of the 'liberal' minority. The Minister of the Interior tried to arrange that of the two deputies to be sent to St. Petersburg from each committee, one should represent the views of the minority. At the same time, Lanskoy warned the Tsar that the deputies of the majorities would attempt to undo the work of the Commission. They might even try to organize a 'planters'' party. The committees, therefore, should be informed that the fundamental principles of the reform were settled once and for all, and that the deputies would discuss only their local application. Alexander expressed agreement; the last struggle with the nobility was approaching.

In September deputies from twenty-one provinces were called to the capital. The arrival of the remainder had been delayed for some months until the departure of the first group. "No notables! I want no 1789," the Tsar exclaimed in conversation with Bismarck. The deputies, moreover, at the first plenary meeting, received from the lips of Rostovtsev an imperial order defining and limiting their functions. They were to have no right of initiative, but would simply answer in writing questions submitted to them by the Commission. If invited to do so, they would attend its meetings for further explanations.

Irked by these restrictions, the deputies gathered at the house of Shuvalov. An address to the Emperor was drawn up, complaining of the Ministry of the Interior and the Editing Commission, and alleging that these bodies were misrepresenting his intentions. The deputies requested permission to lay their views before the Main Committee. In the end, the idea of an address was abandoned. Instead, the deputies asked for permission to hold a joint meeting. They were told that they might meet, unofficially, but must not discuss the general principles of the liberation. They must limit their discussions to the best manner of applying these principles in their respective localities. Any views they might express must deal with individual provinces only. Any representations they chose to make would be placed before the Main Committee.

On September 16 Alexander himself addressed the deputies. "I have called you together", he declared, "to co-operate in a task equally important for all of us and involving Russia's future well-being." When one of the deputies, with greater patriotism than truthfulness, replied that they were ready to sacrifice even a third of their property, the Tsar replied : "No, I don't ask such a heavy sacrifice. I want this great work to be accomplished in a manner not hurtful to anyone and satisfactory to all." This remark, like others made on several occasions, suggests that Alexander either did not fully understand what was involved in the discussions, or was the prisoner of his favourite phrase about a settlement satisfactory to both parties.

In fact, no such settlement lay within the realm of possibility. There was a fundamental clash of interests between the peasants and the nobility. The former considered that all the land rightfully belonged to them. The bulk of the gentry equally claimed all the land for themselves. It was, therefore, absolutely certain from the start that there could be no solution satisfactory to both the main classes of Russian society. The best Alexander could hope to achieve would be to impose by his autocratic power a compromise which, while leaving both classes dissatisfied, would at least safeguard the future of the empire.

Having addressed the deputies, Alexander left St. Petersburg. During his absence, friction between the deputies and the Commission increased. The deputies bitterly resented an announcement from the Ministry of the Interior that, once they had answered the questions

submitted to them, their task would be at an end. Rostovtsev, in a report to the Tsar, explained that while the
Commission looked at the matter from the point of view
of public law and the needs of the state, the deputies
took their stand on civil law and private interests. "They
are right from their own point of view—we from ours."
It was quite untrue—although widely asserted by the
landowners—that the Commission wished to rob them,
and that many of its members were 'reds'. In fact, the
principal object of the Commission was to save Russia;
the best means to that end was to liberate the serfs. No
compromise was possible between the rival points of
view.

The deputies were unable to challenge the Tsar's
authority. However, wishing to place their views on
record, several addressed themselves to the Emperor.
Eighteen declared that the proposals of the Commission reflected neither the general need nor the
principles established by the Tsar. They asked that before the project was finally submitted to the Main
Committee, the provincial deputies should be allowed
to express their views. Another five deputies, representing the liberal minorities, declared that the present proposals would ruin the owners without helping the
peasants. They called for the transfer of land to the
peasants by means of an immediate redemption operation. One deputy appealed to the Tsar to call an
assembly of the Russian nobility which, under his own
presidency, would take the final decisions.

These proposals, especially the ones for an elective
national assembly, were unacceptable to Alexander.
"He has fully convinced me", he wrote on one of the
petitions, "that he and those who think like him wish to
establish in our country an oligarchic form of government." The Tsar decided to transmit the different
addresses to the Main Committee. That body resolved
to silence the inconvenient spokesmen of Russian
opinion. All signatories of petitions, regardless of

the views expressed, received official reprimands. The deputies dispersed.

The meeting of the first group of deputies in St. Petersburg throws a vivid light on one of the basic problems facing the Tsar. From the beginning he had spared no effort to enlist the co-operation of the gentry. He had at every stage encouraged it to take an active part in working out the details of the proposed reform. Yet, however much he would have liked to carry through the measure with the free consent of the nobility, he had never been able to permit real freedom of discussion. The majorities in the provincial committees, like the majority of the deputies, were fundamentally opposed to liberation, and would have obstructed it if they could. The liberal minorities, on the other hand, not only went farther in their sympathy for the peasants than appeared practicable to the government, but were calling for a variety of far-reaching reforms in Russian public life. It might well appear to the Tsar that public participation in preparing the liberation statute, except within the narrowest limits, was incompatible with the orderly introduction of the reform.

The incident also reveals the importance of the autocracy in defending the interests of the serfs. Those interests were safer in the hands of Alexander and Rostovtsev, Lanskoy, and Miliutin, than in those of any elected assembly possible in Russia at that time. It is easy to imagine what would have happened to liberation in a 'constitutional' assembly dominated by the 'planters' and their friends. The truth was that co-operation between the autocrat and the reformers in the Ministry of the Interior against the 'planters' in the provincial committees and on the Main Committee offered the only chance of an effective reform.

The dismissal of the first group of deputies—the second was to be of purely formal importance—marked the discomfiture of the provincial gentry. From now on the battle would be waged at the centre between Rostovtsev's Editing Commission and Orlov's Main Committee. In these circumstances much would depend on the Emperor himself, who held the casting vote between the rival bodies. Rostovtsev was now beginning to take to heart the slanders circulating at Court against himself and the Editing Commission. In a letter to the Tsar, he defended the conduct of his colleagues. Alexander, in his reply, tried to raise his adjutant's flagging spirits. "If these gentlemen consider that they can frighten me by means of these insinuations, they will find they are grossly mistaken. I am far too convinced of the justice of our sacred cause to allow them to arrest me in its accomplishment. The great question is how to carry out the measure. In this, now as always, I place my trust in God and rely on the help of those who, like yourself, sincerely desire the success of the measure. On its success depend the salvation and future well-being of Russia. Do not lose heart, just as I do not despond, although I, too, have much grief to bear. Let us pray God together that he may give us strength. I embrace you with all my heart."

Alexander's sympathetic encouragement could no longer save Rostovtsev. In November, the first symptoms appeared of the illness which was to carry him to the grave. Soon he was confined to his house where, however, he continued to preside over meetings of the Commission. During December he received three visits from his imperial master. Early in the new year he took to his bed. As his illness grew worse, the Tsar's visits became increasingly frequent. Alexander had given instructions that all worry was to be kept from the patient, but Rostovtsev would not hear of it. He had asked his doctor to tell him when his case became hopeless, as there was some work he wished to complete. Thus he devoted his last remaining energies to drawing up a memorandum which would be for the Tsar a clear and non-technical guide to the elaborate statute which was

71

taking shape in the Commission. Early on February 18 he died, with the Emperor praying at his bedside. Alexander himself, together with members of the imperial family, carried the coffin part of the way to its last resting-place.

On the day after the funeral, Semenov, Rostovtsev's closest collaborator, handed the Tsar the latter's memorandum. Alexander confided to Semenov that he did not know whom to appoint in Rostovtsev's place. He had thought of consulting the dying man, but delicacy had stopped him. In any case, whoever succeeded Rostovtsev, the work would be carried on in his spirit. "I ask you to reassure your colleagues. I shall not withdraw from anything laid down in the writings of our late friend, who has so honourably carried out my intentions. Not only will I permit no change in the membership of the Commission, but I guarantee the completion of the work in accordance with the views of the majority. There will be no interference from the new president of the Commission. I ask you, the fellow-workers of the deceased, to complete the work in the spirit in which you have conducted it until now." Four days later, Rostovtsev's successor was named. His name sent a chill down the spine of every supporter of liberation. It was . . . Count V. N. Panin, the Minister of Justice.

Few acts of Alexander II have aroused more criticism than his decision to entrust to Panin the presidency of the Editing Commission. Yet the choice was neither as illogical nor as unreasonable as has been made to appear. Clearly, Rostovtsev's successor must be found among the circle of men who for the last three years had by constant work on emancipation become familiar with the manifold details involved. As the Tsar's representative, he must also be a personage of importance. The choice, therefore, was limited. The aged Lanskoy—hated by the 'planters'—could never have steered the statute through a hostile Main Committee. The Grand-Duke Constantine, owing to his pro-longed absence, was out of touch with the work of legis-lation. In his case also, as in that of Lanskoy, co-opera-tion with the Main Committee was unthinkable. No other prominent 'reformer' existed. If the new president had, on the other hand, to be found among the 'planters', Panin was the obvious choice. Educated and intelligent, he was regarded as a man of honour. His position as Minister of Justice recommended him for a difficult appointment. Alexander felt that he was a man to be trusted. Politically, the appointment had im-portant advantages. It established closer links between the Editing Commission and the Main Committee. It seemed likely to reduce obstruction in the latter body. It helped to calm the apprehensions of the gentry. If Panin loyally carried out the Tsar's orders, the appoint-ment, in spite of its apparent inconsistency, was a wise one.

The Tsar did all in his power to assure that Panin would carry on the work in the spirit of Rostovtsev. He told him that nothing must be changed in the working of the Commission. His predecessor's political testament must be his guide. "I entrust this matter to you on the terms on which we agreed. Conduct it, as it has been conducted. I have always thought of you as an honest man; it never entered my mind that you could deceive me." Panin afterwards assured the Grand-Duke Con-stantine that, whatever his personal views, he would subordinate them to the wishes of the Tsar. Actually, he later made more than one attempt to alter the spirit of the legislation prepared by the late Rostovtsev. If the statute which finally emerged still retained much of its original spirit, the result was due less to Panin's honesty than to the Tsar's vigilance and determination.

In July the Commission began the codification of its project. The Tsar laid down that the work must be com-pleted by October 22, 1860. On that date, the Commis-sion was disbanded after an expression of gratitude from the Emperor. In his closing speech Alexander used a dangerous expression. "It may be", he declared, "that many changes will still need to be made; in any case, however, you have the honour of having done the first work, and Russia will be grateful to you." The Tsar well knew that at least one major hurdle remained—to get the statute adopted by the Main Committee. To do so, he had made an important move. A little while before, Orlov, its aged president, had fallen seriously ill. Alexander, thereupon, had appointed the Grand-Duke Constantine in his place.

Constantine's task in the Committee was not an easy one. Three different views were expressed. Prince Gagarin, an isolated Don Quixote, still spoke for landless liberation. The 'planters' led by Muraviev wished to modify the draft statute in the interest of the owners. Finally, a group led by Lanskoy, Chevkin (Minister of Communications), and Bludov (President of the Imperial Council) wished to accept the draft statute with a minimum of modifications. Panin's attitude was ambiguous. In fact, those who wished to introduce substantial alterations were in the majority. It was the personal influence of the imperial brothers which prevented major changes. At the crucial moment, Constantine succeeded in convincing Panin, and Alexander Adlerberg Junior. Their defection deprived the 'planters' of their majority, and the statute was accepted without major alterations.

Only one further stage of the long-drawn-out legislative procedure now remained—discussion of the statute in the Imperial Council. Before this body the Tsar, in introducing the draft, made an urgent plea for haste. The matter had now been dragging on for four years. On the surface, his good people still showed admirable calm and restraint. But fears and hopes were widespread among serfs and owners alike. He was happy that the first initiative had come from the nobility (a polite fiction), and he had done all in his power to reduce the sacrifices demanded of them. They must not, however, forget that the situation of the serfs must be improved, and not on paper alone. The abolition of serfdom was vital to the future strength of Russia. The matter must be concluded forthwith, as any further delay might prove fatal to the empire. He would listen to different views and was ready to accept amendments. However, he had a right to demand one thing—that they would act not as landowners but as statesmen, disregarding personal interests, and as statesmen, moreover, entrusted with his confidence. Before the agricultural season began, the task must be completed.

With great rapidity, the Council set to work to discuss the one-thousand-odd sections of the statute. Where there was a division, the extreme 'planters' led by Gagarin could muster 8 votes, the moderate critics under Muraviev 16, and the defenders of the statute as it stood 29. On many points of detail, however, the last group was placed in a minority. In that event, the Tsar, as a rule, decided in their favour. However, to speed up the labours of the Council, he accepted one last reduction in the maximum size of allotments. More serious, he failed to veto a proposal introduced at the instance of Gagarin, which created the gratuitous or 'beggarly' allotment. This allotment equalling a quarter of the legal maximum for any given province could, with the peasants' consent, be allocated to them without any redemption payment, while the owner at the same time waived all claim to compensation. Owners of fertile soil would later feel tempted to press these allotments—which meant slow but inexorable starvation for those who accepted them—upon their former serfs.

On February 19/March 3, the sixth anniversary of his accession, Alexander signed the statute. The news was announced to the Russian people in an insincere manifesto drawn up in archaic Russian by the Metropolitan Philaret, an enemy of liberation. On Sunday,

March 17, it was read from the pulpit in all the churches of the capital. In one place it was read publicly by the Tsar himself. Special envoys carried the news to the provinces. On March 24, the Tsar addressed a crowd outside the Winter Palace: "The work was already begun in the time of my father, but he was unable to accomplish it in his lifetime. With God's help, it fell to my lot to complete the task for your good. Now, my children, go and thank God; pray for the eternal repose of my father; prove yourselves useful to the fatherland." All who had taken an official part in the work of liberation received a medal with the inscription 'I thank you'.

Accounts of the way in which the news was received in the capital differ. Kropotkin has left a description of his own impressions. He was in bed at the Corps of Cadets on Sunday, March 17, when his batman, Ivanov, dashed in with the tea-tray, shouting: "Prince, freedom! The manifesto is posted on the Gostinny Dvor" (the block of shops opposite the Corps). "Did you see it yourself?" "Yes. People stand round; one reads, the others listen. It *is* freedom!" In a couple of minutes, Kropotkin was out of bed and dressed. A comrade rushed in: "Kropotkin, freedom!" he shouted. "Here is the manifesto. My uncle learnt last night that it would be read at the early Mass at the Isaac Cathedral; so we went. There were not many people there; peasants only. The manifesto was read and distributed after the Mass. They well understood what it meant. When I came out of the church two peasants, who stood in the gateway, said to me in such a droll way: 'Well, sir? Now—all gone?'" Kropotkin himself read and re-read the manifesto, written in an elevated style in a useless mixture of Russian and Church Slavonic which obscured its sense. The liberty was not immediate, the serfs would remain serfs two years longer. Yet the main point stood out: the serfs were liberated, they would get their homesteads and allotments. They would have to pay a price, but slavery was at an end.

They went on parade. When the military part was over, the Tsar, remaining on horseback, called out: "The officers to me!" They gathered round him. In a loud voice, he addressed them on the great event of the day. Kropotkin and his friends—not yet officers—only heard scraps of the speech: "The officers . . . the representatives of the nobility in the army . . . an end has been put to centuries of injustice. . . . I expect sacrifices from the nobility . . . the loyal nobility will gather around the throne. . . ." There were enthusiastic hurrahs from the officers at the end.

As soon as the parade was over, Kropotkin dashed home to change in time for the Italian opera. Several young cadets dashed lightfooted up to the 'gods'. The house was crowded. In the first interval, the smoking-room was filled with excited young men, who all addressed each other whether acquainted or not. The sound of music reached their ears—they rushed back to the hall. The band was playing the National Anthem, 'God Save the Tsar'—drowned almost immediately in enthusiastic hurrahs from the galleries, the boxes, the pit. There was the same enthusiasm in the streets. Crowds of peasants and educated men stood in front of the palace cheering. Wherever the Tsar appeared, he was followed by cheering crowds.

Kropotkin's impressions were recorded long after the event, and it is possible that his memory deceived him. A Prussian diplomat, at all events, who witnessed the same scenes, wrote to his family shortly afterwards: "When on Sunday, March 17/5, the liberation was proclaimed, I went at noon to the cathedral of St. Isaac. The apathy of the public was positively ridiculous. What the papers write about enthusiasm is untrue. In the theatres the anthem was played, that is all. The following Sunday, outside the Winter Palace, a few thousand muzhiks presented to the emperor bread and salt (the traditional ceremony of Russian peasants welcoming their master) and, last Sunday, some

deputations arrived from Moscow and other towns."
It is more than likely that Kropotkin, regarding the
matter subjectively and in retrospect, exaggerated the
extent of popular enthusiasm.

At all events, as soon as the details of the complicated
emancipation statute began to be understood, any enthusiasm which might have been felt rapidly evaporated. The terms of the liberation were a compromise
which could satisfy neither of the main social groups. In
spite of all modifications introduced for its benefit,
the nobility, at a conservative estimate, lost roughly
one-third of its land. Some estimates, probably exaggerated, put the figure as high as three-fifths. Article 8
of the statute did indeed promise that this act of confis-
cation would never be repeated; but for the landowners
even this single measure was an unprecedented act of
robbery. By this time, the financial situation of many
of them was far from rosy. They were deep in debt;
some seven-tenths of the privately owned serfs on the
eve of the emancipation were mortgaged to state credit
institutions. To pay their debts the owners entered into
agreements with the peasant communities on their
estates for the transfer of land to the peasants; after
which they received from the exchequer government
bonds to compensate them for their losses. During the
first decade following liberation, some 70 per cent of
the owners concluded such agreements. Of the sum of
588 million roubles due to them as compensation, they
received a mere 326—the rest was retained to pay their
debts to public credit institutions. Moreover, the bonds
in which the government paid compensation depre-
ciated in value. This reduced the net proceeds to some
230 million roubles. Thanks to its improvident and
spendthrift habits, the Russian nobility rapidly spent
these and began once again to live on borrowed money.
By 1870 the total indebtedness (some 250 million
roubles) already exceeded the net proceeds from compensation payments. In general, the nobility and

gentry, already deep in debt, were impoverished by the liberation without even the consolation of increased political influence.

The peasants, although as free men they gained greatly in self-esteem, found their economic condition only marginally improved. The charges imposed upon them under the Act of Emancipation were grossly in excess alike of the yield of their land and of its value. The average size of the new allotments, except in the western provinces, fell well below that of their pre-reform holdings. This loss, as might have been expected, was particularly marked in the fertile southern and south-western provinces. In one of these it was esti-mated at 42 per cent, and the average loss may well have been in the neighbourhood of one-third. Moreover, the larger pre-emancipation allotments had occupied only half the serf's time; for three days in the week he had worked on his master's estate. Now the reduced allot-ments should, in theory at least, provide him with whole-time employment. By 1878, according to the figures of the Central Statistical Committee, only 13 per cent of the former private serfs were well-endowed with land. Something over 40 per cent were adequately pro-vided for, whilst the remainder did not have sufficient land to sustain themselves and their families. An added difficulty lay in the fact that by the liberation the peasants lost their customary right to timber and fire-wood from manorial forests, and were denied the use of meadows and pastures which the landowners often re-tained in their own possession. Many peasant families rapidly sank into debt. A particularly sad fate awaited the majority of household serfs. They got no land, and would hardly have known what to do with it had it been given to them. They obtained immediate personal free-dom but nothing else. Most left their former masters to seek employment elsewhere. Some were engaged by merchants, proud to employ the former coachmen and cooks of princes. Those who had learnt a trade found employment in the towns. The rest faced an uncertain and often miserable future.

The peasants soon realized that the land and freedom they had received was not what they had hoped for and vaguely considered their due. Many consoled themselves with the idea that this was not yet the true liberation; another would follow at the end of the two-year period of 'temporary obligation'. Alexander himself had to contradict these rumours. Later in the year he told a group of peasants: "Reports have reached me that you expect a new emancipation. There will be no emancipation except the one I have given you. Obey the laws and the statutes ! Work and toil ! Obey the authorities and the landowners !" It was cold comfort for the peasantry. Acts of insubordination increased immediately after the liberation, often due to misunderstandings. The most serious incident took place at Bezdna in the province of Pensa, where peasants, misled by a religious fanatic, started a demonstration. Unarmed but obstinate, they returned to obedience only in the face of an infantry volley. Fifty peasants were killed and over 300 wounded. However, stern repression, combined with exemplary fairness shown by most of the 'mediators' charged with applying the reform on the spot, usually young noblemen of liberal sympathies, soon calmed the excitement among the peasants. In the years following the emancipation, most experienced some improvement in their circumstances.

The terms of the liberation came as a disappointment to the liberals and radicals who had greeted with such delight the Tsar's decision to liberate the serfs. As early as 1858, Chernyshevsky expressed regret at the premature confidence he had expressed in the Tsar. After the massacre of Bezdna, students in many universities, sometimes encouraged by professors, organized protest demonstrations. They expressed the feelings of the radical intelligentsia. From this disappointment at the terms of liberation can be dated the beginning of the revolutionary movement which would one day kill the 'Tsar Liberator' and finally destroy his dynasty.

Later historians have criticized the terms of the emancipation as placing an undue burden on the shoulders of the newly-liberated peasantry and blamed the Tsar for failing to curb the 'planters'. Others have argued that since serfdom had already become 'un-economical' and was, in any case, beginning to abolish itself from below, the statute of 1861 did little more than register an accomplished fact. Both views overlook the persistent opposition to liberation with land encountered by the Tsar not only in the Main Committee but also in the provincial committees of the nobility. The measure was carried through in the teeth of bitter hostility: to get for the peasants even the terms finally obtained was not an easy matter: without constant pressure from the Tsar, liberation with land was unthinkable. There is much truth in Tolstoy's remark on the occasion of a toast to Alexander II, the 'Tsar Liberator': "I drink this toast with particular pleasure. No others are needed, for in reality we owe the Emancipation to the Emperor alone."

Alexander himself was disappointed at the reception of the Liberation Statute. Less than a month after its publication, Lanskoy was allowed to retire on account of his advanced age. With him went Nicholas Miliutin, the chief architect of liberation. "I am sorry to part with you", Alexander told him, "but I must; the nobility describe you as one of the reds." Lanskoy's place was taken by Valuiev, whose sympathies were on the side of the nobility and its demands for greater political influence.

At the same time, Alexander understood perfectly that the liberation of the serfs must of necessity lead to a series of further reforms. If he had handed over the Ministry of the Interior to the 'oligarchs', this did not mean that the reformers had lost the day. On the contrary, the star of the Grand-Duke Constantine was again in the ascendant. During the autumn and winter of 1861 and in the following spring, several of his followers (the 'Konstantinovtsy') received important appointments. Thus Dimitry Miliutin, the brother of Nicholas, a brilliant and highly educated staff officer of extreme democratic convictions, replaced an aged nonentity as Minister of War. Golovnin, a radical-liberal and the Grand-Duke's right-hand man, became Minister of Education. Reutern, a financial expert and an ardent reformer, became Minister of Finance. Panin's place as Minister of Justice was taken by a reformer, Zamiatnin. Bludov, a supporter of liberation, became President of both the Imperial Council and the Council of Ministers. His place at the head of the Second Division of the Imperial Chancery, which dealt with drafting legislation, was taken by Baron Korff, another friend of reform. With these appointments, the stage was set for the second phase of Alexander's 'great reforms'. In its New Year issue for 1862 the *Northern Post*, organ of the Ministry of the Interior, announced that the government was studying plans for a number of important changes. These included a general reform of the judicial system, a complete reorganization of the police, an improved method of presenting budgets and keeping official accounts, a reform in the administration of imperial domains, and the development of elementary education. A complete transformation of the organs of local government might have been added to the list. It was a programme which would have been unthinkable in the days of Nicholas I.

Chapter Four

The Reforming Emperor

THE liberation of the serfs was undoubtedly the most spectacular achievement of Alexander's reign, yet it was only one of a number of major reforms. In some respects, indeed, it was only a beginning; its repercussions were felt in every department of Russian life. It was the reforms following the Act of 1861 which developed the break with feudalism by reducing the class privileges of the nobility. By the same token, the later reforms raised the status of the non-noble part of the population and paved the way for more rapid commercial and industrial development. The changes brought about in Russia after 1861 'modernized' the *ancien régime* by bringing it more closely into line with western European practices and ideas. They were Russia's response to the challenge of Sevastopol.

In the later reforms, the Tsar's personal share was somewhat less prominent than it had been in the struggle for liberation. This was due principally to the fact that the later changes encountered less opposition. None of the later reforms seriously touched the property rights of individuals and classes. Again, several were the direct and necessary complement to the liberation, and thus no longer the subject of discussion. Alexander's wholesale appointment of reforming Ministers between November 1861 and the following January meant that the reforming party in the government was now stronger than it had been. Finally, between 1861 and 1864 reforming policies were in the ascendant to such an extent that even inveterate 'planters' were carried away by the tide. In these circumstances, direct personal intervention by the Tsar in the legislative process had become less necessary.

This, however, is not to say that the Tsar's over-all influence did not remain decisive. His was the initiative for all new legislation. He normally laid down the scope of the reform it was intended to introduce. After the appropriate Ministry had elaborated in some detail the general principles of the new measure, they would again be submitted to the Tsar. Once the draft had been completed, usually by a ministerial committee, it was again laid before the Emperor, who would sanction its submission to the Imperial Council. Finally, an imperial ukase explaining the scope and intention of the new law would accompany its notification to the Governing Senate. Moreover, whenever differences arose during the preparation of a new measure, the final decision was made by the Tsar. Alexander, therefore, exercised a constant supervision over all the reforms of his reign.

In addition to his administrative supervision, the Tsar exercised political control. He selected his Ministers, who were responsible to him alone. He was his own Prime Minister : in 1861, he dismissed Lanskoy and N. Miliutin, and gave the important Ministry of the Interior to Valuiev, representative of the 'liberalizing' nobility. Some months later, he entrusted to radical reformers the Ministries of Education, Justice, War, and Finance. The political reaction after the attempt on his life in 1866, which might easily have ended all reform, did not, in fact, produce a wholesale dismissal of reforming Ministers. Reformers and 'liberals' did lose control of the 'political' Ministries—Justice, Education, and the Interior. The process, however, was gradual. In the 'technical' departments of War and Finance, reformers remained firmly in control. The radical democrat at the Ministry of War, in spite of severe attacks, was retained by Alexander to the end. Politically, the later reforms no less than the liberation of 1861 were the work of the autocratic power.

The moving spirit behind those reforms, however, was less the Tsar himself than his brother, the Grand-Duke Constantine. Minister of Marine from the beginning of the reign, Constantine had from the start been the protagonist of radical reform. He had instructed his subordinates to give up the 'official lie' of reporting that all was well when the reverse was the case. Naval courts-martial had been reformed, cruel punishments discontinued, educational institutions developed. The *Naval Almanack,* official organ of the Ministry, had, under the editorship of Golovnin, become the most outspoken paper in Russia. It discussed legal reforms and educational changes. Abuses in the administration of the navy were pilloried. In an official circular, Constantine had offered handsome prizes for contributions criticizing 'bravely and effectively' shortcomings of naval life. The Ministry of Marine became "the nursery, the general staff of the entire reforming movement of the sixties". As President of the Geographical Society, Constantine gathered around him a group of ardent reformers—Reutern, Golovnin, the Miliutin brothers. With their appointment to ministerial office late in 1861, the stage was set for major reforms in almost every department of Russian life.

Amongst the most important of these reforms was that of the legal system. Even Nicholas I had recognized the need for this. In 1844 he had heard of some gross abuses in a tribunal not far from the Winter Palace, and had ordered an inquiry. Baron Korff, in charge of the investigation, had discovered "a yawning abyss of all possible horrors, which have been accumulating for years". The Emperor, after studying the report, had written at the bottom : "Unheard-of disgrace! The carelessness of the authority immediately concerned is incredible and unpardonable. I feel ashamed and sad that such disorder could exist almost under my eyes and remain unknown to me." Yet the projects for reform prepared by several committees under Bludov were drawn up unsystematically and no changes were made under Nicholas. A reform of the legal system had been Alexander's first promise to his subjects, contained in the manifesto announcing the conclusion of peace. Until 1861, however, he had been occupied with other matters. The liberation of the serfs made change an urgent necessity, as ways must be found to replace the vanished seigneurial jurisdiction. The reform of the legal system had become the most urgent immediate task facing the Russian Government.

Late in 1861, Alexander set up a commission of officials and jurists to work out the general principles for a radical transformation of the Russian legal system. In his instructions he told members to work out "those fundamental principles, the undoubted merit of which is at present recognized by science and the experience of Europe, in accordance with which Russia's judicial institutions must be reorganized". The direction to follow European theory and practice forms a landmark in the history of Russian law. "The Chinese Wall", a Russian historian has written, "which for forty-five years had separated our legislators from the direct influence of European science and contemporary progress, collapsed. The principles of European public law and science, which till then had penetrated into Russia only as contraband, were at last freely admitted into our legislation." The commission's report was a comprehensive indictment of the existing system, listing no fewer than twenty-five radical defects. To remove these, it proposed that the judicial organization should be completely separated from all other branches of the administration; that the fullest publicity should be introduced into the tribunals; that trial by jury should be adopted for criminal cases; that summary courts staffed by Justices of the Peace should be set up for petty cases; and that procedure in the ordinary courts should be greatly simplified. What was proposed was nothing less than the transformation of an effete and out-of-date system into a modern judicial edifice.

The fundamental principles of the reform were made public on October 10, 1862, and comments were invited from universities, officers of the law, and private individuals. No fewer than 446 observations were submitted, later published in six bulky volumes. These were taken into consideration by a new committee composed of the best jurists of the empire, which was charged with the task of preparing the detailed legislation. In eleven months these specialists had completed their labours, preparing a draft law on the establishment of new judicial institutions and draft codes of procedure in civil and criminal cases. After discussion in the Imperial Council, the judicial statutes received the imperial assent on December 2, 1864. In a ukase to the Senate announcing the fact, Alexander declared: "On ascending the throne of my ancestors, one of my first wishes publicly proclaimed in the manifesto of March 19, 1856, was : 'May justice and mercy reign in our courts !' Ever since that time, amidst other reforms called for by the needs of our national life, I have never ceased to reflect on the manner of achieving this object through a better organization of the judiciary." The present statutes were the outcome of his wish "to establish in Russia expeditious, just, merciful, and impartial courts for all our subjects; to raise the judicial authority by giving it proper independence and, in general, to increase in the people that respect for the law which national well-being requires, and which must be the constant guide of all and everyone from the highest to the lowest".

The new judicial edifice was simple and symmetrical. There were two great sections distinct from and independent of each other. On one side stood the jurisdiction of the Justices of the Peace, on the other the regular courts. Each section contained an ordinary court and a court of appeal; in the case of the peace jurisdiction, this was a counterpart of the English Quarter Sessions. The upper part of the structure, equally covering both sections, consisted of the Senate, organized as a Court of Revision—on the model of the French *Cour de Cassation*. The division of duties between the two sections of the judicature was clear. The peace courts were to decide petty cases which involved no complicated legal principles, and to settle, if possible by conciliation, minor conflicts and disputes of everyday life. The function of the regular tribunals was to take cognizance of more serious cases. In the former courts, the judges were at first chosen from the local inhabitants by popular election (later, this function was transferred to the zemstvos), while in the more formal regular courts the judges were trained jurists nominated by the Emperor.

In 1866, the new courts were opened in the ten provinces which formed the judicial districts of St. Petersburg and Moscow. Their extension to other parts of the empire was spread over decades. There was a great shortage of trained lawyers. Moreover, after auspicious beginnings, public interest slackened. In some instances the statutes were later applied in a modified form. Thus trial by jury was not introduced in Poland, the western provinces, or the Caucasus.

The working of the new courts is described by Mackenzie Wallace, who during a stay in Russia extending from the beginning of 1870 to the end of 1875, had ample opportunity to study these courts in action. One notable feature of the reform was the immediate popularity of the peace jurisdiction. In Moscow, the authorities had calculated that under the new system the number of cases would be more than doubled, and that on an average a thousand cases a year would be heard before each Justice. Great was their surprise when, instead, the number turned out to be 2,800. In St. Petersburg and other large towns, the new courts proved equally popular. The reason for this popularity is not far to seek. Mackenzie Wallace describes the contrast between the old and the new. Under the old system, if two workmen (or peasants) brought their dispute before a police court, "they were pretty sure to get scolded in language unfit for ears polite, or to receive still worse treatment". In the peace court, the Justice, "always scrupulously polite without distinction of persons, listened patiently to the complaint, tried to arrange matters amicably and, if he failed, gave the decision at once according to law and common sense". The popularity of the peace courts increased further when people understood that they acted expeditiously, without unnecessary formalities and—above all—without bribes or blackmail.

Sometimes, indeed, the Justices carried their democratic outlook to extremes. "Imagining that their mission was to eradicate the conceptions and habits of serfage, they sometimes used their authority for giving lessons in philanthropic liberalism, and took a malicious delight in wounding the susceptibilities, and occasionally even the material interests, of those whom they regarded as enemies of the good cause." The number of such cases was not great, and it rapidly decreased. The mere possibility that justice might be partial to the underdog shows how far matters had moved since the days of Nicholas I.

In the regular courts also there was an unmistakable improvement. Wallace observed that it was not easy to find sufficient men with legal training and practical experience of the law to staff the new courts. However, he recorded, "the present generation of judges are better prepared and more capable than their predecessors". Above all, he notes that on the score of probity he had never heard any complaint. No greater contrast to the courts of Nicholas could possibly be imagined. With all their blemishes (and they were numerous), the new courts remained a lasting memorial to

Alexander II and a symbol of the new spirit which was beginning to pervade Russian public life.

The other great organic reform flowing directly from the liberation of the serfs was in the sphere of local government. In the time of serfdom the Emperor Nicholas, when referring to the landed proprietors, used to say jocularly that he had in his empire 50,000 zealous and efficient hereditary police officers. With the emancipation law the authority of these hereditary police masters disappeared; measures had to be taken to replace it. While it was intended from the start that some of the former owners' administrative duties should be transferred to the institutions of peasant self-government, it was clear that an organ would be needed to control an area larger than a village or group of villages.

The reform of the rural police had been intimately linked with the liberation of the serfs and had accordingly been considered in connection with it. In an instruction of April 6, 1859, Alexander set out the principles on which local government was to be reformed. Great administrative activity followed. The local committees on the peasant question submitted to the Main Committee and to the Editing Commission projects for the reform of local self-government, all of which were finally collected by Miliutin's Commission. That Commission soon reached agreement on the reorganization of the police. It proved more difficult, however, to agree on the plan for the creation of new organs of local government, the zemstvos.[1] Two rival views held the field. One favoured the preponderance of the nobility in the management of local affairs, the other equal participation by all the social groups. As long as Miliutin presided over the Commission, the 'democrats' had the upper hand. When Valuiev became Minister of the Interior in the spring of 1861, the balance tilted to the

[1] The word *zemstvo* is derived from *zemlia*, the Russian word for land. It is analogous to the German *Landtag*, and means an 'assembly of the land'.

side of the 'oligarchs'. It was Valuiev's policy to reserve for the nobility the greatest possible influence in local affairs, to place the zemstvos under the control of the Ministry of the Interior, and to limit their activities to the purely economic field. The project, which he steered through the Commission, was inspired by a double preoccupation : to make the zemstvos as innocuous as possible and to ensure the preponderance of the larger landowners.

The struggle begun in the Commission was continued in the Imperial Council. Miliutin himself, Reutern, Baron Korff, and other reformers attacked the principles of Valuiev's draft. A clash occurred over the manner of choosing zemstvo presidents. Should the president be elected by the zemstvo assembly, or should he be the local marshal of nobility? When the matter was discussed in relation to district zemstvos, the Council was evenly divided. Alexander decided in favour of the 'oligarchs'. When it came to the question of the higher provincial zemstvos, the 'democrats' were outvoted. Korff led an impassioned attack on the provisions restricting their functions, and on their subordination to the Ministry of the Interior. "The public desire above all, that, however limited the functions of the zemstvos, they should have *real* independence." Although supported by D. A. Miliutin (Minister of War) and Kovalevsky (a former Minister of Education), Korff was unable to make an impression. Valuiev rejoined that the attacks on bureaucratic interference were exaggerated; independent zemstvos would become 'a state within the state'. When the functions of the zemstvos were discussed, Kovalevsky proposed the inclusion of primary education. Panin opposed the suggestion; he declared that to entrust popular education and the responsibility for health and prisons to these bodies would be to encourage hopes and pretensions which it might not be possible to satisfy. The Council decided against him. Finally, a bitter and prolonged argument arose about the functions of the zemstvos in relation to taxation. Prince Shcherbatov, the mayor of Moscow, supported by Reutern and Kovalevsky, pleaded for a wide zemstvo autonomy in matters of taxation—even for some voice in the disposal of imperial taxes raised in the locality. The proposals provoked a philippic from Valuiev— "To give the zemstvos a voice in matters common to the whole empire would be to break up the unitary executive power of the empire and distribute it among some forty or fifty bodies. This would expose the social order and the entire imperial structure to perils which must be apparent to everyone." After his speech the discussion became so violent that the president had to suspend the sitting. In the end a majority rejected Shcherbatov's proposals.

On January 13, 1864, Alexander II signed the zemstvo statute. The new legislation owed its distinctive character to his personal action in supporting Valuiev against the Miliutins and Reutern. In 1861, he had removed the 'democrats' from the Ministry of the Interior and handed it over to the 'oligarchs'. The new zemstvo statute was the logical and inevitable outcome of that decision, the 'consolation prize' offered to the nobility for the losses of 1861.

The zemstvos were to operate at two levels—district and provincial. They were intended to allow all classes of the population to participate in the conduct of local affairs. Members of the district zemstvo were elected for three years. The electors were divided into three classes, according to a property qualification and on the principle "that participation in the conduct of local affairs should be proportionate to everyone's economic interests". The first class included all landowners, regardless of their social class. In this class, while an estate of a certain size carried one vote, owners of smaller estates had to combine to choose an 'elector' to vote with the larger proprietors. Owners of real property, other than lands attaining a certain value, also possessed a vote.

The second, more numerous, category was composed of townsmen, whose votes also were graded according to wealth. Finally, the peasants elected their representatives by means of a special indirect system. The total membership of each zemstvo was fixed by law in such a way as to prevent the preponderance of any one social group. In fact, for the thirty-three provinces covered by the statute, the total number was fixed at 13,024. Of these, 6,204 were to be elected by the landed proprietors, 1,649 by the townsmen, and 5,171 by the peasants. The landowners, therefore, enjoyed a relative but not an absolute majority. Presently, too, the social composition of the zemstvos would be affected by the fact that non-nobles in increasing numbers were beginning to acquire estates. The provincial zemstvos, dealing with matters affecting a whole province, were elected by members of the district zemstvos from among their own number. At the higher level, there was a marked preponderance of the 'landed element'.

The zemstvos met annually, but their sessions were relatively short. They discussed the outlines of their work, debated and voted the budget, and decided their future policy. To carry out their decisions and direct their permanent secretariat, they elected for three years an executive bureau composed of a president and at least two members. The election of the president was subject to official confirmation by the Governor of the province for the district president, by the Minister of the Interior for the provincial president. The members of the bureau, elected after the president, were not subject to confirmation. The bureaux had the power to engage administrative staff, as well as the specialists necessary to deal with the various branches of regional economy and welfare. As the organization of public instruction and medical assistance required a large number of doctors and teachers, the number of these specialists rose rapidly as the zemstvos extended their activities.

However, the position of the zemstvo executives was not as strong as might appear. They had to carry out orders received from a variety of Ministries on matters like recruiting, billeting of troops, transport. In several branches of regional activity they functioned side by side with organs of the central administration. Contrary to the wishes of Baron Korff, their resolutions had no executive power. To carry out their decisions, and even to collect local taxes, they had, in the last resort, to rely on the ordinary police, which took its orders from the Governor. Only after 1873 were they given the right to make legally binding by-laws with regard to matters like sanitation or fire precautions. The spirit of Valuiev had triumphed; against the wishes of the reformers, the zemstvos had been prevented from growing into fully autonomous institutions of local self-government.

The original intention had been to set up zemstvos without delay in thirty-three provinces. In fact, during 1865 they were opened in nineteen provinces, and during the following year in another nine. By 1875, a further six had come into existence. Mackenzie Wallace, after careful observation of their work, concluded that the zemstvos fulfilled "tolerably well, without scandalous peculation and jobbery", their "commonplace and everyday duties". They had created a new and more equitable system of rating by which landed proprietors and house-owners were made to bear their share of the public burdens. They had done a good deal to provide medical aid and primary education for rural districts. They had 'improved wonderfully' the condition of the hospitals, lunatic asylums, and benevolent institutions committed to their charge. In their efforts to aid the peasantry they had helped to improve the native breeds of horses and cattle, to create a system of obligatory fire insurance, and to make provision for preventing and extinguishing fires—which was extremely important in a country where peasants lived in wooden huts, and where fires were frequent and disastrous.

Something had been done to assist rural industries in the struggle with industrial manufactures. Needs previously neglected were being met for the first time, however inadequately.

More spectacular work was done by the zemstvos in the fields of rural medical and veterinary services—which before had scarcely existed—and, above all, in that of elementary education. In 1856, elementary schools in the empire numbered about 8,000. By 1880 the number reached 23,000 in European Russia alone, of which some 18,000 were financed entirely or in part by the zemstvos. In fact, down to the end of Alexander's reign zemstvo or zemstvo-assisted village schools were created at the average rate of 1,000 each year.

The zemstvo school was beginning to occupy the foremost place in Russian primary education. Wherever the zemstvo village schoolmaster appeared, he came as the agent of progress. As such, he had to fight not only the ignorance of the illiterate peasantry but also the distrust of many landowners and the hostility of officials who regarded him as a dangerous propagandist of democratic ideas. However, in the face of every difficulty, the zemstvo teacher made good his position and soon acquired a reputation for his work.

What the zemstvo statute of 1864 did for the Russian villages, the municipal statute of 1870 did for the Russian towns. The area of local self-government was extended by the creation in all towns above a certain size of elective town councils (dumas) analogous in function and status to the district (and in the largest towns the provincial) zemstvos. The dumas suffered from the same restrictions that hampered the full development of the zemstvos : vexatious supervision over key appointments by the provincial Governors; lack of control over the police; an elective system copied from Prussia, but alien to Russian municipal traditions, based on three electoral groups with a few wealthy citizens enrolled in the first, the bulk of the poorer voters in the third. Yet, in spite of these and other difficulties the dumas, like the zemstvos, did much to revive Russian local life. In Moscow and St. Petersburg in particular a whole network of municipal services was created. Municipal or private enterprises were organized to assure the water supply, to provide for the paving and lighting of roads, to run municipal slaughter-houses. The lesser towns also organized municipal services according to their needs. Everywhere the hospitals were improved and increased.

Above all, the dumas, like the zemstvos, devoted their attention to primary education. Usually the dumas formed education committees, charged with the supervision of municipal schools. The results, especially in the capitals, were spectacular. In St. Petersburg, between 1873 and 1880, the number of municipal schools rose from sixteen to eighty-eight, while the amount devoted to education increased from 27,000 roubles in 1871 to ten times that amount in 1881. In Moscow, the development was equally striking, but even in lesser towns like Kiev or Chernigov the educational budget between 1870 and 1880 increased sevenfold and fifteen-fold respectively. "Beyond a doubt", according to one authority, "if at the end of Alexander's reign the Russian towns awaken from the profound slumber into which they were plunged in the reign of Nicholas, it is thanks to the municipal dumas set up by the law of 1870."

The educational achievements of zemstvos and town dumas had been preceded in point of time by a far-reaching liberalization of the educational system under the auspices of the Ministry of Education. This had become particularly marked during the tenure of Golovnin (1861–6), the trusted assistant of the Grand-Duke Constantine. In 1861, the government, along with the liberation of the serfs, had decided to develop elementary education in the villages. The Holy Synod protested against concentrating the development of primary education in the hands of the Ministry, and claimed for the Orthodox priests "the natural preponderance which is their due". Golovnin vigorously opposed the demand and secured the backing of the Tsar. Early in 1862, an imperial decree laid down that only schools opened by the clergy would be controlled by the Synod; the rest would be supervised by the Ministry of Education. It was the indispensable basis for the later educational work of zemstvos and dumas. Secondary education, previously, had been the virtual monopoly of the nobility. A statute of 1864 proclaimed equality for the future. Anyone would be admitted to a secondary school who could pass the entrance examinations. The Ministry did everything in its power to encourage secondary education. The number of schools and the credits for their maintenance increased, as did the salaries of the masters. The teaching was modernized. Prizes were offered for the best text-books on mathematics, science, and modern languages; the translation of foreign works was encouraged. The 'modernization' of Russian secondary education was largely the fruit of Golovnin's labours.

In higher education the Ministry promoted the autonomy of the universities, severely impaired in the days of Nicholas. The university statute of 1863 crowned Golovnin's efforts in this direction. Every university was to be headed by a Rector, elected for four years from among the professors. The administration was entrusted to a council composed of all the professors. This body was responsible for an extensive field, both academic and administrative. It enjoyed complete freedom in the academic sphere, but many appointments continued to require the approval of the Curator of the educational region, a state official attached to each university. A new institution was created, the university tribunal, with authority over the students in matters of discipline. Its president would be the professor of law, whilst the two remaining members would be elected by the council. At the same time, attempts were made to train the future professors. Scholarships for post-graduate study were awarded to promising students; scientific missions abroad were officially encouraged. Thanks to the régime inaugurated by Golovnin, the Russian universities entered a period of rapid development. The period between 1863 and 1880 has been described as "the most brilliant in the history of the Russian universities".

In the spring of 1865 new 'provisional regulations' for the censorship were promulgated; they remained in operation for the next forty years. These regulations marked a further stage in the 'thaw' which, largely owing to Golovnin, had extended to Russian intellectual life. The preliminary censorship was largely, although not wholly, abolished; judicial procedure was substituted for administrative action in dealing with the bulk of press offences. If the legal protection afforded to the Russian press remained incomplete, and if opportunities for arbitrary administrative action remained, the new regulations yet constituted an undeniable improvement. Indeed, if the 'thaw' continued they would offer adequate safeguards for the freedom of the Russian press.

While Golovnin was restoring a measure of freedom to Russian intellectual life, his colleague, D. A. Miliutin, was revolutionizing the administration of the army. Miliutin was described by Bismarck in 1861 as "the most daring and radical spirit among the reformers" and "the bitterest enemy of the nobility", who thought of the future Russia as "a state of peasants, with equality but without freedom . . . somewhat after the model of Napoleon". Already, as a young officer in the Guards Artillery, Miliutin had attracted attention by publishing numerous studies on mathematical and military subjects. Early in 1840 he had seen active service in the Caucasus and been wounded in action against the mountaineers. In 1845 he had been appointed professor at the Military Academy, and during the next fifteen years he published a number of learned works, the best known of which was a study of Suvorov's campaign in 1799. In 1861 he was appointed Minister of War, a post he filled for twenty years. As Minister he continued to maintain close relations with scientific and literary circles, and his friends included the radical professor, Kavelin. He took a lively interest in all social and educational questions. His military reform bears the imprint of his liberal and egalitarian ideas.

Miliutin's first achievement as Minister of War was effectively to reduce the more cruel forms of corporal punishment. The question had been raised in the spring of 1861 in a letter addressed to the Tsar by N. A. Orlov (son of the celebrated 'planter'), the Russian Minister in Brussels. Both Miliutin and the Grand-Duke Constantine, as Minister of Marine, had thrown themselves heart and soul into the struggle. The leading defenders of branding, flogging, and 'spitzruthen' (flogging through the ranks) were the Minister of Justice, Panin, and the Metropolitan Philaret. Their resistance, however, proved unavailing. On his forty-fifth birthday, April 29, 1863, Alexander signed the celebrated ukase abolishing both in the armed forces and for civil prisoners the crueller and more barbarous forms of punishment. Women, except those sentenced to banishment, were exempted from corporal punishment. For men only the milder forms were 'temporarily' retained for certain offences. It was a great humanitarian reform which completely altered the spirit of the Russian army and navy.

Miliutin's tenure of the Ministry of War was marked by a series of enlightened reforms. He began by reducing the term of military service from twenty-five to sixteen years, and by abolishing the more cruel forms of capital punishment. The Military Code was revised and punishments were reduced. The procedure of military courts was modified to bring it more into line with that established for the civil courts in 1864. The practice of using military service as a form of civil punishment was abolished. The condition of the common soldier was improved. At the same time administrative changes improved military efficiency. The obsolescent weapons of the Crimean War were steadily replaced by up-to-date arms and equipment. The command of the troops was decentralized by the setting up of a number of regional commands. The status of the General Staff was raised, and in 1865 the post of Chief of the General Staff was created. Reforms were carried out in the commissariat and the medical services; military engineering was improved, the construction of strategic railways was speeded up. There was hardly a field of military administration that was not touched by the modernizing spirit.

Nowhere was that spirit more noticeable than in the training of future officers. The old Cadet Corps had been fundamentally hostile to any instruction which was not purely military. Moreover, in their military training they had concentrated on routine and formalism, drill and military ceremonial. Miliutin's changes in this field were far-reaching. The Cadet Corps were replaced by army schools (gymnasia), which were organized like their civilian counterparts, only with the addition of their specialist military instruction. Having acquired some general education, pupils then passed to special schools for officer cadets to prepare for service with their chosen branch of the army. Miliutin's reforms thus provided the Russian army with officers who had both a better general education and a better technical training than their predecessors. The new spirit, moreover, did not stop at the schools for future officers. Thanks to Miliutin's efforts, a beginning was made in teaching recruits how to read and write.

Miliutin's main achievement, however, was the introduction of conscription. Under the old system, the obligation of military service rested exclusively on the 'tax-paying orders', that is, the peasants and the lower middle class. From the moment of his appointment, Miliutin urged the abolition of this system of recruiting as incompatible with the emancipation of the serfs. In 1863 a Commission was formed under the Ministry of War to prepare a new statute on military service. The work advanced slowly in the face of bitter opposition. The nobles, still smarting under the 'insult' of 1861, would not hear of their sons being placed on a footing of equality with those of their former serfs. The wealthy merchants were enraged that their wealth should no longer entitle them, as in the past, to buy their sons exemption from military service. Influential Ministers like Tolstoy, Golovnin's successor at the Ministry of Education, and Pahlen, the reactionary Minister of Justice, bitterly opposed the proposals. With the reaction which set in in 1866, a reform in the system of recruiting became, in fact, impracticable.

Plans for reform, however, received a new impetus from the Prussian victories in 1870-1. Under the impact of Moltke's triumphs, a Commission was set up in St. Petersburg to prepare a further measure of military reform. Miliutin drew up a memorandum embodying the principles he hoped to incorporate in it. "The defence of the fatherland", the first article bravely proclaimed, "forms the sacred duty of *every* Russian citizen." The actual call-up would be determined by ballot; only those unfit for service would be exempt. Temporary postponement would be granted in exceptional circumstances on compassionate grounds or in the interests of the national economy. Substitution and exemption by purchase would disappear. Service would continue to be for fifteen years, of which six would be spent with the colours and the rest in the reserve. Miliutin's basic principles were confirmed by Alexander. Many zemstvo assemblies and town dinners, and even a few assemblies of the nobility, presented addresses welcoming the proposals.

No organized opposition against the introduction of conscription developed, but numerous attempts were made during the legislative stages of the measure to secure special privileges and exemptions for a number of different groups. Miliutin, with the support of Alexander, was able to resist most of these demands for special treatment. On January 1, 1874, Alexander signed the statute on military service, conceived wholly in the spirit of the reform. "Under present legislation the duty of military service falls exclusively on the lower class of town dwellers and on the peasants. A significant section of the Russian people is exempt from a duty which should be equally sacred for all. Such an order of things, which came into being in different circumstances, no longer accords with the changed conditions of national life; nor does it satisfy our military needs. Recent events have shown that the strength of armies is based not only on the number of soldiers but on their moral and intellectual qualities. These attain their highest development where the defence of the fatherland has become the common concern of the whole people and where all, without exception and without distinction of calling or estate, combine in this sacred task." The new statute would carry these principles into practice.

Under the new law all young men on reaching the age of twenty became liable to military service. Only three groups were exempted on compassionate grounds, a concession which applied equally to all classes of the population. Each year the number of conscripts required from each military district was chosen by ballot among those liable for service. These recruits had to serve with the colours for six years, after which for nine years they passed into the reserve. Thereafter they were liable for service in a territorial militia until the age of forty. The length of active service was shortened in accordance with educational attainment. Recruits who had completed a higher education served only six months, those with a secondary education two years. Completion of the higher form of elementary schooling, above the level of the village school, reduced active service to three years. Finally, service would be still further reduced for young men who volunteered for service without being drawn by ballot.

The significance of Miliutin's reforms has been summarized by Florinsky : "The new method of conscription was a step towards social equality, even though shorter terms of service for holders of diplomas favoured proprietary groups. The softening of discipline and emphasis on educational activities gave the army an opportunity of contributing to the enlightenment of the masses. Much of the old brutality in the treatment of men by their officers no doubt remained. But the pre-reform army as a penal institution was gone. Men with criminal records were excluded from the forces. Strange as this may seem, it was in the army . . . that Russian democracy scored one of its first modest yet real successes." If Miliutin was able to carry to a successful conclusion his democratic reforms, this was due in no small degree to the Tsar's personal support. Almost since the beginning of his reforming activities, Miliutin had been bitterly criticized by a group of 'old-fashioned' soldiers, who accused him of destroying the army by undermining its discipline and, more justly, of favouring the Staff at the expense of officers in the field. These attacks were inspired by no less a personage than the formidable Field-Marshal Prince Bariatinsky, the popular and self-willed conqueror of the Caucasus. Miliutin, secure in his master's confidence, could afford to ignore criticisms which, in other circumstances, must have put an end to his reforming career.

Like Miliutin, Reutern, the Minister of Finance, was able to carry out important reforms, thanks to Alexander's constant support. Some of the changes introduced by him were of a technical nature. Before 1862 important sources of revenue had been administered independently by various government departments. Reutern for the first time created a unified Treasury and centralized the accounts of all departments in the Ministry of Finance. He improved the methods of audit, and after 1862 the budget was made public. The following year a system of government excise replaced the pernicious system of farming out the sale of spirits.

Of far greater importance than Reutern's technical reforms, however, were his successful efforts to develop the economic life of the empire. The key to Russia's economic progress lay in railway construction, and under Reutern the Ministry of Finance devoted much of its time and resources to the promotion of railway building by private companies. The results achieved were striking. At Alexander's accession the total permanent way of the empire amounted to some 660 miles —of which a considerable proportion was constituted by the Polish section of the line linking Warsaw and Vienna. When Alexander died, the mileage of Russian railways was approximately 14,000. The peak in railway construction occurred between 1868 and 1874. A special effort was made to construct the new lines in a manner to promote the export of Russian grain. The object was fully achieved. Whereas between 1861 and 1865, the average annual export of grain had amounted to some 76 million poods,[1] it had risen for the period 1876–80 to an annual average of 257 million. Along with the economic revival and with the active encouragement of the Ministry of Finance, a great expansion took place in Russian credit institutions. While at the beginning of the reign private banks had hardly existed, the situation was greatly changed between 1863 and 1877. Towards the end of the reign, Russia possessed not only 278 municipal banks but also 33 joint-stock commercial banks. There were 92 societies for mutual credit, and no fewer than 727 loan and savings associations with a total membership of over

[1] One pood equals 36 lb.

200,000. The number of joint-stock companies in the empire had risen to 566, with a total capital (mainly Russian) of over 750 million roubles. The policy of Reutern laid the foundation for a great commercial and industrial development.

The reforms carried out under the auspices of Alexander II thus touched virtually every department of Russian life. Almost everywhere the preponderance of the gentry was reduced, its exclusive privileges cut down or abolished. Everywhere the autonomy of local bodies was increased, the rigid centralization of Nicholas I relaxed. 'Medieval' survivals disappeared from many walks of Russian life. Education and enlightenment assumed a new importance in the zemstvos and dumas, the army and the navy. At the same time railways, credit institutions, better courts, and reformed fiscal and tariff policies laid the foundation for rapid economic development. Russia was ready to turn from a medieval into a modern state.

Yet the undoubted social and economic transformation was uneven and incomplete. Everywhere the institutions of Nicholas continued to exist side by side with those of the reforming age. The Ministry of the Interior controlling the all-important provincial Governors, whose powers were undiminished, remained in the hands of bureaucratic centralizers. The 'self-governing' institutions created by the reforms had little opportunity to develop any real independence. At every step there was unresolved conflict between the new and the old. "The emancipation", writes the French scholar Leroy-Beaulieu, "was followed by numerous reforms, administrative, judicial, military, even financial; yet all these reforms, prepared by different commissions subject to rival or hostile influences, were undertaken in isolation, in an incomplete manner, without coherence and without a definite plan. The task was to build a new Russia; the edifice was constructed upon the old foundations. Building operations were carried out without a blue-print, without a general plan, without an architect to co-ordinate the different operations. By introducing here and there particular innovations while neglecting near-by indispensable repairs; by incorporating everywhere his innovations into the ancient structure, Alexander in the end succeeded after immense labours in making of the new Russia an incomplete and uncomfortable dwelling where friends and opponents of innovation felt almost equally ill at ease."

The task of reconstructing Russia was gigantic; Alexander lacked the firmness, the vision, and the statesmanlike grasp of detail to be completely successful. He showed the same weaknesses in another important field. Nowhere, in fact, was the need for new beginnings more urgent than in Russia's relations with Poland and Finland, the two autonomous states joined to her. Yet in this sphere also Alexander's success, though promising, was—not entirely through his own fault—partial and incomplete.

Chapter Five

Alexander, the Poles, and the Finns

THE Poles were among the first to benefit from the Russian 'thaw'. Early in 1856 Paskievich, the iron governor of Warsaw, followed Tsar Nicholas to the grave. His successor, Michael Gorchakov, began, with the Tsar's full support, to dismantle the system of repression. The crowded prisons emptied, Paskievich's ubiquitous spies disappeared from public life. The hated military tribunals ceased to function. An amnesty allowed *émigrés* as well as Siberian exiles to return to their native land. In the summer of 1857 a medical school, widely regarded as the precursor of a restored Polish university, was opened at Warsaw. The Concordat, a dead letter since its conclusion in 1847, was put into operation. Finally, the Russian authorities permitted the establishment of the so-called Agricultural Society. With branches all over Poland, it was nothing less than a political organization of the Polish nobility led by Prince Andrew Zamoyski. The Poles, therefore, had every reason to welcome the accession of Alexander II.

However, the new Tsar would no more sanction any form of Polish political autonomy than his father after 1831. This, it was held, would simply pave the way for a demand that the Kingdom should be restored to the frontiers of 1772. The incorporation in a new Poland of Russia's western provinces, however, would destroy the unity of the empire and weaken its strategic position. Alexander therefore rejected the idea of any autonomy for the Poles of the Kingdom. During his first visit to

Warsaw as King of Poland, in May 1856, he told Polish notables that he would not change the government of the country. "I will not change anything; what was done by my father was done well. My reign will be a continuation of his." The happiness of Poland depended on "her complete fusion with the peoples of my empire", and the clergy should impress on their parishioners the need for "union with Holy Russia". To curb the political aspirations of the Poles, Alexander twice repeated his celebrated warning against impossible dreams ('*point de rêveries!*'), followed by a distinct threat against those who would not renounce their hopes. Life would be made easier for the Poles, but they must not attempt to sever the political ties uniting them with Russia.

The policy of a 'thaw' within the existing political framework could not satisfy Polish patriots. The leaders of the Polish national movement regarded Gorchakov's mildness as merely an invitation to prepare for a new revolt. Agricultural societies, societies of students and officers arose everywhere and got into touch with each other and with *émigré* committees abroad. The Catholic hierarchy lent its tacit support. Almost unawares the Polish nationalists passed from organization to demonstration. Memorial services were held to commemorate the deaths of Polish national writers. In June 1860 some 20,000 mourners marched to the funeral of the widow of a Polish general killed fighting the Russians in 1831. In November the thirtieth anniversary of the great rising was celebrated, the streets of Warsaw resounding with patriotic hymns. In February 1861 two great demonstrations were organized, during the second of which demonstrators began to skirmish with the police. Russian troops fired on the crowd, killing five and wounding many more.

Faced with mounting tension, Gorchakov tried to avoid all semblance of provocation. Not only all Russian troops but even the police were withdrawn from the streets of Warsaw. A self-appointed 'Delegation' of twelve prominent citizens was permitted to assume responsibility for the maintenance of public order. For forty days it practically ruled Warsaw with the help of a newly formed municipal guard of 2,000 commanded by an Italian, the Marquis Paulucci. The latter assumed his functions amid cheers for Garibaldi and Italy. Delegations similar to that of Warsaw were set up in other Polish towns. The victims of the shooting affray in the capital, regarded as martyrs for their country, received a public funeral. Gorchakov consented to accept an Address to the Tsar from the Agricultural Society, demanding (in somewhat ambiguous terms) the restoration of Polish autonomy. It seemed clear that Russian authority in Poland was disintegrating and that the Tsar's policy of mildness unaccompanied by political concessions was proving a failure.

In face of this situation, opinion at St. Petersburg was divided. In 'liberal' circles there was widespread sympathy for national movements, not only in Poland but in Italy and Hungary as well. It was widely held that concessions to the Poles would bring nearer the day of constitutional changes in Russia itself. Supporters of moderate Pan–Slavism favoured a policy of leniency towards the misguided Polish brothers. At this time there was a widespread readiness among the Russian upper classes to give freedom to the Poles in the Kingdom. Such were the views of some influential personages —the Grand-Duke Constantine and his wife, Alexander Gorchakov, the Foreign Minister, and Valuiev. On the other hand, a strong conservative and military party wished to reassert Russian authority in Poland, if necessary by force of arms. The Tsar now had to choose between putting Poland under martial law and an extension of his policy of concession and reform.

Alexander's first decision on Polish policy was in favour of conciliation. The 'polonophiles' in his entourage had for some time been directing his attention to a wealthy Polish magnate, Alexander Wielopolski. At one time in favour of complete independence for Poland, Wielopolski was now reconciled to working for more limited ends in co-operation with the Tsar. At most he hoped for a return by gradual stages to the constitution of 1815. After a favourable report by Michael Gorchakov, Wielopolski in the spring of 1861 was appointed director of a national Polish commission for religious and educational matters. Following his advice, the Tsar adopted a policy of internal development for Poland. A ukase of March 26, 1861, outlined a programme of reform. Elections would be held in the autumn both for municipal councils and district and provincial assemblies. A Polish Council of State would be set up. Education, under the auspices of Wielopolski's Commission, would be 'polonized'. There would be new Polish secondary schools, and a 'Main School' in Warsaw, a university in all but name. With these concessions Alexander and Wielopolski hoped to reconcile the more conservative and moderate elements in Polish society to a continuance of the Russian connection.

At the same time, Wielopolski was determined to re-establish the authority of the government in the Kingdom. His first act as the virtual ruler of Poland was to close the Agricultural Society. This provoked demonstrations, during which some demonstrators were killed and a number of others injured. The Tsar, on receiving the news, called on Gorchakov, the Viceroy, to take energetic measures. "Please God", he wrote, "that the lesson given to the Warsaw populace on 27 March may have cured it of the desire for similar demonstrations. I insist that at the first sign of their renewal a state of siege should be declared in Warsaw and the Provinces." While Gorchakov, ailing and pacific, was reluctant to aggravate the situation, Wielopolski was disbanding not only the Warsaw 'Delegation' and Paulucci's municipal guard, but also the oppositional Nobles' Club. The result was a further riot, involving loss of life. Alexander now called for energetic action. Gorchakov, unable to stand the strain, fell seriously ill. At the end of May his deputy, a Russian general, was ordered to take over the civil administration of the Kingdom pending the arrival of Sukhozanet, the Minister of War. Sukhozanet, with the help of the Russian garrison, would restore public order and remain in command until the arrival of a new Viceroy, Adjutant-General Count Lambert. The latter, a Roman Catholic personally close to the Tsar, would carry forward the policy of Wielopolski once order had been restored. The Tsar's course, therefore, would be one of firmness in restoring order, accompanied by the grant of the promised reforms.

While Gorchakov lay dying, unrest in Warsaw increased. Demonstrations in the streets, the singing of patriotic hymns in the churches, and masses for the victims of earlier riots were accompanied by daily clashes between populace and police. Sukhozanet reached Warsaw on June 4, five days after Gorchakov's death. Military courts were once again set up. Rioters were banished without trial to the interior of the empire. Order slowly returned to the streets of Warsaw.

Sukhozanet's policy of repression, however, aroused the hostility of Wielopolski. The real ruler of Poland under the aged Gorchakov, the marquis now found himself pushed into the shade by a ruthless Russian soldier. After repeated clashes, he resigned his post in the Polish administration. Alexander, who regretted this, allowed the marquis to send his son to St. Petersburg for personal explanations. The result was an imperial order that Wielopolski should remain at his post pending the arrival of Lambert. Alexander continued to believe in his policy of combining firmness with conciliation.

Lambert reached Warsaw on August 24, and at once fell under Wielopolski's influence. He observed correct legal forms in all his proceedings, encouraged the new administrative autonomy, and showed respect for Polish nationality. Wielopolski was confirmed in his appointment as President of the Commission of Justice and became Vice-President of the State Council. Lambert's mildness, however, was no more successful than Gorchakov's had been. Street processions and the singing of patriotic hymns were resumed. Mounting excitement greeted the news of disorders in Vilna and the declaration of martial law in Lithuania. Alexander wished to impose martial law on the restive parts of Poland. Lambert, prompted by Wielopolski, tried to dissuade him. The Tsar insisted : "For too long already, the agitators have come to count on our forbearance, which they ascribed to weakness and lack of decision. I repeat once again : this state of things must end." On October 11, in the face of continued disorders, Lambert at last declared a state of emergency. Three days later services to commemorate the death of Kosciuszko were held in three Warsaw churches. Russian troops surrounded the churches; two of the congregations refused to leave. On the following morning Russian soldiers entered the churches and made some 1,600 arrests. The Catholic hierarchy in reply closed all churches in the capital. Lambert was in despair. After a violent scene the military commander, General Gerstenzweig, committed suicide. Lambert resigned. Nothing seemed left but a policy of military repression.

Alexander once more had recourse to Sukhozanet, who was again sent to Warsaw with orders "not to permit any illegal acts on any pretext whatever", to sentence the guilty in accordance with the military code and carry out the sentence on the spot. On hearing of Sukhozanet's impending return, Wielopolski resigned. After refusing to listen to the Tsar's appeal to remain at his post, he was summoned to St. Petersburg for explanations. Sukhozanet's severe measures once more restored order, after which he handed over the command to General Luders, Lambert's successor as Viceroy.

Warsaw was now given over to military rule.

Throughout the winter Russian troops bivouacked in the streets of the city. Offenders were tried by military courts; thousands of rifles and other weapons were confiscated; refractory priests were banished to the interior of the empire. Yet at St. Petersburg the party of moderation remained in the ascendant. Constantine continued to smypathize with Wielopolski; Bludov, Gorchakov, and Valuiev still pursued the forlorn hope of winning over Polish 'moderates'. Wielopolski became a much sought after figure in St. Petersburg society. On his advice Felinski, a young professor of the Catholic Academy in St. Petersburg, was appointed to the vacant see of Warsaw. The new archbishop in a conciliatory spirit reopened the closed churches. Wielopolski received permission to visit Warsaw for deliberations in the Council of State on his project for improving the condition of the peasantry. The Tsar, moreover, accepted his recommendation for the complete separation of the civil and military powers in the Kingdom. However, the new head of the civil administration must be a Russian. The Tsar's choice for the post fell on Nicholas Miliutin. The Grand-Duke Constantine opposed the appointment. In his opinion what was needed was 'not a Russian but a Pole'.

Alexander, ever ready to listen to his brother, determined to make a last desperate effort to pacify Poland without further repression. He decided to recall Luders and appoint Constantine in his place. Wielopolski, under the Grand-Duke, would head the civil administration. "The sad conviction", Alexander wrote in the official instructions to his brother, "that all our efforts for the well-being of the Kingdom will never meet the impracticable aims and desires of the extreme patriotic, that is, revolutionary party, must not deflect us from our course." Once again the basic principles of Russian policy were re-stated. The main object would be the restoration of law and order throughout the Kingdom. At the same time, the distinctive institutions of the country would be developed and the reforms either begun or promised would be carried out. Neither a constitution nor a national army was to be thought of, as either of these would amount to a recognition of Polish independence. On the contrary, Poland must always remain, within her present boundaries, an integral part of the Russian empire. Her advanced geographical position made her a bridge between Russia and the rest of Europe.

Alexander's supreme effort at pacification began under unfavourable auspices. Five days before the Grand-Duke's arrival in Warsaw, Luders was seriously wounded by an assassin. Constantine, the day after his arrival, was fired at when leaving the theatre. The following month two attempts were made on the life of Wielopolski. At the same time popular demonstrations continued. In this unpromising situation Constantine and Wielopolski, with a mere handful of supporters, tried to carry out their difficult task of combining repression and reform. The would-be assassins were hanged; Zamoyski was exiled from the Kingdom; Constantine appealed to the Poles to eschew violence and terror. He received generals and merchants, rabbis and artisans. Martial law was lifted in a number of provinces. In August elections were held for some of the new provincial councils. Poles replaced Russians in many official posts; Polish became the language for all official business in the Kingdom. Polish returned to the schools; the 'Main School' at Warsaw was reopened. Jews were relieved of their legal disabilities. A new land law freed the peasants from compulsory labour services.

It was all to no avail. Patriotic demonstrations continued. Secret leaflets called for resistance to the authorities. Collections were started for a rising. Wielopolski, to save his policy, had recourse to an expedient of doubtful legality. A levy of recruits was decreed. The decree—in violation of a law of 1859 prescribing selection by ballot—was phrased in a way to permit the call-up of youths known to be active in the revolutionary movement. In Wielopolski's own words, it was a proscription rather than a conscription. The intentions of the government were betrayed by Polish officials to the revolutionary leaders. When, in January 1863, an attempt was made to execute the plan, only a quarter of the intended conscripts could be apprehended : the rest had fled to the woods. The unsuccessful conscription became the signal, as well as the pretext, for the long-prepared Polish insurrection. The policy of conciliating the conservative elements of Polish society—first followed by Alexander I and later revived by his nephew—had failed irrevocably. Alexander, who for years had sincerely attempted to apply it, was embittered by what he considered Polish ingratitude. Henceforth, he would show little mercy to Polish nationalism, the Polish upper classes, or the Roman Catholic clergy. From now on, he would seek support from the Polish peasantry. He would return to his father's policy of Russification.

Before the new policy could be applied, it was necessary to suppress the insurrection. In spite of great discrepancy in military forces—10,000 inadequately trained and poorly armed Poles against 80,000 Russian regulars—the rising was not finally suppressed until the spring of 1864. The Poles, disunited and ill-led, fought a bitter guerilla war. The Western powers tried to help them by an unavailing diplomatic campaign. At one moment the movement spread, rather ineffectively, into Russia's western provinces, but whereas in the Kingdom the peasants had at least remained passive, those of Lithuania and the Ukraine tended to side with the Russian authorities. After this double failure, the suppression of the insurrection was simply a matter of time.

The Polish rising led inevitably to the abandonment of Wielopolski's policy. In April Constantine was given an assistant, Count Berg, who represented the party of military repression. In June Wielopolski left Poland, a broken man, to spend the rest of his life in disillusionment at Dresden. Michael Muraviev, the reactionary Minister of Domains, became Governor-General of the six north-western provinces with his headquarters at Vilna. Early in September Constantine resigned and was succeeded by Berg. Nicholas Miliutin went to Poland as Secretary of State with Special Functions, accompanied by his Slavophil friends, Samarin and Cherkassky. Cherkassky was appointed head of the civil administration. Soloviev, the friend of the Russian peasants, became head of a Polish department for peasant affairs.

The new men began the double policy of punishing the Polish upper classes and conciliating the peasantry. Muraviev now gained unenviable notoriety as the 'Hangman of Vilna' by his terror against the Poles. The destruction of insurgent bands in Lithuania was followed by mass executions, punitive expeditions, and the wholesale deportation of Polish families to Siberia. Exorbitant fines were imposed on the rebels; some 1,700 estates were confiscated. Severe penalties were imposed for hostile demonstrations, the wearing of mourning, and the use of the Polish language. Punitive action was followed by administrative measures. Catholic monasteries were closed, priests subjected to various restrictions. Conversions to Orthodoxy were encouraged among the Uniat peasants. Orthodox churches were built. Confiscated estates were given to Russian soldiers and officials. Peasant allotments were increased payments reduced by 2 to 16 per cent. redemption payments reduced by 2 to 16 per cent. Orthodox peasants and villagers of Old Believers were generously endowed with land to pay for the better maintenance of Orthodox priests. When Muraviev left Vilna in 1865, he had done much to 'depolonize' Lithuania. The policy was continued by his successor, General Kaufmann.

In the Polish Kingdom a similar pacification was

meanwhile being carried out by Berg. Miliutin and his friends, moreover, were preparing the measure which would strike the death-blow at the dominant position of the Polish gentry. On 19 February/1 March, 1864 (the third anniversary of emancipation in Russia), an imperial ukase endowed the Polish peasants with allotments more generous than those which had been given to their Russian brethren. One-third of all Polish land became the permanent property of the peasants. Unlike their Russian counterparts, the Poles retained the right to use the pastures and some of the woods belonging to their former masters. Woods in which peasants had rights could not be alienated. Peasant land, moreover, could be sold only to peasants. Redemption payments in Poland were less burdensome than in Russia. The peasants merely paid a moderate land tax, levied on *all* land, by means of which the government recouped itself for the sums paid to the landowners in compensation. Administrative arrangements also favoured the peasants. The noble landowners included in the rural communes were often outvoted, on the basis of the size of holdings, by the peasantry. It was the end of a Poland dominated by the gentry and the beginning of her history as a predominantly peasant country.

Miliutin had come to the conclusion that his 'democratic' policy could be carried out only by Russians. In consequence, the remaining Polish institutions were gradually abolished. In 1866 the Kingdom officially lost its name and became the Vistula Region. Its ten provinces were placed under a Russian Governor-General. Administrative amalgamation was accompanied by cultural Russification. Russian became the language of instruction in Polish schools. In 1869 the university of Warsaw was completely russianized. All this was a reversal of Alexander's earlier policies, yet one which circumstances had forced upon him. His wish had been for a slow autonomous evolution of the Kingdom, not for a policy of violent Russification. Similarly he had hoped to work with the moderate nobility and turned to the peasants only as a second choice. As long as was humanly possible, he had persevered in the course recommended by Wielopolski and Constantine. If he had been finally forced to abandon it, this was due almost entirely to the unrealistic dreams and uncompromising line of the Polish patriots and revolutionaries. If the birth of modern Poland was the result of Russian tyranny rather than peaceful Polish evolution, the fault lies not with Alexander but with the Polish nobles who, like the Bourbons, could neither learn nor forget.

The nature of the development Alexander desired for Poland can be seen clearly in his policy towards the Grand-Duchy of Finland. Already, as Tsarevich, he had acquired considerable popularity as Chancellor of Helsingfors University. When, shortly after the conclusion of peace, he paid Finland his first official visit, he was received with enthusiasm. However, as on the occasion of his visit to Warsaw, he struck a warning note. Alluding to the small separatist movement in favour of a return to Sweden, he declared that it was not sufficient merely to be a good Finn. The inhabitants of the duchy must also feel themselves a part of the great empire headed by the Russian Tsar. As in Poland, Alexander outlined a programme of reform. Its main object was to develop the productive forces of the country by the encouragement of trade and the construction of canals and railways. He also promised an extension of elementary education.

The execution of this policy was entrusted to the recently appointed Governor-General, Count Berg, the later Viceroy of Poland. From the beginning Berg showed a sincere concern for the welfare of Finland. In the autumn of 1856, a committee was formed under his presidency to examine the question of communications. Finnish political opinion was divided : conservative officials of the previous reign opposed the construction of railways and wished to develop water communications instead. The liberals favoured a railway linking Helsingfors with the interior. Berg sided with the liberals and helped them to carry the day both in the Senate, the highest administrative body of the Grand-Duchy, and at St. Petersburg. In 1858 work on the line was begun in earnest : it was completed within four years. The railway, combined with new steamship lines on the lakes of the interior, quickened economic life in regions far away from the coast—agriculture in particular benefited from the new developments.

In 1857 Berg chose an assistant in the person of Fabian Langenskiöld, the Governor of Åbo, whom he introduced into the Senate as Minister of Finance. Under their joint ægis efforts were made to develop the country's natural resources. Finnish-speaking agricultural schools were opened. A beginning was made in developing the vast forests of the country. A German expert was invited to advise on them, an Institute of Forestry was opened, a Forestry Service was formed. Saw-mills were freed from fiscal restrictions, and an expansion of the industry followed. In 1860 a credit bank for agriculture was set up; a year later the first private bank. The inequitable Russian tariff on Finnish goods was revised. Finland got her own coinage. Langenskiöld raised a loan in Russia to finance the railway and the currency reform. Guild regulations were relaxed in the backward countryside. They could not, however, be abolished entirely without the Finnish Diet. In this way, during the early years of Alexander's reign, Berg and Langenskiöld laid the foundations of the modern Finnish economy.

But Finnish liberals, like the Polish patriots, wanted more than economic progress. No Finnish Diet had met since 1809, and there was a widespread demand that one should now be called. Administrative as well as political reasons made this desirable. It was more than doubtful whether the new loan for railway construction was constitutional without the approval of the Diet.

And without its participation it was impossible to remove completely the antiquated guild restrictions. Its absence was holding up a number of other reforms. For these reasons even Berg—no friend to elective assemblies—favoured a meeting of the Diet. There had been hopes at the time of Alexander's coronation, but they had been disappointed. During the coronation ceremonies at Helsingfors, the Rector of the university had discoursed on the functions and constitutional importance of the Finnish Diet. His speech was printed and circulated. As severe censorship still prevented all discussion of the 'Diet question', this created a sensation. The Tsar in annoyance gave orders that the Rector should be reprimanded. However, Alexander was soon pacified owing to the intervention of Alexander Armfelt, the Finnish Secretary of State at St. Petersburg. Armfelt, the 'Finnish Wielopolski', enjoyed the Tsar's confidence and was his trusted adviser on the affairs of the duchy. Alexander declared, peaceably enough, that the Rector's unfortunate speech had helped to delay concessions which he wished to make to the Finns. Pressure from below tied his hands, as he had to consider other parts of his empire. Shortly after the incident, Armfelt—against the advice of Berg—secured the reestablishment at St. Petersburg of a Committee on Finnish Affairs, which was joined by two elected representatives of the Finnish Senate.

In the meantime Berg prevented all further discussion of the 'Diet Question'. However, in the interest of his economic reforms, he from time to time made unofficial inquiries at St. Petersburg. The invariable reply was that, while the Tsar's disposition was not unfavourable, a meeting of the Finnish Diet was inopportune on account of possible repercussions in Russia. However, during 1859, Berg won a preliminary success. In response to one of his inquiries the Finnish Senate was asked to draw up a list of matters requiring legislative action. He was not without hope that this might pave the way for an eventual meeting of the Diet.

The Italian national movement was a stimulus to Finnish aspirations. When it was learnt, too, that the first demonstrations in Warsaw had led to an extension of Polish autonomy, the conviction gained ground in Helsingfors that the Diet would soon be called. In the spring of 1861 the Tsar declared that a Diet in Finland would increase unrest among the Poles and aggravate the agrarian situation in Russia. Langenskiöld in reply suggested the formation, as a first instalment, of a 'skeleton' Diet to study legislation on the questions listed by the Senate. Accepting this, the Tsar invited the four Finnish estates (nobility, clergy, townsmen, and peasants) to elect forty-eight representatives, twelve from each estate, to examine matters to be laid before them by the government. They should then submit recommendations on the basis of which 'interim regulations', valid until the next Diet, would be introduced.

The proposal had a mixed reception in Helsingfors, where it was regarded as an attempt to by-pass the Diet. Five liberal Senators invited the Emperor to declare that the new body would only prepare drafts for submission to the next Diet. Radical students organized a demonstration in support of the Senators. Alexander promised that any measures adopted before the meeting of the Diet would be temporary. In the summer the 'Committee' was constituted, but many of its members had made reservations before agreeing to join. Moreover, Finns at St. Petersburg informed the Tsar that the 'Committee' would function only if Berg were replaced as Governor-General. He had made himself unpopular by his high-handed methods, and in November, at his own request, he was relieved of his duties.

Rokossovski, the new Governor-General, of whose qualities the Tsar himself had a low opinion, was well received in Helsingfors. The appointment had been recommended by Armfelt, who knew that his countrymen would welcome a more 'easy-going' representative of Alexander as Grand-Duke. Rokossovski's appointment marked a turning-point in Finnish affairs. Not only did the new Governor relax the censorship so much complained of under Berg, but he made on the Tsar's behalf a formal promise that the Diet would be called when the 'Committee' had completed its task.

The Tsar's promise was repeated more formally in a letter to the President of the 'Committee' early in 1862. By March that body had completed its labours. In July Alexander authorized the drawing up of new standing rules for the proceedings of the Diet. Even the open sympathy for the Poles shown by much of the Finnish press and public did not deflect him from his course. At the height of the Polish crisis in the summer of 1863, an official decree announced that the new Finnish Diet would meet on September 15. At the elections the more moderate elements among the Finns carried the day. In opening the Diet in September, Alexander proclaimed that "in the hands of a wise nation . . . liberal institutions not only are not dangerous but are a guarantee of order and well-being". He added a promise that Diets should be called at regular intervals.

The sessions of the Diet lasted until the following spring. Liberal deputies constantly raised constitutional points, often of a trivial nature. But, apart from this, the Diet did much to promote the well-being of Finland. Money was voted for elementary education, railway construction, and currency reform. Provision was made for extending village self-government. Laws safeguarding freedom of publication were drafted. The National Bank was placed under the control of the Estates. Alexander was irritated by the aggressive spirit shown by some of the deputies and saw less the solid achievement than the ingratitude of the critics. His closing speech, read in Russian by Rokossovski, was blunt, and concentrated on listing the advantages derived by Finland from her association with Russia.

Yet Alexander's irritation involved no change of policy. Throughout the years which followed the Finnish constitution was scrupulously observed. Diets, called at regular intervals, were enabled to develop Finnish autonomy. In 1865 the Senate decreed that after the first day of 1872 all officials in the duchy must use only the Finnish language. A law introduced in 1869 ended church control over schools, while at the same time reducing the power of the state in Church affairs. In 1874 a reformed conscription law was introduced. Three years later Finland adopted the gold standard.

In this manner, in the reign of Alexander II and sometimes with his personal participation, the foundations of modern Finland were laid. To the Finns, his assassination in 1881 was an occasion of sincere regret and grief. To this day, while other relics of Russian rule have long since vanished from Finland, the statue of the 'Tsar Liberator' dominates the Senate Square in the heart of official Helsinki.

Alexander, therefore, may be regarded as the father of modern Finland as well as of modern Poland. In both countries he endeavoured to pursue a policy of reform and gradual progress towards increasing autonomy. The Poles did not, indeed could not, respond to this approach; the Finns, in spite of a widespread desire for speedier evolution, had the good sense and statesmanship to content themselves with the possible. Wielopolski's policy ended in disaster, that of Armfelt in modest success. Alexander, in Poland and in Finland, pursued his course with tenacity in the face of disappointments and provocation. Ignoring the attacks of Russian nationalists who blamed him for going too far and of radicals who considered his progress too slow, he followed steadfastly the path of reform combined with the maintenance of order and authority. Provided the unity of the empire was maintained—and it is difficult to blame an emperor of Russia for making this proviso —Alexander was eager to promote the well-being of his 'satellite' subjects. In Poland and Finland, as in the rest of the empire, his policy was one of moderate reform and 'modernization'.

Chapter Six

The Tsar Despot

IN the empire proper, as in Poland and Finland, Alexander soon experienced the difficulties inseparable from a 'thaw' accompanied by major reforms. The relaxation of the reins of government following thirty years of Nicholas's stern regime was naturally accompanied by a decline in the imperial authority. A public without political sense or experience, rigidly debarred for decades from all share in public affairs, took advantage of freer conditions to criticize with complete irresponsibility every measure of the Emperor and his government. Again, the modest extension of freedom permitted by the new Tsar inevitably produced a pressing demand for more. Restraints accepted almost without murmur under Nicholas were suddenly felt to be irksome; the public, hitherto largely excluded from state affairs, now protested that the relative freedom given by Alexander was inadequate. Finally, any reform, and in particular one as far-reaching as the liberation of the serfs, must of necessity be a compromise affronting vested interests while disappointing those who had expected more. The liberation as well as his other measures earned the reforming Tsar not gratitude but widespread criticism and hostility. Signs of discontent appeared among all groups of the population. By 1862 Russia apparently was drifting into chaos.

The ferment first began to assume serious proportions shortly after the liberation of the serfs. The trouble—as so often in periods of 'thaw'—started in the higher educational institutions. Student disorders on minor points of discipline began in Kiev in 1857, and subsequently spread to Moscow and other universities. Alexander directed that these first breaches of discipline should be overlooked, but his leniency merely helped to encourage the disorders. Both Polish and socialist influences came to play a part in the unrest. Some professors sympathized with socialist ideas and were subscribers to Herzen's revolutionary publications. From the safety of London, Herzen was preaching fraternization between Russian radicals and Polish patriots. His plea was not without effect. In February 1861 the funeral of the Ukrainian poet Shevchenko was followed by a Requiem Mass for the first victims in Poland. Three hundred Russian students and several professors attended the service held at St. Petersburg in a Roman Catholic church. At a similar service in Moscow, a Russian student declared that Russians and Poles had a common enemy—the Russian government. Polish students in return joined in demonstrations organized by their Russian fellows. The most extensive of these followed the 'massacre of Bezdna', where Russian troops had fired on unarmed peasants. At the same time socialist propaganda was flooding the military schools from the Corps of Pages to the Artillery Academy, where Professor Lavrov combined mathematical instruction with the advocacy of social revolution.

In July *Velikoruss* (The Great Russian), the first of a series of illegal proclamations, began to circulate in St. Petersburg. It was an appeal to the 'educated classes' (whatever the term might mean) to take power from the hands of the incompetent government. The mistakes of the Tsar and his advisers were driving the peasantry to revolt (this was an echo of Bezdna); they would in time provoke another Pugachev rising. Early in September a second issue of *Velikoruss* repeated the earlier warning and called on the educated classes to demand a constituent assembly to reorganize the country. A third issue, some weeks later, gave the text of a proposed

Address to the Tsar. About the same time an appeal *To the Younger Generation* made its appearance, which called for a constitution and a social transformation. Russia should pass directly from a semi-feudal into a socialist state. The manifestoes created an impression : there was a widespread feeling in St. Petersburg that revolution was approaching.

In the spring of 1861 the Council of Ministers debated the state of the universities. Some Ministers wished to close all universities 'for reorganization'. The Tsar rejected the suggestion, but accepted the resignation of Kovalevsky, the liberal Minister of Education. He was replaced by Admiral Putiatin, a rigid disciplinarian. The new Minister put new university regulations into force at the opening of the academic year (early in October). The students of St. Petersburg organized a protest meeting in one of the lecture halls. By order of the authorities, all lectures were suspended and the university was closed. The students assembled in the courtyard and marched, as a body, to the house of the Curator. The police arrested the ringleaders— which produced another mass meeting. The Governor-General called out troops, and the meeting dispersed. Some days later the students organized another meeting; thirty-five were arrested. Another time troops were called out and scuffles developed between them and the students. Some three hundred students were taken to the fortress of SS. Peter and Paul. On the same day the students of Moscow staged a demonstration. These demonstrations found an echo in every institution of higher education in the empire.

When matters had come to this pass, the Tsar intervened in person. Hurrying back to St. Petersburg, he expressed dissatisfaction at the clumsiness of the authorities. He disapproved of the imprisonment of the students. The Governor-General was relieved of his duties and replaced by the humane Prince Suvorov. However, the university was to remain closed until a new statute for all Russian universities had been completed. Funds were placed at the disposal of Suvorov to help needy students forced to move to other universities. The ringleaders among the students were banished to distant provinces to live under police supervision. Soon afterwards, Putiatin's place was taken by the liberal Golovnin.

The 'settlement' of the student problem did little to reduce the general ferment. The demonstrations in the streets of Warsaw were assuming alarming proportions. Moreover, subversion was beginning to affect the Russian army. Late in 1861 a foreign observer noted: "From general to major, all are reliable but of limited intelligence; from major to sergeant-major, all are unreliable. The common soldier is unpredictable and will follow whoever influences him." In May 1862 four junior officers were arrested in Warsaw, together with two non-commissioned officers. Two further officers absconded. A commission of inquiry discovered that two more officers were involved. All were charged with having circulated among the lower ranks "lying and impertinent slanders about the emperor and the ruling dynasty", and with having read and passed to them "books and pamphlets of a subversive nature (*Velikoruss, The Bell,* the *Historical Almanack*) with the object of undermining their loyalty and obedience to the lawful authorities". Of the accused, three were sentenced to death, one (an N.C.O.) to flogging through a double row of soldiers. If he survived (which was doubtful) he would serve twelve years' hard labour in the mines. On July 28 the sentences were carried out in the Polish fortress of Modlin.

Even more alarming to the authorities were certain developments in another sphere. In May 1862 there circulated in St. Petersburg another clandestine leaflet, the most violent of them all. *Young Russia* demanded not only elective national and provincial assemblies as well as elected judges, but also publicly owned fac-

tories, the dissolution of monasteries, universal education, and the abolition of marriage. The object of the
recommended changes was to "change radically and
without exception all the foundations of contemporary
society". The ruling classes would resist; the people
must pitilessly strike them down. Some weeks after the
appearance of *Young Russia*, a series of devastating
fires broke out all over Russia. In St. Petersburg itself a
week of outbreaks culminated in a conflagration which
gutted two thousand shops and warehouses. "If there
had been wind on that day, half the city would have
perished in the flames." There was evidence to suggest
that the fires were started deliberately. Those guilty
were never discovered, but public opinion attributed
the outbreaks to Poles and socialists—who, in their turn,
asserted that the fires were started by right-wing *agents
provocateurs*. Whoever was responsible, the fires greatly
increased the prevailing feeling of insecurity and alarm.

The unrest of 1861-2 which ended the honeymoon of
Alexander's reign profoundly affected the Tsar's temperament and outlook. In the first place, his health was
beginning to be affected. Already in 1860 he had returned from a visit to Warsaw in a state of near-prostra-
tion which led foreign diplomats to speculate whether
he might not be suffering from tuberculosis. By 1862 his
nerves were on edge. In a letter to the Grand-Duke
Constantine he dwelt on the need to attain calmness of
spirit in the face of daily disturbing rumours. "Un-
happily I know from my own experience that this is
difficult; I am often seized by an internal trembling
when particularly stirred by anything. But one must
control oneself, and I find prayer the best means to this
end." An instance of Alexander's loss of control is recorded by one of his pages. It was on the day before the
disloyal officers were shot at Modlin. The Tsar had
given a final examination to cadets about to be commissioned. At the end of the parade he called together the
newly commissioned officers. On horseback, he con-

gratulated them quietly and said a few words about
military duty and loyalty. Then, changing his tone,
"distinctly shouting out every word, his face suddenly
distorted with anger", he continued : "But if anyone
among you—from which God preserve you—should
prove himself in any circumstances disloyal to the Tsar,
the throne, and the fatherland—take heed of what I say
—he will be treated with the full se-ve-ri-ty of the law
without the slightest com-mi-ser-a-tion !" His
voice failed. With an expression of blind rage on his face, he
violently spurred his horse and galloped away. Yet at
other moments his page was struck by "that problematic, absent-minded gaze, which I had often begun to
notice".

Alexander's anger found expression in the policy of
his government. In September 1861 Mikhailov, a poet,
was arrested as the reputed author of one of the clandestine handbills. He was tried and sentenced to penal
servitude in Siberia, where he died four years later.
This was the first political trial since the days of Nicholas, a landmark in the history of Alexander's reign. The
great fires provoked further repressive action. The leading radical journals were suspended for eight months.
Chernyshevsky, the editor of one of them, was arrested
together with some other journalists. Detained for two
years, he was finally brought to trial and sentenced—on
inconclusive evidence—to fourteen years of hard labour
in the Siberian mines and exile for the rest of his life.
In the meantime, a special Commission had been set up
in the Third Division to unearth the authors of illegal
leaflets and members of secret revolutionary organizations. The Tsar himself based high hopes on the results
of this Commission; its discoveries were negligible. It
did, however, report that the Sunday-school movement (classes run by students and journalists for artisans
and workers), which had greatly developed in the last
two years, was dangerous. All Sunday schools were
closed. Such was the beginning of the duel to the death

between Alexander II and the Russian revolutionary movement.

The first round in the struggle went decisively in favour of the Tsar and his Ministers. The great fires produced a change in Russian public opinion. That part of society at St. Petersburg, and especially at Moscow, "which carried most weight with the government, suddenly threw off its liberal garb, and turned not only against the most advanced section of the reform party but even against its moderate wing". The Polish insurrection completed the conversion. Herzen's stand in favour of the Poles cost him the support of all patriots among the Russian reformers; the circulation and influence of *The Bell* rapidly declined. Herzen's loss was the gain of Michael Katkov, a 'repentant liberal', who now stood forth as the champion of Great Russian nationalism. From this moment his *Moscow Gazette* replaced Herzen's paper as the mouthpiece of Russian opinion. Western diplomatic intervention fanned Russian patriotism to fever heat. Gorchakov, by expressing popular opinion with uncompromising firmness, became the hero of the hour. Nationalism rather than radicalism had become the fashionable creed.

The temporary eclipse of Russian radicalism did not, however, put an end to the Tsar's anxieties. His struggle with the radical intelligentsia appeared, for the moment, won; that with the upper classes was continuing without respite. Constitutional demands were not confined to the Poles and Finns but were voiced with increasing insistence among the Russians themselves. As early as 1859 the delegates sent to St. Petersburg by the provincial committees on liberation had demanded a national assembly. Oligarchs who desired to increase the influence of the nobility and genuine believers in constitutionalism alike supported the movement. It possessed the sympathy of Valuiev, who wrote: "On 19 February [the day of liberation], the sun of imperial favour warmed the bottoms of the valleys; now it must illumine and warm the summits and the slopes."

The spearhead of the constitutionalists had lain at first in the assemblies of nobility. At the turn of 1861 several of these had discussed general political questions. At St. Petersburg a proposal calling for a national assembly with advisory functions was defeated by only two votes. In Moscow and Tula similar demands were raised. More drastic was the action of thirteen noblemen of Tver, all of whom had taken part in putting the liberation statute into effect. In an address to the Tsar, after criticizing in undiplomatic language the defects of the statute, they called for a national assembly representing the whole Russian people. The Address was printed and circulated in the countryside; it was even read at village meetings. The Tsar—against the advice of Valuiev—decided to make an example. After a sojourn in the fortress of SS. Peter and Paul, the signatories appeared before a special court, which condemned them to detention in a lunatic asylum and the loss of civil rights. The first part of the sentence was carried out for four days, the second proved permanent.

Alexander's views on the problem of a constitution were expounded in conversation with Bismarck late in 1861. The idea of receiving advice from subjects other than his officials, the Tsar explained, was not in itself objectionable. Greater participation in public affairs by respectable notables could only be an advantage. The difficulty was that it had never in practice been possible to stop liberal development at an appropriate point. This would be particularly true in a country like Russia, where the indispensable political sense and training were confined to a narrow circle. Constitutionalism was not in accord with Russia's political tradition. Throughout the interior of the empire common people still regarded the monarch as their 'paternal and absolute God-given ruler'. This sentiment, which amounted to a religious belief, was quite independent of any personal attachment. The veneration with which the Russian people surrounded the throne of its emperors could not be shared. To call representatives of the nobility or the nation to share his absolute power would be to diminish, without compensating gain, the authority of the government. In particular, God alone knew what would become of relations between landowners and peasants if the imperial power was no longer strong enough to exercise a dominating influence. Views like these were not without foundation; they forbade major concessions to the constitutionalists.

After the pacification of Poland the constitutional movement received a new impetus from the newly created zemstvos. In December 1865 the zemstvo of St. Petersburg demanded the creation of a central zemstvo office; the following year the demand was repeated with even greater insistence. Alexander felt unable to give up his autocratic power. He explained his reasons during a paternal talk with one of the constitutionalists. "And now", said the emperor, "I suppose you consider that I refuse to give up any of my powers from motives of petty ambition. I give you my imperial word that, this very minute, at this very table, I would sign any constitution you like, if I felt that this would be for the good of Russia. But I know that, were I to do so to-day, to-morrow Russia would fall to pieces." There can be little doubt that the Tsar was sincere in his belief. Considering the interest of Russia to be at stake, he decided to act after the second demand of the St. Petersburg zemstvo. The assembly was dissolved, and several of its more prominent members were exiled. The constitutional movement of the zemstvos died down and did not revive until 1875.

The suppression of the St. Petersburg zemstvo was only part of a wider policy following the first attempt on Alexander's life. On April 16, 1866, while taking his daily walk in the Winter Garden in the capital, he was fired on and saved only by the prompt action of a bystander (a *muzhik*). The would-be assassin turned out to be Karakozov, a member of the lesser nobility, expelled from Kazan university. A special Commission under Muraviev, the 'Hangman of Vilna', was set up at once to investigate the attempt. Little was discovered, but Muraviev was forced to admit that in that very social group—including the government itself—there were individuals who wished to overthrow the monarchy. Karakozov was hanged; thirty-four members of secret groups suffered lesser penalties; numerous innocent people were arrested.

Muraviev's report drew attention to the fact that many members of revolutionary circles were students. This was attributed to the state of Russian education. Teachers at all levels were politically unreliable; insubordination was rife in the schools as in the universities. The younger generation was steeped in atheism, materialism, and socialism, inculcated not only by the teachers but also by the radical 'progressive' press. Impressed by this report, the Tsar resolved to change the spirit of Russian youth. A Rescript to the President of the Council of Ministers called for the suppression of subversive activities in all educational establishments. Golovnin was forced to resign and replaced by D. A. Tolstoy, the obscurantist Procurator of the Holy Synod. Katkov bitterly attacked the nihilism of the younger generation. His educational ideal was the 'gentleman' produced by English public schools. He agreed with Tolstoy that the harmful spirit among the young sprang from the teaching of science, which produced a superficial, materialistic outlook. He objected also to the manner of teaching history and Russian literature, both of which were largely in the hands of liberals. The remedies against the 'bad spirit' were to be found in discipline, inculcated through Greek, Latin, and mathematics.

In the teeth of fierce opposition in the Imperial Council, Tolstoy and Katkov 'reformed' the educational system. The teaching of science was excluded from 'grammar schools', that of other 'suspect' subjects reduced. Ancient languages, with a heavy emphasis on grammar, received pride of place. Teachers became officials and were forced to act as spies and policemen. Under the mask of strict obedience, hypocrisy and time-serving were encouraged. Moreover, thousands of pupils failed to pass the new severe examinations in classics and had to leave the schools without diplomas. Many others were excluded from schools and universities for trivial breaches of discipline and went to swell the ranks of the malcontents. The excluded student would soon become the most typical figure in the ranks of the revolutionaries. An ultra-conservative Russian publicist noted that Tolstoy had created dozens and even hundreds of secondary schools, but his system— even more than that of his liberal predecessor—had made them into 'hotbeds of political subversion'.

The educational sphere was not the only one affected by Karakozov's shot. Immediately after the attempt the aged chief of the Third Division tearfully offered his resignation and proposed as his successor Peter Shuvalov, his former chief of staff. Shuvalov's first act after his appointment was to demand the replacement of Annenkov, the chief of the St. Petersburg police. Annenkov was a protégé of Suvorov, the liberal Governor-General of the city. A fierce struggle began between the 'new men' and the surviving 'liberals' for the body and soul of the Tsar. The weak emperor became the central figure in an incident which, in his father's time, would have been unthinkable.

On hearing Shuvalov's demand, Suvorov rushed to the Tsar and declared that, without Annenkov, he could not answer for the security of the capital. Alexander agreed with Suvorov. Egged on by Shuvalov, Berg, the Governor-General of Poland, recommended General Trepov, the chief of police in Warsaw, for a similar appointment in St. Petersburg. Alexander promptly offered Trepov Annenkov's place. Trepov accepted on condition that he should not be responsible to the Governor-General but report directly to the Tsar. (This was the Russian equivalent to a seat in the Cabinet.) Alexander declared angrily that he would not accept such terms: Trepov must accept the post as it was. The general had the courage—some might say the impertinence—to reply : "At your Majesty's command. Your orders will be carried out, but I must warn your Majesty that I cannot accept responsibility for the safety of St. Petersburg. That responsibility must remain with the Governor-General." The Tsar did not have Trepov arrested—as his father would certainly have done.

Trepov at once went to Suvorov to report his conversation with the Emperor. Suvorov threatened to repay him. Shuvalov now decided to destroy the inconvenient Governor-General. Three times he represented to the Emperor that in the interest of public order the office of Governor-General of St. Petersburg must be abolished. Alexander replied : "I am ready to do anything, but this, never !" At Shuvalov's fourth attempt the Tsar gave ear without signs of irritation. A few days later, at a hunting party, he informed Suvorov of his decision to abolish the post of Governor-General. After the interview Suvorov pointedly declared that he would retire to the estate where his grandfather, the great Suvorov, had lived in exile under the tyrant Paul. "Trepov", a conservative nobleman recorded, "became the unchallenged ruler of St. Petersburg, and people began to breathe more freely under his firm yet intelligent administration."

During a visit to Paris in the summer of 1867, the Tsar was fired at again, this time by a Pole named Berezowski. This second attempt finally established the ascendancy of Shuvalov. The Chief of Police had the manners of a gentleman (always an important point with Alexander II) and combined ability with tact.

Shuvalov alone could give the harried Tsar a feeling of calm, security and confidence. He became indispensable to his master, and soon enjoyed the reputation of being all-powerful in domestic affairs. On his advice, the Ministries of Justice and the Interior were handed over to conservatives. In 1867 Zamiatnin, the patron of the judicial reforms, made way for Count Pahlen, a reincarnation of the late Panin. The following year Valuiev fell victim to an unscrupulous intrigue mounted against him by the Tsarevich (the future Alexander III, advised by his ultra-conservative tutor, Pobedonostsev) with the enthusiastic support of Katkov. With the transfer of his Ministry to General Timashev, the establishment of the reactionary régime was complete.

The Tsar, under the impression of two attempts on his life, resigned himself to police rule. Personally brave, he had not flinched under the fire of Berezowski, but his peace of mind was disturbed. If Trepov now appeared at the palace with his daily report a few minutes after the appointed time, he was met with the anxious question whether all was quiet in the city. Indeed, Alexander had become almost a prisoner of the police. Kropotkin records how, one day, a senior official of the Third Division repeated in a private house a conversation in which the Emperor had reprimanded a member of the imperial family. Asked how he could know the details, the policeman replied: "The words and opinions of his Majesty must be known to our department. How else could a delicate institution like the state-police be managed? Be assured that the Emperor is the most closely watched person in all St. Petersburg."

By this time Shuvalov's police were much concerned with the Emperor's private affairs. During 1865 the Tsar, a connoisseur of female charms, had developed a passion for a young aristocratic girl, Catherine Dolgoruky, then eighteen years of age. The following summer she became his mistress. Alexander, in his delight, made a solemn promise: "To-day, alas", he declared, "I am not free; but, at the first opportunity, I will marry you; for from now onwards and for ever I regard you as my wife before God." In the autumn, the liaison became regularly established. Three or four times a week, the princess would come secretly to the Winter Palace. Through a low door, of which she had the key, she would make her way to a secluded room on the ground floor. The connection was soon known in St. Petersburg society. Relatives hurried Catherine to Naples. The two lovers wrote to each other every day. They met again in Paris during Alexander's visit. After his return to St. Petersburg, Catherine was established in a luxurious flat. Appearances were preserved—but with increasing difficulty. The need to maintain at least a pretence of secrecy subjected Alexander to increasing personal strain; it multiplied the responsibilities of those charged with his protection.

In May 1872, Catherine bore Alexander a son, christened George; other children followed. The event caused indignation in the imperial family and in aristocratic circles in the two capitals. A romantic liaison had been accepted; it was different when the matter became a public scandal. There was indignation that a ruler of fifty-four, already a grandfather, should thus lower the prestige of the dynasty. The disparity in the ages of the lovers caused comment. More serious, the health of the Empress was known to be failing. Would Catherine Dolgoruky be one day legitimate wife, consort, empress? Might not even the order of succession be imperilled? Filled with anxiety and foreboding, Russian society rallied behind the heir-apparent and his wife. The future Alexander III abhorred moral laxity and soon became the bitter enemy of Catherine and her friends. The female members of the imperial family shared his indignation. Alexander's liaison with Princess Dolgoruky had become a matter of public concern. It finally alienated from the Tsar the respect of Russian society, destroyed his moral prestige, and split the imperial family.

Moreover, it was not long before Princess Dolgoruky began to exercise a political influence. At first she had been simply a sympathetic listener, offering her lover opportunities to unburden himself of the cares of state. Inevitably, however, she became the rallying-point for a group opposed to the conservatives and the Tsarevich. Like the heroine of Tolstoy's *Anna Karenina*, her equivocal position forced upon her a life of semi-seclusion. Both Catherine and Alexander, therefore, were more than grateful to those who, disregarding a strict official boycott, were willing to join in the couple's modest social life. These, apart from the Tsar's closest friend, Sasha Adlerberg, came to include some men of 'liberal' views—Valuiev, steadily returning to favour; Abaza, a future Minister of Finance, and, later, Count Loris-Melikov.

Among those who refused to pay court to Catherine Dolgoruky was Peter Shuvalov, the all-powerful chief of police. Some of his remarks—duly reported in the highest spheres—were far from favourable to the princess. Finally, he had the unwisdom to oppose some of her friends in a doubtful railway speculation. In 1874 Shuvalov—against his wishes—was suddenly appointed ambassador in London. He was replaced by Potapov, a nonentity. The results of his disappearance were not long in showing themselves. The efficiency of the police organization deteriorated. Soon the government would enter—with weakened forces—its mortal combat with the revolutionary movement. The infatuation for Catherine Dolgoruky was closely connected with the decline in the Tsar's authority and his inability to curb effectively the dangerous influences at work in Russian society.

Chapter Seven

Alexander II
and the Russian Expansionists

IT is in the field of foreign policy that in the later
years of the reign, Alexander's inability to control the
more explosive forces in Russian society is most clearly
revealed. In his dealings with the representatives of
Russian expansion, he showed in the fullest measure the
ambiguity and weakness characteristic of so many of
his undertakings. Alexander's approach to problems of
foreign policy had been fundamentally one of caution,
based on an overriding desire to preserve peace. The
reasons for this were not primarily humanitarian.
Russia after the Crimean War clearly needed a prolonged period of recuperation, and no one understood
this better than the Tsar. Soon a second imperative
reason had been added. The Austro-French war of 1859
—originally encouraged by Russia—was seen before
long to have opened the floodgates of revolutionary
nationalism. The risings in central Italy, followed by
Garibaldi's famous expedition, stimulated national
movements in Germany, Hungary, Denmark, and
Poland. Moreover, Napoleon III in 1863 showed an unmistakable desire to intervene on the side of the insurgent Poles. Any war in Europe threatened to produce results unwelcome to the Russian government.

The resurgence of the revolutionary tide during 1860
suggested to the Tsar not only closer relations with
Prussia but even a measure of reconciliation with 'per-

fidious' Austria. The British government, estranged from France after the Polish crisis of 1863, seemed inclined to associate itself with a conservative defensive grouping. Such a system, dear to the heart of Alexander and Gorchakov, demanded the preservation of peace in Europe. Miliutin and Reutern, in the interest of their military and financial reforms, strongly supported a cautious and pacific diplomacy. In pursuit of this policy, the Russian government went to the length of repeatedly warning the Balkan Christians against 'premature' insurrections. Russia, during the period of her transformation, must preserve friendly relations with both England and Austria; she must not give cause for alarm in either Central Asia or the Balkans. Such, in brief, was the official policy of Alexander II and Gorchakov.

This policy of caution failed to satisfy important expansionist forces in Russian society. It was precisely during the reign of Alexander II that Russian imperialism assumed a 'modern' form. The bearers of the new imperialism were, in the first place, energetic and ambitious proconsuls in the outlying portions of the empire. They were supported by colonial soldiers eager for fame and booty. Indeed, the desire for conquest was well-nigh universal among the military forces stationed in 'colonial' territories. A contemporary Russian observer noted: "A positive fever for further conquest raged among our troops—an ailment to cure which no method of treatment was effective, especially as the correctives applied were frequently interspersed with such stimulants as honours and decorations. Not only the Russian Generals but even the youngest Lieutenants craved after further extension of territory, while those of the officers who were entrusted with any sort of independent command carried into effect their individual schemes. It was, indeed, impossible that such desires should be resisted when by gratifying them it was possible for a Lieutenant in four years to become a General."[1]

Military ambition was reinforced by commercial aspirations. "Almost hand in hand with the conquering generals", writes B. H. Sumner, "went the Khludovs, Moscow textile millionaires, Pervushin with his lead mines, Kolesnikov with his gold and coal scandals . . . and the big trading firms of Pupyshev and Bykovsky."[2] In 1876, the Governor of Transcaspia noted that recently the eastern shores of the Caspian had attracted attention from capitalists and various big companies. He was approached on all sides with applications for concessions for fishing, salt, sulphur, and oil. A high-placed court official headed a particularly important salt company. The military and commercial interests favouring expansion were not without support in official circles. The influential Asiatic Department of the Ministry of Foreign Affairs looked with favour on a policy which might easily come into conflict with that adopted by Alexander and Gorchakov.

The Tsar's attitude towards the movement for expansion had been from the start ambiguous. While favouring caution and restraint, he yet delighted in any extension of Russian territory and influence. Already in 1850 he had sided with 'imperialism' when supporting the annexation of the Amur region in opposition to Nesselrode, the Foreign Minister. Nicholas Muraviev, the celebrated Governor-General of Eastern Siberia (1847–61) came to St. Petersburg to fight in person the Ministers who vetoed Far Eastern expansion in order to avoid clashes with China and Great Britain. It was the Tsarevich's personal intervention that had turned the scales in his favour. Muraviev left St. Petersburg with authority to extend the area of Russian occupation. The fruits of the new policy were seen in the foundation of

[1] Quoted in B. H. Sumner, *Russia and the Balkans 1870–1880*, (O.U.P., 1937), p. 48.
[2] Ibid., p. 46.

Vladivostok (July 1860) and the signing of the Treaty of Pekin, negotiated at the same time by Colonel Ignatiev (the future Pan-Slav leader). By that treaty China finally ceded the regions of the rivers Amur and Ussuri, which became the Russian Maritime Province. Thanks in no small degree to Alexander's support, a great new province had been added to the Russian empire.

The Tsar gave similar encouragement to colonial expansion in the region of the Caucasus. In this instance it was a question of completing a conquest begun many years before. In 1857 Prince Bariatinsky had been appointed Viceroy at Tiflis with orders to complete the subjugation of the area. After two years of heroic resistance Shamil, the leader of the mountaineers of the eastern Caucasus, had been forced to surrender to the Russians. Thereafter had come the turn of the proud Circassians defending their mountain fastnesses above the Black Sea. By 1864 they also were subdued, and those who would not accept Russian rule had migrated to the territories of the Sultan of Turkey. The Caucasus was firmly in Russian hands.

The conquest of the Caucasus left large Russian armies unemployed and longing for further action. Under Alexander's brother, the Grand-Duke Michael (Bariatinsky's successor as Viceroy), Russian forces began to cross the Caspian and to advance southwards along its eastern shores towards northern Persia. In 1869 the important base of Krasnovodsk was established 150 miles from Baku across the Caspian Sea. In 1874, under the control of headquarters in Tiflis, an elaborate Trans-Caspian Military District was established. Its creation had been preceded by one of the periodic clashes between the colonial proconsuls and the civil authorities at St. Petersburg. Gorchakov and Reutern, fearing political complications with Great Britain, opposed expansion in this area. The Grand-Duke Michael, supported by Miliutin, persuaded the Tsar to sanction the move. As on other occasions, Alexander finally gave his vote in favour of expansion. Once the new command was set up, the 'Caucasians' began to press forward towards Merv and the Afghan border. In 1879 army engineers began work on the Trans-Caspian Railway along the northern frontier of Persia. Relentlessly, the Russians were advancing into the area of ill-defined border territories with Persia and Afghanistan.

In the meantime, other Russian forces were advancing further to the east. In 1864, virtually on his own initiative, Colonel (later General) Cherniaev captured the cities of Turkestan and Chimkent. The following year he took the important city of Tashkent, provoking an armed conflict with the Amir of Bokhara. The Russians occupied part of his territory. In 1866 the extensive territories seized by Russia since 1847 were formed into the Governor-Generalship of Turkestan. General Kaufmann, one of Russia's great empire-builders, became its first ruler. During his proconsulship (1867–83), the conquest of Central Asia was completed. A protégé of Miliutin, Kaufmann had from the start enjoyed full political and diplomatic powers for dealing with the independent states of Central Asia. Under his direction operations against the khanates of Kokand and Bokhara were prosecuted with vigour. In 1868 the key cities of Bokhara and Samarkand fell to the Russians. Kokand and Bokhara became Russian vassal states. In 1873 Khiva, the last independent khanate, acknowledged Russian suzerainty. This was followed by the subjugation of the independent Turcomans and a rapid advance towards Herat and Afghanistan.

The Russian expansion in Central Asia raised the question of a possible clash with Great Britain. The alarm felt by British administrators in India was beginning to communicate itself to the home government and British public opinion. Repeated inquiries from London forced the Tsar and Gorchakov to recognize the international implications of the Russian advance in Asia. Alexander was faced with a dilemma. At heart an expansionist, he appreciated that failure to respect British susceptibilities might in certain circumstances provoke an anti-Russian coalition. He therefore resolved to restrain the colonial hotheads and calm British apprehensions.

In a lengthy circular of November 1864, Gorchakov tried to justify the Russian advance in Central Asia. The needs of security and the interests of trade, he argued, compel any major state bordering on areas occupied by warlike tribesmen to bring them under its control. "The United States in America, France in Africa, Holland in her colonies, England in India were all forced to take the road of expansion dictated by necessity rather than ambition, a road on which the chief difficulty is to know where to stop." For Russia, the farthest point of advance would be Chimkent. In making this declaration, Gorchakov was unaware of the fact that already, several weeks before, General Cherniaev had made a first unsuccessful attempt to capture Tashkent. This was a city far beyond the line designated in the circular as the limit of Russian penetration. The incident was typical of many. From 1865 onwards a continuous stream of 'mollifying' assurances issued from the Russian government. Each advance was the last; the most categorical instructions had been issued to prevent any forward movement. Yet each year saw another expedition and another Russian advance.

In 1865 Lord John Russell tried to negotiate an agreement defining British and Russian spheres of influence. All he was able to obtain were vague assurances of Russia's peaceful intentions. Four years later Clarendon, the British Foreign Secretary, met Gorchakov at Heidelberg and taxed him with his failure "to control the ambition of military Commanders". At the same time he proposed that Afghanistan should become a neutral buffer state. Gorchakov accepted the principle, but negotiations dragged on for several years; the two countries could not agree on the boundaries of Afghan-

istan. Finally, in January 1873, agreement was reached.
The Russian government acknowledged that the
khanate of Khiva lay outside its sphere of influence.

The agreement was not effective; Kaufmann insisted
that an expedition against Khiva could no longer be
deferred. In 1875 the campaign was opened. The
Russian ambassador in London explained that its sole
object was to rescue enslaved Russians (there were some
Russian slaves in Khiva), to punish brigandage (a legitimate objective), and to teach the khan a lesson. Not only
was it far from the Tsar's intentions to occupy the
khanate but positive orders had been given to prevent
it. The conditions imposed would be such as could not
produce a prolonged occupation. By June Kaufmann
was in control. The treaty imposed by him reduced the
khanate to complete dependence on Russia.

The Russian treaty with Khiva formed the climax
of the numerous episodes in which the professions of
Gorchakov and the Tsar were belied by the men on
the spot. Tashkent had been captured by Cherniaev
contrary to instructions. A Chinese province had been
occupied (it was later restored) against the wishes of the
Foreign Ministry; the treatment of Khiva ran counter
to the Tsar's formal assurances. Soon Kokand would be
annexed, allegedly against his wishes. Small wonder
that by the middle seventies neither the British government nor the British public attached the slightest value
to Russian assurances and protestations.

Yet Alexander's unfulfilled promises were the result
of weakness as much as trickery. The government at St.
Petersburg had, in a large measure, lost control over its
energetic agents in faraway Central Asia. Gorchakov
lamented, "I am an outspoken opponent of any Russian
extension whatsoever; but I can do nothing against the
ambition of our generals." Miliutin was able to break
Cherniaev, but could do little to assert his authority over
Kaufmann and the Grand-Duke Michael. As for the
Tsar himself, he was too indolent, and probably too ill-

informed, to swim against the tide of Russian imperialism. Not only were his orders ambiguous, but the men on the spot knew only too well that they would never be enforced. For instance, in 1875 the Tsar had vetoed ambitious plans submitted by the Caucasian Viceroy. He had given special instructions that nothing should be done to inflame British susceptibilities. Yet his orders were phrased in such a way as to sanction in advance any step the local commanders might see fit to take. They were "to avoid as much as possible any measures of aggression" and "not to cross our present frontiers without absolute necessity". Did Alexander seriously believe that instructions such as these would restrain his colonial soldiers? In the event, the Grand-Duke Michael acted as though the orders did not exist. However much the advances in Central Asia might increase Russo-British tension, Alexander either would not or could not control the imperialist elements in Russian society.

In a similar manner, the Tsar failed to check Pan-Slavism, the other great expansionist force of the day. Pan-Slavism had begun as an academic doctrine elaborated by publicists like Pogodin and Ivan Aksakov. It had gained a foothold in the Ministries of Education and Foreign Affairs. Ignatiev, who in 1860 negotiated the Treaty of Pekin, was one of its active exponents. Head of the influential Asiatic Department of the Foreign Ministry since 1861, in 1864 he became Russian Minister at Constantinople. Among the most active Pan-Slavs was the unfortunate Empress. Ailing, devout, and suffering in proud silence her husband's notorious infidelity, she gave herself heart and soul to the cause of the brother Slavs. Encouraged by her confessor, she surrounded herself with a circle of pious elderly ladies of Pan-Slav views. The heir-apparent also staunchly supported the 'cause'. Finally, Pan-Slavism attracted a number of adventurers, including several retired soldiers. Of the latter, Fadeev and Cherniaev were perhaps the most important. Fadeev had served in the Caucasus for twenty years under Bariatinsky, and had become an ardent supporter of Russian expansion in Central Asia. In 1867 he attacked Miliutin's reforms in a series of articles, and this ended his military career. He subsequently joined forces with Cherniaev, the conqueror of Tashkent, another soldier who had fallen foul of the powerful Minister of War. In 1869 Fadeev published a celebrated work, *Opinion on the Eastern Question*, which became, almost at once, the most widely accepted exposition of Pan-Slav doctrine.

The keynote of Fadeev's work was a violent attack on Austria-Hungary in the spirit of Paskievich's celebrated dictum that the road to Constantinople lay through Vienna. In his opinion Russia's interests in the Balkans were fundamentally opposed to those of the Dual Monarchy. It was Russia's mission to liberate the Slavs—Austria-Hungary was the chief obstacle to its accomplishment. "Austria can hold her part of the Slavonian mass as long as Turkey holds hers and vice versa." Turkey had ceased to count either as a military or a naval power. With a force of one hundred thousand men to cover the Bulgarian fortresses and a striking force of one hundred and fifty thousand, Russia could reach Constantinople within six weeks. However, the Russian lines of communication would be threatened by Austria's strategic position on the Russian flank! (Fadeev remembered the lesson of the Crimean War; his warning was not a bad forecast of the situation which would arise in 1877.) For this reason the 'Austrian question' must be solved before it was possible to liberate the Slavs.

Here was a political programme differing profoundly from the conservative policy favoured by Alexander and Gorchakov. The Tsar disliked not only its disturbing effect on international relations but also its revolutionary implications. He was, therefore, far more wholehearted in his condemnation of Pan-Slavism than in his attempts, inspired by *raison d'état* alone, to limit the

Russian advance in Central Asia. On many occasions he criticized Pan-Slav ideas. In 1862 in his instructions to the Grand-Duke Constantine before the latter's departure for Warsaw, he uttered a warning against Pan-Slav dreams. "These ideas, however attractive they might be for the future, I consider at the present moment extremely dangerous for Russia and for the principle of monarchy. I see in their triumph a division of Russia not merely into a number of states but into separate and even hostile republics. The union of all Slavs under one head is a utopia unlikely ever to become a reality." Two years later he assured the Austrian Minister at St. Petersburg : "People fear Pan-Slavism. So far as I am concerned, I am a Russian before I am a Slav." (A recognition of realities, since hardly a drop of Slav blood flowed in Alexander's veins.) In 1867, in addressing delegates to the Moscow Slav Congress, the Tsar spoke in terms to which even the Austrian government could hardly have objected. Pan-Slavism was unacceptable to him because it spelt a (probably republican) federation including as autonomous units both Poland and the Ukraine. Moreover, as Gorchakov sensibly wrote in 1872, it was difficult to believe in "a sincere sympathy of the Slav races for *Autocratic Russia*". The Pan-Slav movement, therefore, could expect no sympathy from either the Tsar or his Minister. Yet, in the end, Alexander could control Pan-Slavism as little as 'Asiatic' expansion. A variety of circumstances drove him into the Balkan war of liberation desired by the Pan-Slavs, against the warnings of Reutern and Shuvalov, and perhaps also against his own better judgment. Once again, Alexander proved himself unable to control events.

The developments which provoked the Russo-Turkish War of 1877 began without the active participation of the Russian Pan-Slavs. In the summer of 1875 agrarian unrest developed among the Slav populations of Herzegovina (a Turkish province). Outside Slav societies—Serbian, Austrian, Russian—began to feed the flames. Ionin, the Russian consul-general at Ragusa (Dubrovnik), an ardent Pan-Slav, later told a British colleague : "I did not create the situation but I profited from it. It began as a small stream, which might have been lost for want of direction; so I put up a stone here and a stone there, and kept the water together." As 1875 turned into 1876 Russian agents made their appearance at Ragusa; the insurgents received financial support; they were encouraged by the knowledge that they did not stand alone.

The burning issue at this stage was the attitude of Serbia and Montenegro, the two neighbouring Slav principalities. In Serbia a rising tide of nationalist senti-ment urged war on the side of the insurgents. Prince Milan inquired of the Tsar whether, in the event of intervention, Serbia could count on Russian protection against Austria-Hungary. Alexander replied that Serbia would have to bear alone any consequences of a possible war with Turkey. Yet, characteristically, the Russian answer was rather less definite than it was made to appear. Kartsov, the consul-general in Belgrade, was a man of little personality or ambition. A visit to St. Petersburg showed him that Gorchakóv and the Tsar had not formulated a clear policy. He was instructed to tell the Serbs that Russia, in conjunction with Austria-Hungary, was working for peace. At the same time, Russia would view without disfavour Serbian defensive armaments if attempts to preserve peace should fail. Returning to Belgrade, Kartsov judiciously tried to strike a balance between these official views and the Pan-Slav promptings of Ignatiev, his superior at Con-stantinople. There is little doubt that the Serbs believed him to speak his true mind when he told them that, if they went to war, they could in the last resort rely on Russian support.

In May 1876 Cherniaev arrived in Belgrade. Neither Milan nor the Serbian public could be expected to know that he came without the blessing of the Russian government. Yet when Kartsov was summoned to Ems early in June, he found the Tsar determined on peace and angry at Cherniaev's unauthorized mission. Gorchakov, however, reminded the consul : "All the same, don't forget that, although the Tsar is against war, the heir-apparent stands at the head of the movement." Russian opinion in fact was divided; Russian diplomacy spoke with two voices. Indeed, shortly after his return to Belgrade, Kartsov received a letter from Giers, the Acting Minister of Foreign Affairs, breathing a Pan-Slav spirit and telling him not to ignore the state of Russian opinion. On June 7 Kartsov informed the Serbian government that the Tsar did not want war; within twenty-four hours he delivered a thinly disguised encouragement from Ignatiev for Serbia to go to war. Cherniaev was never disavowed. Serbia, confident of Russian support, placed her forces under his command; at the beginning of July both Serbia and Montenegro declared war on Turkey. Alexander's peace policy had been defeated by Serb impetuosity and Pan-Slav machinations. It is impossible not to feel that the Tsar had lost control of the situation.

By this time Russian opinion was in a ferment. The Bulgarian atrocities (there had been risings in Bulgaria in May cruelly suppressed by the Turks), publicized by Ignatiev and the western press, inflamed Pan-Slav indignation. Serbia's declaration of war raised excitement in St. Petersburg and Moscow to fever heat. Exaggerated reports of Serbian strength and successes appeared in the Russian press. On July 13 a special service was held by the Metropolitan of Moscow for the success of Serb and Montenegrin arms. Relief funds were set up by Slavonic Benevolent Committees. Church collections formed the largest source of funds. Khludov (who had already financed Cherniaev's mission to Belgrade) and other Moscow millionaires made impressive contributions. Whereas public collections by unofficial bodies had previously been prohibited, society ladies—including members of the Empress's entourage—began to collect money in trams, on steamboats, and in the streets. The authorities refused to intervene.

With the outbreak of fighting in the Balkans, a new field of activity opened up before the Pan-Slavs. The Red Cross, under the active patronage of the Empress, began to organize medical work on a large scale. More serious, a movement of volunteers (somewhat more genuine than some of its modern counterparts) was started. A recruiting office was opened without interference from the authorities. The chief of staff of the Corps of Guards, an ardent Pan-Slav and confidant of the Tsarevich, encouraged Guards officers to volunteer for service in Serbia. They had to resign their commissions, but were promised reinstatement. The departure of volunteer trains (vividly described at the end of Tolstoy's *Anna Karenina*) was accompanied by patriotic manifestations fully reported in the Russian press. The actual number of volunteers is estimated at 4,000 to 5,000, including some eight hundred officers. Some of the latter were regulars and highly placed in society. The movement had developed without the sanction of the Tsar and his Ministers, a fact almost unheard of in the annals of Russian history. Ivan Aksakov, looking back on the Pan-Slav campaign, wrote: "Public opinion conducted a war apart from the government and without any state organization, in a foreign state." It was a challenge to the authority of the Tsar and his advisers.

Alexander and Gorchakov returned to Russia from Germany in the middle of July, when the Pan-Slav campaign was in full swing. Katkov, in alliance with the Moscow merchants and the cotton millionaire Tretiakov, was appealing for funds for the Serbs and Bulgars. Cherniaev and his doings were exploited; when his personal failings and military defeats could no longer be concealed, Katkov demanded that the European powers should save the Serbs. This, however, did not prevent him from publishing violent attacks on England and later on Austria. In the face of these vociferous activities, the Tsar and his Ministers tried —ineffectually—to assert their authority. In August Alexander assured Reutern of his determination not to go to war. Early in September the first half-hearted steps were taken to curtail the activities of the "Slavonic Benevolent Committees". Cherniaev's proclamation of Serbian independence was followed by a prohibition of 'volunteering' from the active army. Gorchakov attempted to check Katkov's hysterical anti-British campaign. None of these measures proved very effective. Restrictions imposed on the "Slavonic Benevolent Committees" were soon withdrawn, it was believed, at the instance of the Empress. In October the press, led by Katkov, resumed its attacks—this time against Austria.

During the autumn foreign observers began to express doubts whether the Tsar would be able to resist Pan-Slav pressure. The 'activist' forces were impressive: the Orthodox Church linked in unnatural alliance with the Old Believer millionaires of Moscow; the Empress and her coterie; the Tsarevich with all those who looked to the coming reign; soldiers and sailors who swam with the tide, whether from conviction or interest; last, but not least, the press, led by the indefatigable Katkov and the able propagandist Aksakov. Against this formidable array stood a handful of pacific Ministers (Reutern, Valuiev, Miliutin, and Timashev, the Minister of the Interior, occasionally supported by the senile Gorchakov) and the German element among the soldiers and bureaucrats. Yet the Pan-Slav Movement, however impressive in appearance, was a movement of 'public opinion' rather than of the masses. Few of the volunteers came from the ranks of the peasantry. In September the abject failure of Cherniaev and the Serbs produced second thoughts even amongst the upper classes.

The star of Pan-Slavism was waning. The Tsar was free to determine Russian policy almost independently of Pan-Slav effervescence.

At Livadia in the Crimea in the autumn, Alexander conferred with his closest advisers. Adlerberg and Gorchakov, Miliutin and Reutern with their assistants, were in attendance. Ignatiev came from Constantinople. The Tsarevich was summoned to attend. The Grand-Duke Nicholas, the Tsar's soldier brother, was called in. The Empress was present, attended by her ladies and by a chaplain in close touch with the Moscow "Slavonic Benevolent Committee". The question of war or peace was debated. Reutern submitted a secret memorandum explaining that war would ruin his financial reforms. Miliutin and Totleben, the hero of Sevastopol, were lukewarm. The majority of those present recommended a 'national' policy from which at least the possibility of war was not excluded. The Tsar, influenced by "a feminine atmosphere of exalted nationalism", agreed to partial mobilization. A plan of campaign was approved; the Grand-Dukes Nicholas and Michael were appointed commanders-in-chief respectively of the Danubian and Caucasian armies. If this was not yet a decision for war, it was a long step towards it.

In fact, Alexander still hoped to secure 'peace with honour', by which he understood far-reaching concessions to the Balkan Christians. If this proved impossible to attain, Russia would go to war. Such was the programme announced to the Russian public in the celebrated Moscow speech of November 11. "I know", Alexander told an enthusiastic gathering, "that all Russia shares with me the deepest interest in the sufferings of our brothers in faith and origin; but for me the true interests of Russia are dearer than everything else, and I would do my utmost to avoid the shedding of precious Russian blood. That is why I have tried and am still trying to bring about by peaceful means a real improvement in the life of all the Christian inhabitants of the Balkan peninsula. Discussions among representatives of the six great powers will shortly open at Constantinople to arrange conditions of peace. I sincerely desire agreement. If, however, there is no agreement, if I see that we cannot obtain such guarantees as will ensure the satisfaction of our just demands ... then I am determined to act independently. I am convinced that in such an eventuality all Russia will respond to my appeal ... May God help us to fulfil our sacred mission." Two days later the Tsar ordered the mobilization of six army corps and the corresponding reserves.

The Russian government was now committed to a policy which must result either in substantial guarantees for the Balkan Christians or in military intervention. For several months the Tsar continued to work for a pacific solution. The six powers agreed on a settlement, setting up autonomous states in eastern and western Bulgaria. The Porte rejected the proposals. Thereupon, Alexander, in a manifesto of April 24 (1877), informed his subjects that Russia was at war with Turkey.

How far was Pan-Slav agitation responsible for driving Russia into war? It is certain that the Pan-Slavs played an active part in the early stages of the crisis, first by keeping alive the rising in Herzegovina and later in encouraging Serbian intervention. In this phase, Pan-Slav activities ran counter to official policy, and Alexander and Gorchakov were faced with a *fait accompli*. On the other hand, it would be wrong to say that the Russian government itself was driven into war. The Pan-Slav Movement in Russia reached its peak during August and September (1876), after which enthusiasm began to wane. Moreover, the decisions of Livadia—reminiscent of similar decisions taken by Nicholas I on the eve of the Crimean War—were taken at a spot far removed from noisy Pan-Slav pressure. If Alexander was subjected to moral pressure it was mainly from members of his own family. The evidence suggests that, even after partial mobilization, he still hoped for a peaceful outcome. The decision to go to war was in the end taken in cool deliberation by the Tsar and his official advisers.

The war, tardily but not unwillingly begun, brought the Russians a series of disappointments. The Grand-Duke Nicholas proved himself an incompetent commander. The hospital and commissariat services, in spite of Miliutin's reforms, proved scarcely more satisfactory than they had been in the Crimean War. The Turks' heroic defence of Plevna held up the Russian advance for several crucial months. During this delay, Anglo-Austrian hostility began to crystallize. When the Russians finally reached the outskirts of Constantinople and Ignatiev imposed on the defeated Turks the Treaty of San Stefano, it was already too late: a British squadron was securely anchored in the Bosphorus. England and Austria appeared ready to declare war; nothing beyond a benevolent neutrality was to be obtained from Bismarck. Faced with the danger of a powerful coalition, the Russian government surrendered to the pressure of Europe. During tense weeks of negotiation, agreement was reached to 'revise' Ignatiev's treaty. The main change, agreed to at the Congress of Berlin, was that Russia should give up her big Bulgarian state. The other major decision was that Bosnia and Herzegovina were to pass under Austrian control. This settlement—although accompanied by considerable Russian gains (in Asia Minor and Bessarabia) and the creation of a small Bulgarian state—caused bitter disappointment in Russia. A general feeling of disillusionment succeeded the Pan-Slav fervour of 1876 and the patriotic enthusiasm of the war. The settlement of 1878 was considered—unjustly—a Russian defeat like that of 1856. The net result of Pan-Slav dreams was an apathy and irritation dangerous to the Tsar.

Alexander's attitude towards expansionist forces in Russian society had been, from the start, ambiguous.

Too cautious to approve unreservedly the dangerous schemes of a Kaufmann or an Ignatiev, he at no time took effective steps to curb their expansionist ardour. Apart from a few officers removed for their opposition to Miliutin, not a single one of the empire builders or Pan-Slav enthusiasts was ever dismissed from his post or even reprimanded. As a moderate imperialist, Alexander welcomed any development conducive to the power and greatness of Russia. Desiring the ends without the means and torn by conflicting sentiments, his orders lacked vigour and firmness. In consequence, they were disregarded—usually with impunity—alike by empire builders and Pan-Slav publicists. Resolute agents of expansion would adopt the policy of the *fait accompli*—knowing in the event of success that their actions would be condoned and even praised. Yet it is difficult to blame Alexander too severely for his weakness. While trying half-heartedly to curb the more flagrant acts of men who, after all, remained his loyal subjects, he was engaged in a deadly struggle with forces of subversion which threatened to undermine his authority and the security of the state.

Chapter Eight

The Tsar Martyr

FOR some years after the establishment of police rule in 1866, the revolutionary movement in Russia was at a low ebb. By 1869 there were signs of a revival. Groups of revolutionaries were coming into being in many parts of the empire. The most important of these, composed mainly of young intellectuals of the upper and middle classes, students and army officers, had agents in some thirty provinces. Their ranks were swelled by students expelled from the universities after the disorders of 1869. Then in 1873 the Russian government had the unwisdom to order all Russians studying at foreign universities (especially Geneva) to return. By this decision further reinforcements were provided for the revolutionary groups.

During the late sixties and early seventies revolutionary leaders had given out the slogan 'to the people', to increase contacts of the revolutionaries with workers and peasants. In consequence, in the summer of 1874, thousands of young men and women invaded the countryside, clad as peasants, in an attempt to convert the villagers to socialism. Their efforts met with little success : the peasants proved apathetic and even hostile. Shuvalov's police were active in breaking up the movement. Some 800 agitators had been seized by the end of the summer. After prolonged investigations two groups of 193 and 50 were held for trial.

Undeterred by their first failure, the revolutionaries still at large attempted a second 'going to the people' in 1876. This time, to gain the respect of the peasants, they went as petty officials, teachers, artisans, and shop-keepers. The peasants again remained almost wholly indifferent, and the movement, like its predecessors, exhausted itself without effect. The revolutionaries then decided to create a more effective organization. 'Land and Liberty' was directed by a 'basic group', divided into a number of sections. The 'administrative section' located in St. Petersburg issued general political directives and was responsible for the issue of false passports. There were three separate sections for propaganda among the intelligentsia, the factory workers, and the peasants. The 'disorganizing section' was responsible for the rescue of arrested comrades from prison, the protection of 'revolutionary honour' (which meant the assassination of traitors and police spies), and the protection of members against the police. 'Land and Liberty' owned a secret press bought abroad but operated in St. Petersburg. Provincial groups were autonomous in the conduct of their own affairs but responsible to the 'basic group' for their activities. The 'basic group', whenever necessary, would summon a meeting of the 'council', composed of all members present in St. Petersburg at the time. Such was the body which now began to pit its forces against the Tsar and his government.

In December 1876, on the eve of the Turkish War, a small revolutionary demonstration was organized in a snowstorm outside the Kazan Cathedral in St. Petersburg. It was easily dispersed and many arrests were made. In February and March 1877 the government staged the first mass trial of revolutionaries. Another major trial, that 'of the 193', opened in the autumn. As the accused were tried by the new courts, sentences were comparatively lenient. Of the 193 accused, no fewer than 153 were acquitted. Many of those found guilty received only light sentences. The Tsar was displeased and increased many sentences; a number of those acquitted by the courts were sent into exile away in the interior. The trial of the 193 was followed by a *cause célèbre* which marked the beginning of open war between the revolutionaries and the government.

Among those arrested after the demonstration outside the Kazan Cathedral was Bogoliubov, an ex-student and 'veteran' revolutionary. One day in prison he refused to salute Trepov during an inspection. The all-powerful police chief thereupon ordered Bogoliubov to be flogged for insubordination. The flogging provoked a demonstration among the other prisoners; several revolutionary groups prepared to punish Trepov. They were anticipated by a woman revolutionary, the famous Vera Zasulich, who on her own initiative fired at and severely wounded him in January 1878. She made no attempt to escape and stood her trial in April. Amid tremendous excitement the jury, after brief deliberation, returned a verdict of 'not guilty'. There was enthusiastic applause from the packed galleries, those demonstrating their approval including generals and high officials. There was a tumult outside the court building when the police tried to rearrest her. She was spirited away by her friends, and after hiding for some time in the capital was able to escape to Switzerland. The government, in impotent fury, decreed that in future all matters of 'resistance to the authorities, rebellion, assassination or attempts on the lives of officials' would be tried by military courts. It was a declaration of war against the revolutionaries.

The growing ferment was not confined to the capital. At Odessa some days after Zasulich's attempt on Trepov, Kovalski, a prominent revolutionary, defended himself with revolver and dagger when trying to resist arrest. At Kiev an unsuccessful attempt on the life of the assistant prosecutor was followed by the armed efforts of two revolutionaries to resist arrest. Leaflets were distributed, signed by 'the Executive Committee of the Russian Social Revolutionary Party'. The students of Kiev demonstrated. Large numbers were excluded from the university and fifteen banished from the city.

Their passage through Moscow provoked demonstrations and scuffles. A police officer in Kiev was fatally injured.

Unrest at Kiev and Odessa was followed by a daring stroke in the capital itself. In broad daylight, in one of the city's busiest thoroughfares, Kravchinski (alias Stepniak), a former artillery officer, cut down Mezentsev, the head of the Third Division, with a sword. Kravchinski managed to escape and lived to publish his memoirs in London. 'Land and Liberty' distributed a leaflet entitled 'A Death for a Death', justifying the murder. (During the summer, political prisoners in the fortress of SS. Peter and Paul had organized a hunger strike, when several had died. Kravchinski's action was justified as a reprisal.)

Other acts of violence followed. Early in 1879 a revolutionary killed Prince Kropotkin (a cousin of Peter Kropotkin, the anarchist), the Governor-General of Charkov, where student riots had been suppressed with severity. As usual, the assassin was able to make good his escape. A subsequent attempt on Drenteln, the new head of the Third Division, was unsuccessful. The climax of the campaign came in April, when Soloviev (without the official consent of 'Land and Liberty') fired on the Tsar himself outside the Winter Palace. Five shots missed Alexander, who escaped unhurt, Soloviev paid the penalty of his crime.

The most alarming feature for the government, however, were not the acts of revolutionary violence— striking though they were—but the attitude of the Russian public. The acquittal of Vera Zasulich had been a 'slap in the face' for the government, and the applause of the public had underlined the fact. Again, had the public felt the slightest sympathy for the authorities, Kravchinski could never have escaped after killing Mezentsev in broad daylight in the centre of St. Petersburg. The escape of other revolutionary terrorists was made possible only by the complete apathy of the public. When the government turned to the zemstvos for support, it received the reply that, until the Russian public received greater freedom to express its views, it could take no part in the struggle. Indeed, certain zemstvo leaders were engaged in abortive negotiations with 'Land and Liberty' about joint action in favour of constitutional government. Revelations of corruption in the supply services of the Russian armies and the diplomatic defeat at the Congress of Berlin increased the hostility of wider sections of the Russian public. There was widespread opposition to the police system of Shuvalov's incompetent successors. The mood of the Russian public favoured the activities of the revolutionaries.

Even within the charmed circle of Court and official society the Tsar had by this time become very unpopular. His relations with Catherine Dolgoruky were public property. To help the police protect his life, his second family was now moved to the Winter Palace itself. There the Empress Mary was approaching the term of her unhappy life. As she lay dying she could hear playing in the room above her her husband's children by his 'second wife'. By this time conservative circles in the two capitals, led by the Tsarevich, hardly forbore even in public from showing their detestation of Catherine and her children. The Grand-Duchesses in particular repulsed any attempt of the Tsar to introduce the princess into the domestic circle. The unhappy Emperor was surrounded by tension and strife even in his intimate private life. A palace revolution seemed not at all impossible.

Alexander now lived in semi-isolation, surrounded by a small group of personal friends, of whom the amiable gambler Sasha Adlerberg was the most conspicuous. To these were added some 'liberal' politicians like Abaza and Valuiev, protégés of the princess. Finally, some faithful but insignificant officials loyally stood by their master. The Tsar was isolated from the Russian people, unpopular with the educated public, and cut off from the bulk of society and the Court. His fate had become a matter of indifference to the majority of his subjects.

This situation was bound to have its effects on a personality as impressionable as the Tsar's. In the summer of 1878 he returned to his capital, after a prolonged absence, looking exhausted and suffering from a nervous collapse which he tried to conceal. He was drained of energy at a moment when he needed it more than ever. The Empress continued to play her difficult role with dignity, but she had aged even more rapidly than her husband. Receptions were held as before, but the atmosphere had changed. Everywhere in the vicinity of the Court police precautions were in evidence. On ceremonial drives the Tsar was accompanied by an escort of Cossacks. "One feels", noted an observer, "that the ground is shaking and the building threatened with collapse; the inhabitants behave as if they did not notice the fact; the masters perceive darkly the coming disaster but conceal their innermost fears."

Alexander himself had become cynical and disillusioned. When told that someone had spoken ill of him, he observed : "Strange, I don't remember ever having done him a favour; why then should he hate me?" When asked if that was really his opinion of people, he replied : "Yes, that is what I have learnt in the bitter school of experience; all I have to do to make an enemy is to do someone a favour." Sunk in bitterness and disillusionment, Alexander now felt more than ever the need for affection which he could hope to find only in the bosom of his second family. His love for Catherine and her children increased with every day; to provide for their future, to give them a legitimate status in the eyes of the world, to make the woman who had sacrificed everything for him Empress, became the object of his every thought. Compared to this, matters of state were of secondary importance. In this frame of mind,

Alexander was ill-fitted to lead the forces of authority in their life-and-death struggle with revolutionary terrorists.

Soloviev's attempt was followed by renewed efforts to stamp out the revolutionary movement. Governors-General with emergency powers were appointed for the whole of Russia. Under their direction military courts began to operate; within a few months some dozen revolutionaries had ended their lives on the gallows. Gurko, the new Governor-General of St. Petersburg, went about his business with calm determination. He expressed the well-founded conviction that the number of active revolutionaries was small. The new measures appeared to produce results. During the summer of 1879, acts of revolutionary violence ceased. Superficially, the streets of the capital resumed their normal appearance. It was the calm before the storm.

'Land and Liberty', in fact, was passing through a crisis. Soloviev's attempt had been made without orders from the organization. Its members were profoundly divided between those advocating terrorist methods (the followers of Bakunin) and those who preferred the earlier policy of peaceful propaganda. Among the chief advocates of terror were Mikhailov, the leader of the movement, and Zheliabov from Odessa. In the summer of 1879 the old 'Land and Liberty' was dissolved and replaced by two daughter organizations, the 'Black Partition', which favoured peaceful methods, and the terrorist 'People's Will'. The latter group was led by the formidable Mikhailov. He was the security expert of the terrorists. An adept at secret correspondence and the manufacture of false documents, he had thoroughly familiarized himself with the geography of St. Petersburg. He knew most of the connecting passages and houses with more than one entrance, and was an expert at shaking off police agents. He succeeded in introducing one of his followers, Kletochnikov, into the headquarters of the Third Division. In this way he learnt of the existence of a police spy in his own organization, who was promptly 'liquidated'. On September 7, 1879, the Central Executive Committee of the 'People's Will' formally condemned Alexander Romanov to death. From now on every effort of the movement was directed to his assassination.

The first attempt was to be made on the train in which the Tsar returned from a visit to the Crimea. Preparations were made in three places to blow up the train. Alexander did not pass the first (in Odessa). At the second the mine failed to explode. But on December 1 a train was overturned by an explosion a few miles outside Moscow. However, it was not the train in which the Tsar was travelling, but only a baggage train sent in advance of the imperial party. If the Tsar escaped with his life, so did the terrorists in each of the three attempts. Three days after the Moscow explosion, the paper of the 'People's Will' published an appeal to the Tsar. The organization, it declared, had vowed merciless war against him as the embodiment of reaction and repression. However, he would be 'pardoned' if he agreed to call a Constituent Assembly. It is hardly surprising that the offer met with no response.

The authorities were perplexed and the Third Division was powerless. A German historian who has examined its records remarks on "the incredible powerlessness and incompetence of the institution". In 1878 Alexander called for the names of ringleaders of the revolutionary movement : the Third Division could name only one. For the rest the Tsar was informed that the number of the revolutionaries seemed to have unaccountably grown. It would continue to do so until the leaders were destroyed. Another report described the situation as serious but not hopeless. Final victory was guaranteed by the boundless affection of the entire people, the army, and the landowning nobility for His Majesty's sacred person. Later, the head of the Division reported 'with sad and heavy feelings' the appearance of the first issue of 'The People's Will'. Forty-three searches had failed to reveal a single copy of the paper. At last several copies were discovered in the pockets of a careless Jewish revolutionary in the public library at St. Petersburg. After an investigation lasting eighteen months the secret terrorist press remained undiscovered. The revolutionaries were aided by Kletochnikov, who repeatedly gave warning of impending police raids. When the Tsar taxed the head of the Third Division with his lack of success, he received the reply that the revolutionary party was vigilantly watched. To soften the reproach Alexander observed amiably that his criticism applied to all branches of the administration 'since we are inclined to go to sleep'.

But the revolutionaries were not 'inclined to go to sleep'. With feverish energy they were preparing a new attempt. Khalturin, one of the founders of the Moscow Workers' Union, was a skilful carpenter with numerous acquaintances among the St. Petersburg workers. In the autumn of 1879, thanks to several high recommendations, he secured employment in the Winter Palace. In the disorganization during the Emperor's absence, he managed to introduce a quantity of explosives into the Palace. These he stored under his pillow in a basement room. The German government warned the Russian government that an attempt was impending. It drew attention to the basement as a danger spot. A revolutionary arrested by the Russian police was found carrying a sketch of the Palace, with a spot in the basement marked with a red cross. The special police in the Palace were reinforced; surprise checks were carried out day and night. Again everything was inefficient and nothing was discovered.

On the evening of February 17, 1880, a violent explosion shook the Winter Palace. The dining-room, where the imperial family were about to entertain the Prince of Bulgaria, was only slightly damaged. In the room below some forty Finnish soldiers of the guard lay in their blood. Khalturin got away to continue his revolutionary activities in southern Russia. The reaction of the upper classes to the attempt was one of utter indifference. Schweinitz, the German ambassador, has described the fatal evening. The fashionable world of the capital was gathering for dinner at the residence of the French ambassador. As the guests were assembling, Giers (the effective head of the Foreign Ministry) told Schweinitz that, on entering his coach, he had heard an explosion from the direction of the Palace. He had sent a servant to inquire. Schweinitz was horrified at the conduct of Giers, the Tsar's 'best and most honourable' Minister, who had calmly driven past the Palace to his dinner after hearing a violent explosion. When the servant arrived with the news of what had occurred, Schweinitz left the dinner in disgust—not before having given 'a piece of his mind' to a general of the imperial suite who was calmly sipping his coffee by the fireside. When, a few hours later, the ambassador presented himself at the Palace, he found the Tsar enjoying his usual game of whist. "God has saved me again", he said, embracing Schweinitz. The Empress, who knew nothing of the attempt, had slept quietly all night. The public was apathetic: there was not the slightest movement in the streets. The middle classes were completely indifferent, while society was pursuing its pleasures. "One is tempted", Schweinitz observed, "to regard as moribund a social body which fails to react to such a shock."

The apathy of the Russian public in the face of repeated terrorist attempts led the more intelligent and responsible of the Tsar's Ministers to seek a way of conciliating public opinion. Both Valuiev and the Grand-Duke Constantine brought forward again proposals for advisory constitutional bodies which they had first suggested in the sixties. After some hesitation, Alexander agreed that the subject should be discussed, and, early in 1880, held several meetings in private with his confidential advisers. Valuiev's and Constantine's proposals were rejected. The Tsarevich bitterly attacked their 'liberalism' and demanded that all government departments should be placed under one central directing authority. He recommended a Supreme Commission, similar to the commissions of inquiry set up in 1862 and 1866 but with vastly extended powers. The Tsar accepted the idea. At the head of the new Commission he placed an Armenian, General Loris-Melikov, who since 1879 had been Governor-General of Charkov. In this office he had succeeded in combining sternness in the struggle against revolution with consideration for the population at large. These appeared to be qualities desirable in the new 'dictator'.

The powers now granted to Loris were almost 'autocratic'. The Commission was to exercise supreme power in the empire: all civil and military authorities had to carry out its orders. Loris himself had chosen his own colleagues on this all-powerful body. His 'cabinet' included Pobedonostsev, ideologist of reaction and confidant of the Tsarevich, two generals, and a number of senators and high officials. Moreover Loris, like Shuvalov before him, had accepted office on his own terms. He wrung from the reluctant Tsar permission to unite the different police administrations. The Third Division lost its autonomy and was absorbed into a general police department headed by Plehve, a conservative official. Loris also secured the dismissal of the obscurantist Tolstoy and his replacement as Minister of Education by a liberal, Saburov. The incompetent Minister of Finance (the successor of Reutern, who had resigned in protest against the Turkish war) made way for the liberal Abaza. There were other changes of lesser importance in the personnel of the government. For the second time in his reign Alexander had abdicated his powers, this time into the hands of an 'unnatural' coalition between conservative critics (the Tsarevich, Pobedonostsev, Plehve) and 'liberals' grouped around Catherine Dolgoruky (Loris and Abaza). Thus began what critics soon came to describe as the 'Dictatorship of the Heart'.

The policy of the new government was essentially one of relaxation and concession to moderate opinion. Once again, as at the beginning of the reign, prisoners were released. The press was given greater freedom. Abaza's first act was the removal of the oppressive tax on salt. The basis of Loris's programme was the belated application, in the spirit as well as the letter, of the great zemstvo and judicial reforms. Restrictions imposed on the zemstvos were eased, so that even the radical zemstvo of Tver expressed satisfaction at the dictator's efforts to improve relations between government and public. Such repression as there was became unobtrusive : only a few revolutionary leaders were quietly arrested. Early in May the German ambassador noted that ten weeks of the new administration had produced a general relaxation of tension, however ephemeral it might prove to be.

A new crisis, however, was approaching, provoked by the Tsar's irresponsible infatuation. In June 1880 the Empress died, and forty days later (the minimum prescribed by the Orthodox Church), Alexander married—morganatically—the lady who for many years had been his wife in all but name. In December she was raised to the rank of Princes Yurievskaya (the family name of the Romanovs). Early in the new year, in the company of eight-year-old 'Gogo' (her oldest son, Prince George), she began to share the meals of the imperial family. During these meals the Tsar (now sixty-three years of age) behaved like a lover of eighteen. When he invited those around him to share in his happiness, the response of the imperial family was icy. The Grand-Duchesses detested the princess as an upstart, but her bitterest enemy was the Tsarevich. It had been anticipated that, when the Empress died, Alexander would not only marry Catherine but secure her coronation. (Catherine considered that, as a descendant of St. Vladimir, she was entitled to this honour.) An impassioned protest against any such proceeding was registered by Alexander Alexandrovich; there were reports of violent altercations between father and son.

While Alexander was storing up new troubles for himself, Loris had successfully—or so he thought—completed his policy of pacification. Six months after its creation, the Supreme Executive Commission was dissolved. Loris now assumed the functions of Minister of the Interior. His position resembled that of a prime minister or, as Valuiev jokingly called it, a 'First Boyar'. At a 'press conference' in September 1880, Loris asked editors not to excite the public with speculations about constitutional changes. Some months later he asked provincial Governors to encourage the zemstvos to discuss the state of the peasantry. He also ordered senatorial inspections in various provinces, and let it be known that the results would be examined by the government in conjunction with representatives of the public. Loris submitted to the Emperor that it was his policy to satisfy the loyal elements among the liberals. To do this, he proposed the formation of two Commissions to prepare legislation: one to deal with administrative and economic, the other with financial matters. The Commissions would be composed of officials, zemstvo representatives, professors, and publicists. Their drafts would come before a General Commission, to be composed of the two Preparatory Commissions together with two elected 'experts' from each provincial zemstvo and major city.

The inspiration of the proposal, which might have paved the way for a peaceful transition from autocracy to a semi-constitutional monarchy, came not from Loris but from Abaza. The Minister of Finance worked on the Tsar through Princess Yurievskaya by representing to her—possibly with some justice—that a concession of this kind would reconcile some of the public to the proposed coronation. The two events might well be announced in the same manifesto. Alexander was willing to pay this price to obtain public acquiescence in the achievement of his dearest wish. At a special meeting of advisers under Valuiev's presidency even the Tsarevich did not veto the Abaza proposals.

While these 'constitutional' plans were being matured, the government had been winning its long-drawn-out battle with the terrorists. Misled by the police about the extent of their knowledge, a captured terrorist had inadvertently given detailed information about their organization. As a result of the numerous arrests and deportations which followed, the terrorist organization shrunk to a mere handful. The surviving leaders felt that the sands were running out. A last grand attempt was planned. For months a detailed study had been made of the Emperor's movements. One of the principal arteries of St. Petersburg was mined, and a shaft driven under a lesser street used by the Emperor. It had been filled with enough explosives to blow the near-by buildings sky-high. To make doubly sure, four young terrorists volunteered to throw bombs at the Emperor. The plans were in an advanced stage when, on March 11, 1881, Zheliabov, the leader of the organization, was arrested. The arrest of the remainder might now be a matter of hours. The terrorists, led by a woman, Sophia Perovskaya, resolved at the earliest opportunity to carry out their attempt.

Loris also knew that the situation was becoming critical. "There need only be another unfortunate shot", he had told a high official, "and I am lost and with me my entire system." On 12 March Loris reported to the Emperor the results of Zheliabov's first interrogation. The prisoner had refused to give any information and boasted that his arrest would not prevent another attempt. Loris warned the Tsar, in the presence of the Tsarevich, not to attend the usual Sunday parade the following day. If he insisted on doing so, special precautions must be taken. In fact, all that was humanly possible had already been done in the streets he was likely to pass. For the last three weeks, Princess Yurievskaya had dissuaded her husband from attending the Sunday parades. Now, seeing him completely calm after his talk with Loris, she made no effort to do so again. A visit to the ailing Loris at his home confirmed her in a sense of security. That night, taking her arm to lead her to dinner, Alexander remarked: "I am so happy at present that this happiness frightens me." He spent the evening—as on several previous occasions—telling his son George what to do if he suddenly lost his father.

Alexander had taken a decision. On Sunday, March 13, he received Loris to give his personal approval to the constitutional changes now recommended. Having signed the document, the Tsar went to inspect the parade. His wife had specially asked him to avoid two streets—which happened to be the streets mined by the conspirators. After the parade, he paid a call on his cousin, the Grand-Duchess Catherine. He imparted to her his decision to sanction the participation of elected members in his legislative commissions, and took his leave.

It had long been the practice for the Emperor to return to the Palace by a different route from that by which he had come. The return route he would announce only at the last moment. This time his return drive took him through Catherine Street along a canal of the same name. As the sledge entered this quiet street —which, contrary to the assurances of the Minister of Police, had not been closed to the public—a mining student, Ryssakov, threw a bomb. Alexander was unhurt. Against the advice of his driver, he stepped out of the sledge to look after the wounded cossacks of the escort. "Thank God, no", he replied to a question from bystanders if he was wounded. "Thank God?" exclaimed at that moment another terrorist (Hriniewicki, a Polish student at the Technological Institute), and hurled a bomb directly at the Emperor's feet. Both the

Tsar's legs were shattered. To his brother Michael, who arrived upon the scene, he could only whisper : "Home to the Palace, to die there." In Michael's arms the dying Emperor was taken by sledge to the Winter Palace, escorted by bleeding cossacks on bespattered horses. The Princess Yurievskaya was waiting for her husband, expecting to accompany him on a stroll through the Summer Garden.

Any emotion felt in Russia at the news of the assassination was neither widespread nor sincere. The popular attitude at St. Petersburg was a blend of indifference and curiosity. No indignation was felt against the terrorists, there were no lamentations or expressions of grief. For a little while a few hundred people gathered each day at the place of the attempt; some wept and brought flowers and wreaths. The funeral cortège from the Palace to the fortress was hasty and disorderly; the conventions of common decency were barely maintained. The populace remained stubbornly unmoved. The feeling of the upper classes was, perhaps, best expressed by the honest Schweinitz. Asked why he did not show more grief at the death of a sovereign to whom he had been sincerely devoted (Schweinitz and Alexander had been inseparable hunting companions), the German ambassador replied : "We have already grieved for him" ("*nous en avons fait notre deuil*"). "After the war and through his fatal relationship with the woman he loved, he was too greatly changed. God has saved him from losing still more of his dignity and self-respect. His death we should regard as a blessing, if only the circumstances had been less cruel."

The circumstances of Alexander's death underline his tragic personal failure. Except at brief moments during the liberation struggle, and later during the Polish insurrection, he had never been a popular ruler. His personality—however charming in an intimate circle, and particularly in the company of children—was reserved and haughty. The pleasantness and suavity of his manner was broken all too easily by outbursts of temper. Both the Tsar's private life and that of his entourage brought the dynasty reproach. Nor did Alexander possess many of the qualities indispensable to a successful ruler. From his childhood he had tried to evade difficulties, to find an easy escape from complex situations. What had been a venial sin in the pupil of Merder and Zhukovsky, became a serious fault in the autocratic Emperor of All the Russias. A sense of duty instilled by his father had prevented the Tsar from becoming *Alexandre le Bien Aimé*—another Louis XV—but the tenacity and concern for the public welfare shown in the struggle for liberation later evaporated. A sense of insecurity and apprehension made Alexander the 'prisoner' first of Shuvalov and Trepov, later of Loris-Melikov. His ill-starred infatuation for Catherine Dolgoruky became a scandal to the state which undermined his own authority and destroyed the respect of his subjects.

Alexander's personal failings aggravated his already difficult task of reconciling the increase of freedom with the preservation of imperial authority. Peter the Great, Nicholas I, and Lenin did not experience this conflict: they were autocrats who knew not the meaning of liberty. Alexander, on the other hand, although not a liberal himself, was born into an age when liberalism was in the ascendant. The teachings of Zhukovsky, reaction against the régime of Nicholas, popular expectations and demands, combined with the impetuosity of the Grand-Duke Constantine, carried him into concessions to the liberal *Zeitgeist* against his inclination. These concessions, half-hearted though they were, produced the general ferment of opinion inseparable from a Russian 'thaw'. Alexander's 'mildness' led to a general loosening of the reins of government. The Russian public, unprepared for freedom, indulged in extravagant criticism which threatened to undermine the authority of the Tsar and his government. By 1861, with student and peasant unrest, subversion in the army, incipient rebellion in Poland, and incendiarism in the capital, it appeared that Russia was slipping into chaos; liberty was degenerating into licence.

Yet Alexander was a pupil of Nicholas much more than a pupil of Zhukovsky. He was at heart a believer in order, authority, and autocracy. In his view everything at home must come from above and be carefully controlled and supervised; abroad, there must be order, authority, and a respect for existing rights and obligations. With a disposition in itself autocratic, Alexander naturally turned to reaction—some would say the defence of his legitimate authority—when subversive movements made their appearance.

It was, however, precisely as an autocrat that Alexander was the greatest failure. Throughout his reign order was not effectively maintained, authority never secure. Characteristically, he flouted the wishes of his parents by his marriage to the Princess Mary. Again, in his private and family life he failed to set an example of order. Leading an irregular life himself he was unable to rebuke others—in this way very much unlike his father. The absence of a firm paternal or fraternal authority in the imperial family became notorious. Nor could the Emperor's entourage—from the gambler Sasha Adlerberg to Catherine's stock-jobbing friends—inspire much respect. The Tsarevich consistently opposed Alexander in his later years, and did not scruple to criticize his father's private and public conduct. The Tsar was never master in his own house. A court rent by factions and intrigues can be no secure basis of authority for an absolute government in troubled times.

The disorder spread outwards from the centre. There was no unity in the government. Ministers of divergent views fought and intrigued against each other; important political decisions were made according to the constellation of the moment. The Emperor, it was said, gave his voice to whoever had spoken to him last. Alexander had no Richelieu or Bismarck, but only a Gorchakov. Shuvalov, his ablest Minister, fell victim to an intrigue engineered by the Princess Catherine. Loris's power was based on a precarious coalition brought about by an emergency. If there was no cohesion in the government in distant St. Petersburg, there could be no order among its local agents scattered over the vast empire. Alexander could exercise effective control neither over the powerful proconsuls in Tiflis and Tashkent, nor yet over Katkov, the eloquent demagogue, ambitious liars like Ignatiev, or even a windy adventurer like Cherniaev. Acts of defiance and insubordination enough to cause Nicholas I to turn in his grave were committed with impunity every day.

Alexander proved himself not only a disappointing 'liberal'—if indeed that term can be applied to him—but, more seriously, an inefficient autocrat. While he would not give his educated subjects the constitution for which they clamoured, he failed to use to advantage the autocratic powers which he felt impelled to retain. He merely succeeded in proving that a pseudo-liberal autocrat is an unhappy hybrid unlikely to achieve political success. The narrow principles of Nicholas I or Alexander III, for whom Alexander's problems did not exist, proved—on a short-term view—more effective than the unsuccessful attempt to combine authority and freedom.

Yet Alexander's policy of combining reform with control from above was not, in itself, unsound. He was right in initiating long-overdue reforms; one cannot blame him for trying to carry them into effect through the existing machinery of government. Such a policy, however, was likely to be opposed from two different directions. Reform could not but hurt the vested interests of landowners, merchants, and officials; refusal to admit the participation of the public in government could not but antagonize the liberals. Alexander's reign combined reform and repression; the combination pleased no important section of the population. Conservatives would have preferred less reform and more control; the liberals the opposite. Alexander, working for the public welfare according to his lights, succeeded in antagonizing both groups at the same time. A gulf began to open between the Russian government and the public never again to be closed. Loris's administration—so nearly successful yet, in the event, so tragically abortive—was the last attempt of tsarism to come to terms with liberal Russian opinion. Could Loris have succeeded in his policy of organic institutional development? Could even he have successfully counteracted the effects of the Tsar's unpopular liaison and Catherine's probable coronation? It seems more than likely that, had Alexander once again escaped the assassin, he would have fallen to a peaceful palace 'revolution' and abdicated in favour of his son. The end would still have been Alexander III, Pobedonostsev, and Katkov.

If the seeds of Alexander's tragedy lay in his personal character and the resulting inability to combine freedom and authority, it is true that unfavourable circumstances made his difficulties almost insuperable. The Tsar was fated to preside over one of the recurring and normally abortive 'liberal' interludes in the history of Russia. After the reign of Nicholas, as after those of Peter III, Paul I, or Stalin, a 'thaw' had become an imperative necessity. The new government must throw off the odium accumulated by the preceding despotism. Yet as soon as Alexander lifted the tight lid of repression, the compressed steam began to escape with powerful effect. Conditions developed enough to frighten even a ruler less naturally insecure than Alexander. Not for nothing did the great Tocqueville observe that the most dangerous moment for a bad government usually comes when it begins to reform itself. By 1862 the dangers of the 'thaw' were clearly apparent to all, and repression, never completely abandoned, again came into its own.

Alexander has been criticized for 'abandoning' his earlier course. Yet what could the Emperor have done? The establishment of a democratic form of freedom was surely out of the question in the conditions of nineteenth-century Russia. Oligarchic rule, as demanded by the disgruntled gentry? Complete freedom for the radical press and its revolutionary supporters? Could the Poles be given their freedom—within the boundaries of 1772 which they claimed? If not, what course was left but repression once Wielopolski's policy had failed? Real freedom in the Russian empire was an impossibility. So, regrettably from Alexander's point of view, was a policy of effective repression—except in Poland and Lithuania after the suppression of the insurrection. Alexander was not by nature a 'stern reactionary' like his father or his son. His hankering after popularity sometimes introduced an element of weakness and hesitation into a repressive system. In any case, the zemstvos and the new courts, supported by the weight of public opinion, made 'black repression' of the type Muraviev and Panin might have favoured a practical impossibility. Finally, except for a time under Shuvalov, the police organization was weak and inefficient. The weapons of the modern totalitarian state were not at the Tsar's disposal. Complete repression was no more practicable than complete freedom. Only a compromise policy was possible.

It is here that the Tsar's course is open to criticism. The compromise to which, under pressure, he consented at the end of his reign might have been greeted with acclamation if it had followed the introduction of the zemstvo and judicial reforms. Instead, frightened by Karakozov's attempt, the Tsar, rather than listen to Valuiev and the Grand-Duke Constantine, handed over power to Shuvalov and Trepov. It was a fateful decision. The wiser course *might*, if adopted, have led

Russia along the road of peaceful constitutional development.

Could Alexander have prevented the Turkish War which finally helped to destroy his system? The conclusion would appear to be that the pressure for warlike action, although powerful, was not irresistible. The Tsar —half-unwillingly—allowed himself to be dragged along the road which might lead to Constantinople. Public opinion did not force him into war; when he made his decision the Pan-Slav agitation had passed its peak. What Alexander hoped for—perhaps understandably—was a military walk-over to bolster up his shaken régime. A century-old ambition of the Russian people might be realized. Osman Pasha's unexpected resistance at Plevna upset the Russian plans. What might have been a brilliant Russian triumph became a disappointing compromise. Circumstances, as well as the flaws in his personal character, were responsible for the failures of Alexander's reign.

And yet even though Alexander cannot be termed a successful ruler, the results of his reign challenge comparison with the more spectacular achievements of Peter the Great and Lenin. The policy of 'modernization' applied to almost every sphere of Russian life made Alexander one of Russia's great 'westernizers'. In his reign, and in no small degree as the result of official policy, the Russian empire passed from the semi-feudal to the early capitalist stage of its development. Far-reaching social changes resulted. In a different sphere, the reforms of Alexander II helped to assure Russia's survival as a major power after her collapse in the Crimean War. Under him, the bounds of the empire were enlarged. Finland and Bulgaria were set on the road to nationhood, the economic and social structure of Poland was transformed. Finally, although Alexander was not himself a distinguished patron of the arts, it was in his reign that Turgeniev, Dostoevsky and Tolstoy, Mussorgsky, Chaikovsky and

Rimsky-Korsakov, wrote and composed their master-pieces. The foundations were being laid for Russia's cultural 'conquests'.

In fact, there was more than a little truth in the remarks made by one French diplomat to another during Alexander's funeral :

"Have a good look at this martyr. He was a great tsar and deserved a kinder fate. . . . His was not a great intellect, but he had a generous soul, very upright and very lofty. He loved his people and his solicitude for the humble and the suffering was unbounded. . . . Remember the reforms he introduced. Peter the Great was the author of none more deeply reaching, and he put into them less of his heart. . . . Think of all the resistance he had to overcome to abolish serfdom and restore the foundation of rural economy. Think that thirty million men owe their affranchisement to him. . . . And his administrative reforms ! He aimed at nothing less than the destruction of the arbitrary bureaucracy and social privilege. In the judicial sphere he established equality before the law, assured the independence of the magistrates, abolished corporal punishment, instituted the jury. And this was done by the immediate successor of the despot Nicholas I ! . . . In foreign politics his work is on the same scale. He followed the line taken by Catherine II on the Black Sea; he wiped out the humiliations of the Treaty of Paris; he brought the eagles of Muscovy to the shores of the Propontis, the very walls of Constantinople; he delivered the Bulgar; he established Russian dominion in the heart of Central Asia. . . . Finally, on the morning of his death, he was working on a reform which would have surpassed all the others, would have launched Russia irrevocably along the track of the modern world: the granting of a parliamentary charter. . . . And the Nihilists have killed him ! . . . But mark the odd coincidence of history, the strange irony of things. Lincoln, the emancipator of the American negroes, was also assassinated. Now, it was the deliverance of the negroes which brought in its train, on the other side of the world, the affranchisement of the *moujiks*. Alexander did not intend that Russia should remain the only serf-holding nation in the Christian world.[1] . . . Oh, a liberator's is a dangerous job !"[2]

[1] de Vogüé is at fault here. Alexander's resolution to free the Russian serfs preceded the abolition of negro slavery in the U.S.A.

[2] M. Paléologue, *The Tragic Romance of Emperor Alexander II* (London, n.d.), pp. 27 ff.

NOTES ON BOOKS

THERE exists no adequate biography of Alexander II in any language. The fullest life is the official biography of S. S. Tatishchev, *Imperator Aleksandr II* (St. Petersburg, 1903, 2 vols.), which, however, suffers from the defects inseparable from the work of a court historian. In English there is a popular biography by S. Graham, *Tsar of Freedom: Life and Reign of Alexander II* (New Haven, 1935). A French diplomat, M. Paléologue, has produced a romanticized account of Alexander's relations with Catherine Dolgoruky (published in English as *The Tragic Romance of the Emperor Alexander II,* London n.d.).

Neither is there an adequate account of Alexander's reforms. G. A. Dzhanshiev's standard work on the subject (*Epokha velikikh Reform,* St. Petersburg, 1907), is little more than a useful quarry. A. A. Golovachev's *Desjatj let reform* (St. Petersburg, 1872), is slight, but interesting as giving the views of a contemporary observer. A. A. Kornilov's *Obshchestvennoe dvizhenie pri Aleksandre II* (Moscow, 1909), contains an analysis of public reaction to the reforms. In English there is a comprehensive study of the liberation of the serfs in G. T. Robinson's *Rural Russia under the Old Regime* (New York and London, 1932). A Leroy-Beaulieu's *Un homme d'état Russe: Nicolas Milutine* (Paris, 1884), remains a useful biography of one of the moving spirits of the reform movement.

Alexander's foreign policy can be studied in several works. Ch. Friese's *Russland und Preussen vom Krimkrieg bis zum Polnischen Aufstand* (Berlin, 1931), is indispensable for the early years of the reign. Relations with France are analysed in F. Charles-Roux's *Alex-andre II, Gortchakoff et Napoléon III* (Paris, 1913). Russian policy in the early and middle years of the reign can be studied in W. E. Mosse's *The European Powers and the German Question 1848–1871* (Cambridge, 1958), while the later years are covered in B. H. Sumner's *Russia and the Balkans 1870–1880* (Oxford, 1937).

There are a number of interesting contemporary accounts. The system of Nicholas I is vividly portrayed in *The Memoirs of Alexander Herzen,* translated by J. D. Duff (New Haven, 1923), and in A. de Custine's *La Russie en 1839* (Bruxelles, 1843), edited and translated into English by P. P. Kohler as *Journey for our time: the journals of the Marquis de Custine* (London, 1953). A lively picture of the beginnings of the reign emerges from P. Kropotkin's *Memoirs of a Revolutionist* (London, 1899), and the Prussian diplomat K. v. Schlözer's *Petersburger Briefe* (Stuttgart u. Berlin, 1922). The latter years of the reign are covered by the memoirs of the ultra-conservative Prince V. P. Meshchersky, *Moi Vospominanija* (St. Petersburg, 1898), and the invaluable reminiscences of the German ambassador, General v. Schweinitz, *Denkwürdigkeiten des Botschafters General v. Schweinitz* (Berlin, 1927). Two thoughtful foreign observers produced detailed accounts—D. Mackenzie-Wallace, *Russia* (revised edition, London, 1905), and A. Leroy-Beaulieu, *L'Empire des Tsars et les Russes* (Paris, 1881).

The two leading histories of Russia in a non-Russian language contain admirable surveys of the reign: M. T. Florinsky, *Russia* (New York, 1953, 2 vols.), Vol. II, Chapters XXXIII–XXXVII, and K. Stählin, *Geschichte Russlands* (Königsberg Pr. u. Berlin; completed 1939, 4 vols.), Vol. IV, part 1, Chapters I–IV.

Of works more readily accessible to the British reader, H. Seton-Watson's *The Decline of Imperial Russia* (London, 1952) and Bernard Pares's *A History of Russia* (4th edn., London, 1944) also contain useful accounts of the reign.

Index

INDEX

INDEX

INDEX